DATE			

AIRPORT
FINANCE

AIRPORT FINANCE

Norman Ashford
Professor of Transport Planning
Loughborough University
Leicestershire, United Kingdom

Clifton A. Moore
Executive Director
Los Angeles Department of Airports
Los Angeles, California

VNR VAN NOSTRAND REINHOLD
_____ New York

Library of Congress Catalog Card Number 91-44701
ISBN 0-442-00192-4

Printed in the United States of America

Van Nostrand Reinhold
115 Fifth Avenue
New York, New York 10003

Chapman and Hall
2–6 Boundary Row
London, SE1 8HN, England

Thomas Nelson Australia
102 Dodds Street
South Melbourne 3205
Victoria, Australia

Nelson Canada
1120 Birchmount Road
Scarborough, Ontario M1K 5G4, Canada

16 15 14 13 12 11 10 9 8 7 6 5 4 3 2 1

Library of Congress Cataloging-in-Publication Data

Ashford, Norman.
    Airport finance / by Norman Ashford, Clifton A. Moore.
        p.   cm.
    ISBN 0-442-00192-4 : $64.95
    1. Airports—Finance.   I. Moore, Clifton A.   II. Title.
HE9797.4.F5A84   1992
387.7'36'0681—dc20   91-44701
                                                    CIP

REF

Contents

Preface

This book was written as an introductory text discussing the basic elements of airport finance. The material presented and the matters discussed are drawn from an international scene, reflecting the international nature of aviation and the need for those involved in the airport industry to understand the structure of airport finance in this context. The authors have selected the content based on their joint knowledge of airport administration and postexperience aviation training.

The draft manuscript was used as a teaching text at the airport finance course at Loughborough University in May 1990 with twenty-four postgraduate/postexperience participants. Based on that experience and comments from a number of readers and reviewers, the final form of the text is that presented here.

Chapter 1 deals generally with the patterns of airport ownership on a worldwide basis and describes the sources of revenues and expenditures, the manner in which they are reported, and the form in which airport accounts are reported. Because systems and practices vary among countries, the material is presented on a comparative basis.

In Chapter 2, Harry Kluckhohn describes the manner in which U.S. airports are financed. Not only will this be of interest to U.S. readers, but it will serve as a useful guide for others who may have little knowledge of how this highly developed financing system works.

The financing of non–U.S. airports is covered in Chapter 3. Because the methods vary greatly among different countries, the approach taken is of a broad brush nature to provide examples on a comparative basis. Chapter 4 is a primer of the various types of commercial financing that exist. These may or may not be available to individual airports depending on the regulatory structure under which they operate.

Robert W. Poole has contributed Chapter 5, which draws on his extensive experience in studying privatization and examining how well such a system could be applied to the U.S. case. It is expected that U.S. readers will be especially interested in this chapter. Other readers should examine the points made and apply the lessons drawn to the peculiarities of their own system.

The position of concessionary agreements is examined from an international position in Chapter 6, with much of the discussion based on material published by the then International Civil Airports Association (ICAA) through the activities of its Commercial Activities Commission. The ICAA became defunct in 1991 on its merger with the Airport Operators Council International (AOCI), forming a joint organization Airports Association Council International (AACI). Its work continues in the international context under its new structure.

Chapter 7 presents a general discussion of the purpose and format requirements of a financial management information system. Such systems in computerized form were expensive rarities ten years ago. By the turn of this century, even very small airfields will have such systems available to them. It is, therefore, important that readers should obtain a reasonable grasp of the objectives and contents of such systems.

Financial management of any airport should involve a clear understanding of project financial appraisal methods. Chapter 8, "Life-Cycle Costing," encapsulates the concepts of financial appraisal in the airport context and uses simple case studies to show how the principles are applied.

Chapter 9 describes how financial performance indicators are computed and how they are used. In an increasing "commercial" airport industry, such indicators are becoming more widespread in use.

In the final chapter, "Business Plans," the principles of setting up a business plan are exemplified by a case-study approach, which is based on the actual business plan of a real airport. However, to protect commercial confidentiality, the figures have been systematically modified so that the case study shown is still realistic.

From the comments of both postexperience and postgraduate students, the authors believe that this text will be of use as a teaching text both in airport and aviation industry training programs and in postgraduate programs that specialize in aviation studies.

We would like to express our sincere appreciation to many individuals who have made significant contributions to the final production of this book. We are greatly indebted to Harry Kluckhohn and Robert Poole, who contributed Chapters 2 and 5, respectively. Their recognized expertise in the areas in which they have written has been especially useful in completing this work. We would also wish to thank the following individuals for their provision of data and helpful comments on the early drafts of the manuscripts.

D. Benham	Heathrow Airport Ltd., London
L. Cousins	Georgia Department of Transportation, Atlanta
P. Coutu	IAMTI, Montreal
A. Duff	Heathrow Airport Ltd., London
L. Jackson	Manchester International Airport
T. Lovett	East Midlands International Airport
G. Watson	Formerly Scottish Airports Ltd.

We would also wish to express appreciation of the invaluable work carried out by Vivien Grove in her help in editing and preparing the manuscript and to T.L. Parker and B. Trnavskis who reviewed the entire work.

Norman Ashford
Loughborough

Clifton A. Moore
Los Angeles

1

The Structure of Airport Finances

1.1 THE OWNERSHIP PATTERNS OF AIRPORTS

In common with other enterprises, it is normal for airports to publish their accounts at yearly intervals. These accounts indicate on a yearly basis the size of annual turnover, the sources of income and expenditure, the nature and size of profit and loss, and the sources and status of capital. The exact format of the published annual financial report varies significantly among airports within individual countries and among different countries. Often the form of accounting is determined by the form of ownership, which itself varies significantly among different countries.

In the United States, more than 4,500 airports are overwhelmingly in public ownership. The majority of airports are owned by counties and municipalities, with a number belonging to the states themselves. In some cases, formal ownership is vested in an airport authority, such as the Port Authority of New York and New Jersey and SeaTac, which may or may not have powers to levy taxes directly. These authorities are creations of the states, counties, or municipalities and ultimately each is responsible to the governmental body that created it. In many cases, the members of the governing authority are publicly elected, although in some cases these positions are filled by appointment. With few exceptions the federal government in the United States does not, in general, own civil airports, and private ownership of airports is principally limited to general aviation facilities. The private sector of the airport industry has, therefore, very limited influence on civil air transport.

The United Kingdom has recently taken a very different approach to the ownership of airports. When the Airports Act 1986 came into force in September of that year, all airports with an annual turnover of more than £1 million were required to become private companies as part of the Thatcher government's political goal of denationalization. Prior to 1986, most large- and medium-sized air transport airports were owned either by local authorities or by the British Airports Authority (BAA), an autonomous government-owned airport authority that reported through its board to a minister of central government. The BAA, which owned only seven of the more than forty air transport airports of the United Kingdom, accounted for approximately three-fourths of all passenger traffic in the United Kingdom. A large proportion of the BAA's traffic was handled at the two large London airports, Heathrow and Gatwick, and the profits from these two facilities, especially Heathrow, were used to cross-subsidize the operation of less profitable airports, particularly Stansted and Prestwick. In 1987, BAA plc[1] was floated on the London Stock Exchange as a quoted company in which the public could buy shares.

Since then BAA plc has diversified its activities to include hotel and property operations. As a private company, responsible only to its shareholders, there is little limitation on the scope of BAA's activities outside the airport field. The remaining affected local authority airports in the United Kingdom became private companies, but by 1992 all shares in these companies continued to be held by the original local authorities. These regional airports now have a private-company status that resembles the public corporation status of a number of West European airports, notably Schipol Amsterdam and the regional German facilities such as Düsseldorf, Hamburg, and Munich.

Within continental Western Europe and the Irish Republic, ownership patterns vary. Airports such as Schipol Amsterdam, Munich, Frankfurt, and Hanover are public corporations, the shares of which are owned by the state and municipalities. In France, Aéroports de Paris dominates air transport, owning Charles de Gaulle and Orly airports in Paris as well as Le Bourget and eleven other general-aviation airports. Aéroports de Paris is owned entirely by the French government. Similarly, the Rome, Milan, and Turin airports are owned by the Italian government. Scandinavian airports are owned directly by the national governments, and Aer Rianta owns and runs Dublin, Cork, and Shannon airports as a government-owned airport authority.

Airport authorities responsible directly to government are widespread throughout the world (1): Nigeria (Nigerian Airports Authority); Brazil (INFRAERO); Saudi Arabia (International Airports Project for Jeddah, Riyadh, and Dharhan and the Presidency of Civil Aviation for other airports); Canada (Airport Authority Group); Australia (Federal Airport Corporation); Portugal (Aeroportos e Navigaçao Aerea, ANA); Vienna (Vienna Airport Authority). Equally widespread are arrangements whereby airports are run as part of the

---

[1] The term *plc* in British company law is similar to the term *incorporated* in the United States. A plc or PLC (either is permissible) has more than fifty registered shareholders.

civil aviation authorities either within or outside a department of transportation: Norway, Sweden, South Africa, Algeria, Zimbabwe, Singapore, and Oman, for example.

The financial structure of an airport and the form in which it is reported are greatly dependent on its relationship either with government or with its shareholders.

1.2 AIRPORT REVENUES: OPERATING AND NONOPERATING

The total revenues of an airport are frequently divided into two principal categories (2):

Operating revenues. Operating revenues are revenues that are directly associated with the running and operation of the airport, including the operational areas, terminals, leased areas, and grounds.

Nonoperating revenues. Within the category of nonoperating revenues are included all income items derived from activities that are not directly associated with the running of the airport and would continue even if the airport were closed down.

Operating Revenues

In that operating revenues are generated by the facilities or services provided by the airport in the course of the activity of running the airport, the sources of these revenues are generally easily identified. Although the method of classifying these revenues is not universally agreed upon, the following format is not atypical for most airports:

1. *Landing area revenues.* Income from the landing area is generated directly by the operation of aircraft. It includes the following:
   a. *Landing fees.* These are associated with the use of runways, taxiways, landing strips, clear zones, clearways, safety zones; traffic control and guidance; temporary parking and servicing areas; emergency services, including rescue and fire-fighting services (RFFS), ambulance and medical services, and so on.

      Landing fees can be charged in a variety of ways: by *gross landing weight, gross take-off weight,* or even as a *percentage of the airline's gross revenue at the airport.*

      At some small airports, no landing fee is required; revenues to support the airport are generated in other ways—often, for example, from sale of aviation fuel. At general-aviation airports, fixed flat-rate fees for all aircraft are common, as are rates dependent on gross landing weight. Whereas at large airports, the depth of administration permits complex charge structures, at most general-aviation airports, for administrative convenience and simplicity the landing fee structure is necessarily un-complicated.

The landing fees may also be structured to encourage airlines to move scheduled service out of the congested peak hours by charging different and higher rates during the congested hours. This has been the practice for a number of years at London's Heathrow and Gatwick air-ports. Because of the strong customer preference to travel at convenient times of the day, differential tariffs have little effect in spreading opera-tions across the day for short- and medium-haul traffic. Long-haul oper-ations are usually also constrained by "windows" of service opportunity, which must avoid curfews and periods of congestion at enroute and destination airports. Their flexibility to move schedules to less-con-gested periods is therefore severely restricted (1). Charter operators also face difficulty in moving their operations from peak to noncongested hours. By the nature of their operation and the cost structure of their fares, such operators attempt to achieve more than sixteen hours of equipment utilization per day during the busy periods. The loss of in-come that would accrue from lost flying hours due to moving operations out of optimally timed slots would far outweigh any gains from lower landing fees at nonoptimal times.

b. *Passenger load supplement.* At many non–U.S. airports, the landing area revenues are partly made up of charges that are related not only to the aircraft size or weight but also to the number of passengers actually carried. In this way, aircraft operating during peak operational hours with high-load factors pay higher airport charges than the same aircraft with low-load factors, which are more likely in the nonpeak hours. This form of charging structure is common in Europe, where in some coun-tries a security charge is also levied on a per-passenger basis; such a charge permits the airports to finance the special security arrangements that have become necessary in civil aviation due to a sustained and continuing threat of terrorism from many sources.

c. *Passenger head tax.* Until relatively recently, passenger head taxes at federally aided U.S. airports were illegal. However, in October 1990 the Congress passed legislation that permitted U.S. airports to institute such taxes, should they desire to do so, in the form of a Passenger Facility Charge (PFC). Although differing legally and constitutionally from the passenger load supplements used elsewhere in the world, in practice they will work in very much the same way. Both the passenger head tax and the passenger load supplement are ways in which the airport can recoup the varying costs of terminal and landside operations that accrue from the number of passengers handled rather than the number of aircraft, the airside costs of which are, to a degree, independent of the passenger loading.

d. *Parking ramp fees.* The structure of fees charged for parking on the apron in the terminal area vary considerably among airports. They include the following:

   i. No charge

   ii. Fixed charge for a limited time, with additional charges for stays beyond the time limit. To encourage airlines to attain a high aircraft turnover at terminal gates, these additional charges are sometimes punitive. Other airports operate a towing policy to achieve the same end.

   iii. Variable weight-related charge for an unlimited time

   iv. Variable weight-related charge for a limited time with additional charges for extended parking

At some airports, the apron parking charge includes a charge for the use of an air bridge at pier-served gates; in other airports this charge is separate.

2. *Terminal area concessions.* Within this classification, it is usual to include the revenues from all nonairline sources within the terminal. These include the following:

a. Bars, restaurants, snack bars, coffee shops, and other food and drink concessions

b. Travel-related services and facilities: left-luggage checkrooms, lockers, porter service, hotel reservation desks and phone insurance booths and machines, airline club lounges, commercially important passenger (CIP) facilities, business centers, rest rooms, bedrooms, showers, and other toilet facilities. In the case that a charge is made to the airline for facility use, this category would also include VIP facilities and handling of handicapped persons and unaccompanied minors.

c. Personal services, including, for example, barber shops and beauty salons, valet services such as pressing and cleaning, manicures, and shoeshines

d. Airport speciality shops: duty- and tax-free shops, newsstands, local specialities, flower stalls, banks, postal facilities, and telecommunications

e. Amusements and games: cinemas, pay television, computer games, gambling machines, and observation area equipment

f. Other terminal building facilities: office rental, advertizing space, rental of terminal for special services (e.g., television and filming)

g. Facilities outside but closely related to the terminal building (e.g., ground transport, parking, hotel, and car valet services)

3. *Airline-leased areas.* It is frequently convenient to group together revenues from leasing arrangements with the airlines. As major users of airport space, the airlines account for a very significant proportion of the total airport revenue. Typically these revenues are derived from the following:

   a. *Ground rentals.* Bare ground is provided on which the airlines construct their own facilities. Such arrangements are usually in the form of a long-term lease, with provisions for renegotiations of rental terms at various stages of the leasing period.

   b. *Cargo-area rentals.* In such cases, the airline leases all or part of a constructed cargo facility. Leases of constructed property are frequently of a shorter-term nature than ground rentals.

   c. *Office rentals.* Constructed offices both within or outside the terminal are frequently provided on short- or medium-term leases.

   d. *Check-in desks and ticket counters*

   e. *Rental of operational and maintenance areas.* At various parts of the airport, both within the terminal apron area and elsewhere, the airline will have need for dedicated space or facilities for its operational and maintenance requirements. If not provided via a ground-rental arrangement, these requirements can be provided by leasing directly from the airport. The operational areas required within a main terminal building would come into this category in a terminal belonging entirely to an airport authority.

   f. *Hangars*

4. *Other leased areas.* Depending on the nature of the airport complex, there can be a variety of other revenue-producing leases from nonairline operations, including manufacturing, warehousing, freight forwarding, and even farming. Revenues from these areas may be categorized in the following way:

   a. Fixed-base operator leases

   b. Ground rentals

   c. Cargo-area rentals (freight forwarders, etc.)

   d. Industrial areas

   e. Other buildings

   f. Fuel and aircraft servicing

   g. Agriculture

5. *Other operating revenue.* This category of revenue can be used for all sources of revenue not conveniently covered by previously mentioned categories. Typically, such income as equipment rental, the resale of utilities, and the provision of miscellaneous services to airport users can be drawn together in this category.

TABLE 1-1. Relationship between Operating Income, Total Income, and
Airport Size

	Ratio of Operating Income to Total Income
Airports with less than ½ million enplanements	0.957
Airports with ½ to 2 million enplanements	0.985
Airports with 2 million or more enplanements	0.922

Source: Adapted from Reference 2

Nonoperating Revenues

Nonoperating revenues include all income to the airport operator derived from
activities not directly associated with the operation of the airport. These revenues would presumably continue even if the airport were to shut down. The
sources of such revenues, therefore, can be extremely varied. Typically, they
can include income from investment and securities and the leasing of nonairport properties and equipment. Also in this category are the fees from sales of
services, training, and consultancy. There is evidence that as the size of an
airport operation grows—either in terms of passenger enplanements or in
terms of annual financial turnover—the proportion of nonaviation activity
increases. This increase is reflected in a decreasing ratio of operating income to
total income. See Table 1-1 (2).

1.3 AIRPORT EXPENDITURES: OPERATING
AND NONOPERATING

The *operating expenditures* of an airport are those expenditures incurred in
the course of the running of the airport. These expenditures can disappear if
the airport portion of the business or operation is closed down. *Nonoperating
expenditures* are those expenses incurred even if no operations are carried out.
Typically, they include the interest payments on outstanding capital debt and
amortization charges on the fixed assets, such as runways and buildings. Also
included in this category are expenditures incurred in the generation of nonoperating income.

Operating Expenditures

There are two common ways of reporting operating expenditures:

1. According to the function of the facility or operation for which the expendi-

tures occurred, where expenditures are typically grouped under the two general headings, such as *traffic handling* and *commercial activities*
2. According to a categorization of type of expenditure, such as *salaries, premises, supplies and services, transport and plant, administrational expenses,* and *miscellaneous items*

The consequences of these different forms of reporting are discussed further in Section 1.5.

Nonoperating Expenditures

As already stated, nonoperating expenditures are usually regarded as those expenditures that would continue even if the operation of the airport were to cease. As such, this category of expenditure includes interest payments on outstanding capital debt, amortization on fixed assets (such as runways, buildings, and equipment), expenditures incurred in the generation of nonoperating income, fees for various nonoperating purposes, and the like.

1.4 ACCOUNTING PRINCIPLES FOR AIRPORTS

When reference is made to trading and profit and loss accounts and balance sheets, it is important to bear in mind that there is no "mysticism" in such terms and that, effectively, all that is being talked about is simply the presentation of a set of facts that flow from an orderly process of keeping financial records, known as *bookkeeping*. In practice, such records are kept in permanent form so that there is a record of each transaction or each group of transactions of a similar nature, with a view to ensuring that any particular transaction made during a given period can be ascertained relatively easily.

It is interesting to note that modern trading accounts, which are based on a system of what is known as *double-entry* bookkeeping, had their origins in the fifteenth century and are believed to have been devised, in fact, by Venetian Merchants. In the double-entry system of bookkeeping, two *actions* are required by a firm for each separate transaction and these two actions can be defined as "for each debit entry a credit entry is required."

Effectively, therefore, in a firm's books the receiver is debited and the giver is credited; in the simplest form—for example, in the case of a cash transaction for the sale of goods—the cash account of the seller receives money and, therefore, the cash account is debited and the goods account is credited with the value of the sale. It is important to remember, however, that for each transaction there are really four entries made, that is, *two entries* in the seller's books as indicated above and *two entries* in the buyer's books. These "actions" form the whole basis of modern accounting systems.

To understand the basis of the trading, profit and loss account, and balance sheet, it is also important to remember that in bookkeeping the debit columns of accounts are always on the left of the vertically divided page and the credits are always on the right of the page.

A company does not necessarily want to know the profit or loss on each particular transaction; instead, it wants the data only over a given period of time, which is, of course, normally a period of one year. To enable this type of reporting to be achieved, a *nominal account,* called the *profit and loss account,* is utilized. At the end of the predetermined period, the *gross profit*— that is, the excess of the amount charged for the sale of goods or services over that paid for the goods or for providing the services—is transferred from the trading account to the credit side of the profit and loss account.

Accordingly, the profit and loss account will have, on the right-hand side (that is, the credit side of the account), the gross profit on trading, together with any other income or gains, whereas the left-hand side of the profit and loss account will show expenses together with any losses, including a gross loss on trading, if such has occurred. The balance—that is, the difference between the totals of these two columns in the profit and loss account—will represent the *net profit or loss for the period of the account.* If the total of the credit side is greater than the total of the debit side, a net profit results, whereas if the total of the debit side is greater than that of the credit side, a net loss results.

To "balance" the two columns of the profit and loss account in the case where a net profit has been made, a balance entry is made on the credit side of the capital account, as the value of the capital account has increased. Alternatively, if a net loss has occurred, a balance entry is made on the credit side of the profit and loss account and a similar entry is made on the debit side of the capital account, since the latter has, effectively, decreased in value.

As was pointed out before, a profit and loss account covers a given period of time, normally one year, and is, therefore, referred to as the *Profit and Loss Account for the Year Ended* 31 *December* 1992, for example.

However, with regard to the balance sheet, a major point to bear in mind is that whereas the profit and loss account is for a given period of time, normally twelve months, the balance sheet is drawn up at a particular date and should bear the words "Balance Sheet as of 31 December 1992," for example. The balance sheet is normally either divided into left- and right-hand columns, with one side showing the *liabilities,* including the capital account balance and the other side showing the *assets.* Alternatively, it may be set out in a "vertical" manner, with the assets set out first and totaled and the liabilities set out next. It is also important to remember that the *balance sheet is, in effect, only a statement.* It is not an account and is not, therefore, part of the actual double-entry system, as no transfers are made to or from the balance sheet.

These, then, are the major basic principles that must be understood fully before a proper appreciation of a set of accounts is possible.

The main role of the trading account is to determine the gross profit (or loss) for the period under consideration. However, if the position in the trading account of various items is standardized, this account can also be used for the purposes of comparing one year with another. In the simplest "trading" form, the trading account shows, on the debit side, the stocks at the commencement of the period, the cost of purchases made during the period, and other costs directly involved in placing the product in a marketable condition. On the credit side of the trading account is shown income from sales or, in the case of a nonmanufacturing organization, income from services or facilities provided, together with the stocks at the end of the period.

The function of the profit and loss account is to determine the *net profit (or loss)* arising out of the trading period. This account is credited with the gross profit from the trading account or debited with the gross loss from the trading account. On the debit side of the profit and loss account will therefore be gross loss, establishment costs such as rates, rent, heating, and electricity, administration costs such as salaries, wages, fees, and commissions, and other expenses, including finance costs. On the credit side of the profit and loss account will be shown any gross profit from the trading account and all income, such as rents and income from services provided.

Whereas the profit and loss account gives a historical view of the business for a given period of time, the role of the balance sheet is, as was pointed out, to give a statement of the financial position at a particular date. The balance sheet also allows comparisons to be made between the state of the business at the end of various accounting periods. The entries on the balance sheet in the "classic" presentation are, on the right-hand, or asset, side of the balance sheet, goodwill, land and premises, plant, fixtures and fittings, stock, debtors, and cash; on the left-hand, or liability, side of the balance sheet, entries are capital and long-term and current liabilities, such as creditors.

These points describe, in a somewhat simplified manner, the roles of the trading account, profit and loss account, and balance sheet, but the principles set out are those effectively used in practice. Of course, a considerable number of other aspects must be taken into account, one of the most important being the question of provision for the depreciation of assets.

Depreciation is the diminishing value of an asset over a period of time, and in each financial period, depreciation is an expense that must be provided for in the profit and loss account. A number of methods may be used to depreciate assets; one is by determining the number of years over which the asset is to be depreciated and dividing the capital cost into equal amounts of depreciation for each year. This is known as the *straight-line method.* Another method frequently used is the *reducing balance method,* where a fixed percentage of the book value of the asset is used. This latter system results, of course, in larger charges for depreciation in the early years of the asset than in later years. However, maintenance costs might be expected to be lower in the early years of the asset than in later years, and the argument frequently used in the defense of this system is that net costs tend to equalize over the period of depreciation.

1.5 CONSOLIDATED PROFIT AND LOSS
STATEMENTS: U.K. EXAMPLES

The exact form of the *profit and loss account* or the *statement of revenue or expenses* varies among countries and also varies among airports in the same country. In the postwar period 1945–1985, most airports around the world were entirely in public or quasi-public ownership. Accounting procedures, therefore, reflected public-accounting procedures, where the concepts of cost centers and profit centers had significantly less meaning than in the private sector and where accounting procedures designed to provide information about such centers is inappropriate. The precise form of the profit and loss statement will depend on a number of factors:

1. Whether the airport has a liability for corporate taxation or its equivalent
2. Whether depreciation on fixed assets is to be charged as an expense
3. Whether the airport is a privately owned company and there is the expectation of dividend payments to shareholders

In the United Kingdom, all airports of significant size were *privatized* in the late 1980s under a government policy of denationalizing central and local government operations. Tables 1–2, 1–3, and 1–4 show the same profit and loss account in the form in which it could appear either prior to privatization (Table 1–2), after privatization using the old local-authority form of expenditure accounting (Table 1–3), and, finally, after privatization using an accounting system that is more amenable to cost-center accounting and profit-center accounting (Table 1–4).

In the first case, Table 1–2 shows the profit and loss account of an airport operating as a department of a local authority. No depreciation is included in the accounts, and the operation has no liability to pay corporation tax. Fixed assets are constructed with direct grants to the airport from central and local government funding, and the largest portion of surpluses generated are returned directly to the local government. The form of accounting used in this table reflects the form of accounting used in local government.

Table 1–3 shows a profit and loss account that might have been produced

TABLE 1–2. Example of a Profit and Loss Account for a Publicly (Local Authority) Owned Airport in the United Kingdom

	× 1,000	
Revenues		
Operational Revenues		
Traffic: Fees and Charges		
Landing fees	$ 2,236	
Navigational services	2,320	
Passenger load supplement	4,814	
Apron services	828	
Aircraft housing and parking fees	177	
Other operational revenue including government security grant	1,024	
	$11,399	
Commercial Activities		
Aircraft fueling	$ 200	
Car parking	1,220	
Car hire	220	
Catering	134	
Flight catering	150	
Duty-free shop	900	
Bonded store	56	
Cargo terminal	220	
Industrial estate	200	
Other ancillary services	66	
Rents, airlines, and other airport tenants	950	
	$ 4,316	
Total operational income		$15,715
Nonoperational Revenues		
Income from securities	$ 320	
Interest	22	
Total Nonoperational Income		$ 342
Total Income		16,057

for the same year if the airport had been operating as a private company. In this case, depreciation would be charged, there would be a tax liability, and the decision would have to be made as to whether or not a dividend would be paid to shareholders. The general form of accounting for expenditures conforms largely to that shown in Table 1–2, which is common for public authorities. In this form of accounting, variously called the *subjective analysis* or *financial accounting procedure,* expenditures are related to types of expenditure rather than to the areas in which these items occur.

TABLE 1–2. *(Continued)*

Expenditures	× 1,000	
Operational Expenditures		
Salaries and wages, social security, pensions	$ 5,222	
Premises, airfield, repairs, and maintenance	2,254	
Supplies and services	770	
Transport and plant	361	
Administration overhead expenses	1,088	
Contribution to aviation security fund	910	
Total Operational Expenditure	$10,605	
Nonoperational Expenditures		
Fees	$ 102	
Total Nonoperational Expenditure	$ 102	
Total Expenditure		$10,707
Surplus on activities		$ 5,350
Surplus returned to local authority		$ 4,000
Retained surplus		$ 1,350

The form of reporting shown in the expenditure section of Table 1–4 groups expenditure by source or location in the airport, more closely reflecting the activities of cost or profit centers. This is known as the *objective analysis* or *management accounting* approach.

1.6 CONSOLIDATED PROFIT AND LOSS STATEMENTS: U.S. EXAMPLES

In the United States, airports are overwhelmingly owned by local or state governments or by public authorities that are creations of governments at these levels. Such airports are free to borrow funds in the open market by the mechanism of revenue bonding, subject to authorization by the appropriate level of government. It is, therefore, unlikely that privatization in its present form, which has become popular within Britain and its former Dominions and dependencies, will spread widely within the United States. Within the British system, public borrowing secured only by future incomes is not legal. Publicly owned airports must, therefore, secure capital funds for infrastructural expansion by local-authority assets within the limits of public-sector borrowing set

TABLE 1–3. Example of a Profit and Loss Account for a Privately Operated Airport in the United Kingdom (Subjective Analysis or Financial Accounting Method)

	× 1,000	
Revenues		
Operational Revenues		
Traffic: Fees and Charges		
Landing fees	$ 2,236	
Navigational services	2,320	
Passenger load supplement	4,814	
Apron services	828	
Aircraft housing and parking fees	177	
Other operational revenue including government security grant	1,024	
	$11,399	
Commercial Activities		
Aircraft fueling	$ 200	
Car parking	1,220	
Car hire	220	
Catering	134	
Flight catering	150	
Duty-free shop	900	
Bonded store	56	
Cargo terminal	220	
Industrial estate	200	
Other ancillary services	66	
Rents, airlines, and other airport tenants	950	
	$ 4,316	
Total operational income		$15,715
Nonoperational Revenues		
Income from securities	$ 320	
Interest	22	
Total nonoperational Income		$ 342
Total Income		16,057

by government. In inflationary times, governments have set very strict public-sector borrowing limits, making difficult the acquisition by airports of the necessary expansion capital. This does not apply in the United States; therefore, the present widespread public ownership of commercial transport and general aviation airports is likely to continue much in its present form. Even though airports are generally publicly owned, their form of presenting profit and loss statements can vary as widely as those previously shown for British airports. This is demonstrated by Tables 1–5 and 1–6, which show the profit and loss statements for Memphis-Shelby County Airport in 1986 and the four-airport

TABLE 1–3. *(Continued)*

	× 1,000
Expenditures	
Operational Expenditures	
Salaries and wages, social security, pensions	$ 5,222
Premises, airfield, repairs, and maintenance	2,254
Supplies and services	770
Transport and plant	361
Administration overhead expenses	1,088
Contribution to aviation security fund	910
Total Operational Expenditure	$10,605
Nonoperational Expenditures	
Fees	$ 102
Depreciation of tangible fixed assets	3,015
Amortization of goodwill	50
Total Nonoperational Expenditure	$ 3,167
Total Expenditure	$13,772
Profit on activities	$ 2,285
Taxation	618
Profit on activities after taxation	1,667
Profit attributable to shareholders	1,667
Dividends	—
Retained profit	$ 1,667

system of the city of Los Angeles, comprising Los Angeles International, Ontario International, Van Nuys, and Palmdale. Table 1–7 shows how the consolidated revenue and expense statements have been published in a more expanded form.

1.7 THE BALANCE SHEET: U.S. EXAMPLE

The forms of balance sheets differ only in detail between various airports. As stated in Section 1.4, the asset side of the balance sheet shows facilities, land, fixtures, goodwill, stock, debtors and cash, and so on. Liabilities include capital, long- and short-term liabilities, and the like. Viewing the balance sheet from year to year enables an analyst to assess trends in liquidity and debt. The annual report of an airport gives a statement of the assets and liabilities at the end of a particular trading year at an airport. Table 1–8 shows the consolidated balance sheet of a large regional airport in the United States.

TABLE 1–4. Example of a Profit and Loss Account for a Privately Operated Airport in the
United Kingdom (Objective Analysis or Management Accounting Method)

	× 1,000	
Revenues		
Operational Revenues		
Traffic: Fees and Charges		
Landing fees	$ 2,236	
Navigational services	2,320	
Passenger load supplement	4,814	
Apron services	828	
Aircraft housing and parking fees	177	
Other operational revenue including government security grant	1,024	
	$11,399	
Commercial Activities		
Aircraft fueling	$ 200	
Car parking	1,220	
Car hire	220	
Catering	134	
Flight catering	150	
Duty-free shop	900	
Bonded store	56	
Cargo terminal	220	
Industrial estate	200	
Other ancillary services	66	
Rents, airlines, and other airport tenants	950	
	$ 4,316	
Total operational income		$15,715
Nonoperational Revenues		
Income from securities	$ 320	
Interest	22	
Total nonoperational Income		$ 342
Total Income		$16,057

TABLE 1–4. *(Continued)*

	× 1,000
Expenditures	
Operational Expenditures	
Terminal building	$ 2,217
Ground transportation	501
Airfield and navigational services	5,209
General administration	572
Security, including contribution to aviation security fund	1,477
General maintenance	271
Other aviation areas	151
Other	207
Total Operational Expenditure	$10,605
Nonoperational Expenditures	
Fees	$ 102
Depreciation of tangible fixed assets	3,015
Amortization of goodwill	50
Total Nonoperational Expenditure	$ 3,167
Total Expenditure	$13,772
Profit on activities before taxation	$ 2,285
Taxation	618
Profit on activities after taxation	1,667
Profit attributable to shareholders	1,667
Dividends	—
Retained profit	$ 1,667

TABLE 1–5. Consolidated Profit and Loss Account
          Memphis-Shelby County Airport

Statements of Revenues and Expenses Year Ended June 30	1986
Operating Revenues	
Terminal building	$ 4,404,837
Ground transportation	6,133,935
Airfield	6,528,108
Other aviation areas	4,147,133
Industrial park	100,391
Other nonaviation	546,355
Total Operating Revenues	$ 21,860,759
Operating Expenses	
Terminal building	$ 5,066,453
Ground transportation	1,109,023
Airfield	2,085,413
General administration	1,847,534
Security	869,905
General maintenance	622,403
Other aviation areas	126,339
Other	16,074
Total Operating Expenses	$ 11,743,144
Net Operating Income	$ 10,117,615
Nonoperating Income (Expense): Interest expense	
Special facilities revenue bonds	$(21,110,758)
General obligation bonds	(2,339,291)
General revenue bonds	(1,996,121)
Other	(1,120)
Total Interest Expense	$(25,447,290)
Interest Income	
Net investment in financing lease	$ 21,110,758
Other	759,473
Total Interest Income	$ 21,870,231
Total Nonoperating Expense	$ (3,577,059)
Net Revenues Before Depreciation	$ 6,540,556
Depreciation	5,069,947
Revenues Over Expenses	$ 1,470,609

TABLE 1–6. Consolidated Profit and Loss Account
City of Los Angeles Airport System

City of Los Angeles
Department of Airports
Operating Statement by Airport
For the Year Ended June 30, 1989
(Dollars in Thousands)

	Los Angeles International Airport	Ontario International Airport	Van Nuys Airport	Palmdale Regional Airport	Total
Operating Revenue					
Aviation revenue	$ 77,089	$ 8,827	$5,050	$ 496	$ 91,462
Concession revenue	93,600	9,544	2,721	0	105,865
Airport sales and services	1,634	33	9	0	1,676
Miscellaneous	829	46	1	2	878
Total Operating Revenue	173,152	18,450	7,781	498	199,881

(continued)

TABLE 1–6. *(Continued)*

City of Los Angeles
Department of Airports
Operating Statement by Airport
For the Year Ended June 30, 1989
(Dollars in Thousands)

	Los Angeles International Airport	Ontario International Airport	Van Nuys Airport	Palmdale Regional Airport	Total
Operating Expense					
Maintenance and repairs	58,830	5,070	2,041	140	66,081
Administrative expense	31,129	6,132	1,863	191	39,315
General operating expenses	16,875	4,690	2,131	835	24,531
Cost of sales and services	1,957	5	6	0	1,968
Depreciation	26,824	2,009	474	87	29,394
Depreciation, grants and other aid	1,588	707	5	0	2,300
Total Operating Expense	137,203	18,613	6,520	1,253	163,589
Income (loss) from Operations	35,949	(163)	1,261	(755)	36,292
Nonoperating Revenue					
Liquidated damages	35	1	0	0	36
Interest income	21,451	1,327	0	0	22,778
Gain on condemnation of land	39,048	0	0	0	39,048
Income (loss) before Other Deductions	96,483	1,165	1,261	(755)	98,154
Other Deductions					
Interest expense	36,945	2,059	29	1,433	40,466
Loss on extinguishment of debt	8,496	637	0	0	9,133
Net Income (loss) for the Year	$ 51,042	$ (1,531)	$1,232	$(2,188)	$ 48,555

TABLE 1–7. Revenue and Expense Statement
Los Angeles International Airport

Department of Airports
Operating Revenue
for the Year Ended June 30, 1989
(Dollars in Thousands)
Los Angeles International Airport

	1988–1989	
Aviation Revenues		
Flight Fees		
Scheduled passengers	$26,287	
Scheduled cargo	1,428	
Nonscheduled	674	28,389
Building Rentals		
Passenger terminal	23,752	
Air freight terminal	3,490	
Shop, storage and other	1,443	28,685
Lease of Ground Areas		
Airline	12,191	
Manufacturing and service	1,311	
Transportation	1,573	
Governmental	1,080	
Others	2,405	18,560
Other Aviation Revenues		
Fuel fee	601	
Miscellaneous	854	1,455
Total Aviation Revenues		$ 77,089
Concession Revenues		
Terminal Sales		
Auto park	39,437	
Food and beverage	7,823	
Gift and newsstand	9,153	
Duty-free sales	12,628	
Insurance	101	
Telephone and telegraph	1,047	
Parcel locker and other	1,256	$ 71,445
Land Transportation		
Rent-a-car	19,127	
Bus and limousine	2,433	
Hotel-motel service	595	22,155
Total Concession Revenue		$ 93,600
Airport sales and Services		
Water	196	
Electricity	700	
Accommodation sales	100	
Airfield bus	578	
Telephone	60	$ 1,634
Other Operating Revenues		829
Total Operating Revenues, Los Angeles International Airport		$173,152

(continued)

TABLE 1–7. *(Continued)*

Department of Airports
Operating Revenue
for the Year Ended June 30, 1989
(Dollars in Thousands)
Los Angeles International Airport

	1988–1989
Maintenance and Repair of Field Areas	
Security, field area	$ 6,591
Runways, taxiways, aprons	2,984
Concourses, other	578
Total Maintenance and Repair of Field Areas	10,153
Maintenance and Repair of Public Areas	
Security, public area	8,796
Parking lot	7,039
Roads, streets and walks	2,087
Landscaping	1,347
Total Maintenance and Repair of Public Areas	19,269
Maintenance and Repair of Buildings	
West imperial terminal building	200
Inflatable structure 1—Customs	1
Inflatable structure 2—Bag claim	8
Inflatable structure 3—tktg 3	1
Terminal building 1	2,830
Terminal building 2	1,051
Terminal building 3	1,466
Terminal building 4	1,448
Terminal building 5	1,332
Terminal building 6	1,772
Terminal building 7	1,838
Terminal building 8	1,023
Tom Bradley International Terminal	4,754
Theme complex	255
Administration and control tower	677
Shops, storage, and miscellaneous buildings	7,845
Air freight buildings	728
Total Maintenance and Repair of Buildings	27,229
Maintenance and Repair of Equipment	
Tractors and other heavy-duty equipment	989
Autos and trucks	636
Other equipment	554
Total Maintenance and Repair of Equipment	2,179
Cost of Sales and Services	
Water sales	590
Electricity	443
Accommodations	716
Airfield bus operations	208
Miscellaneous	0
Total Cost of Sales and Services	1,957

TABLE 1–7. *(Continued)*

Department of Airports
Operating Revenue
for the Year Ended June 30, 1989
(Dollars in Thousands)
Los Angeles International Airport

	1988–1989
General Operating Expense	
Field operations	134
Insurance	1,294
Bus operating expense	10,192
Miscellaneous	2,888
Loss on disposal of assets	2,367
Total General Operating Expense	16,875
Administration Expense	
Management services	16,149
Expansion and development	3,246
Advertising and publicity	825
Airport tours	179
Employee benefits:	
Workers' compensation	916
Vacations	2,979
Sick time	2,108
Bereavement	55
Jury duty	213
Holidays	2,237
Military leave	21
Miscellaneous	2,201
Total Administrative Expense	31,129
Total Operating Expense (Excluding Depreciation)	
LOS ANGELES INTERNATIONAL AIRPORT	$108,791

TABLE 1–8. Consolidated Balance Sheet for San Francisco International Airport as of
December 31, 1988

	Year Ended June 30, 1988
Assets	
Current Assets	
Cash and investments held in City Treasury—	
Airport Operating Fund	$167,419,775
Cash—Revolving Fund	20,000
Accounts receivable (less allowance for doubtful accounts:	
1988, $1,152,134; 1987, $1,206,573)	9,527,476
Accrued interest	
City and County of San Francisco	2,876,134
Other	442,600
Federal grants receivable	967,620
Other	429,878
Total Current Assets	181,583,483
Restricted Assets	
For capital outlay	
Cash and investments in City Treasury	82,412,208
Accrued interest	4,039,420
For revenue bond reserves	
Investment with Trustee	41,905,192
Other	92,023
Total Restricted Assets	128,448,843
Property, Plant, and Equipment—Net	530,614,705
Deferred Financing Costs	807,708
Total	$841,554,739
Liabilities and Equity	
Current Liabilities	
Current maturities of bonded debt	$ 9,250,000
Accounts payable	2,921,514
Claims payable	3,402,716
Accrued bond interest payable	5,632,806
Accrued payroll and related costs	8,989,170
Payable to City and County of San Francisco	1,525,018
Rent collected in advance and other	2,529,611
Aviation revenue collected in advance	23,461,717
Total Current Liabilities	57,712,552
Payable from Restricted Assets	
Contractor retentions payable	294,764
Payable to contractors and other	1,336,427
Total	1,631,191
Bonded Debt—Less current maturities	410,159,846

TABLE 1–8. *(Continued)*

Assets	Year Ended June 30, 1988
Equity	
Contributed capital	105,632,584
Retained earnings	266,418,566
Total Equity	372,051,150
Total	$841,554,739

1.8 SUMMARY

Because of the nature of accounting practices, which vary greatly among countries, and because the sources of finance also vary greatly according to national jurisdiction and airport size, it is not possible to lay down definitive rules on the methods of reporting airport financial structure. Neither is it possible to draw up firm methods of assessment. In this chapter, an attempt has been made to give the general guidelines for interpreting the financial structure of airports based on the generally accepted principles of financial reporting.

REFERENCES

1. Ashford, N.J., H.P.M. Stanton, and C.A. Moore. *Airport Operations.* London: Pitman Longman Press, 1991.
2. Bauml, S. "Airport Revenue and Expenses," in *Airport Economic Planning,* edited by G.P. Howard. Cambridge, Mass.: M.I.T. Press, 1974.

2

Financing U.S. Airports

Harry Kluckhohn

President, Harold B. Kluckhohn and Associates

2.1 OVERVIEW

Within the United States, airports providing air-carrier service are public-sector enterprises. That is, they are owned and operated as governmental facilities. The level of government involved differs from airport to airport. For some airports, the governmental entity is the city in which the airport is located. For others, the entity is the county; in still other jurisdictions, the governmental entity is the state. In some circumstances, the sponsorship by a single city, county, or state does not reflect the nature of the passengers using the airport and an alternative form of sponsorship is employed. This is the airport authority, a quasi-governmental entity formed for the sole purpose of operating airport facilities or airport properties in combination with other transportation facilities. Regardless of the form of sponsorship, the premise remains that transport airports are largely publicly owned.

The topic of bonds is discussed subsequently, but in the context of airport sponsorship, one point bears mentioning here. Given the fact that U.S. airports are governmentally owned, U.S. federal tax legislation grants favorable treatment to bonds issued to finance airport-improvement programs. For federal income tax purposes, the interest income provided to investors from airport bonds is not calculated as an item of gross income. Airport bonds are thus said to be *tax-exempt* bonds. The effect of this tax-exempt status is that, in comparison with a taxable investment alternative, investors can obtain an equivalent after-tax yield with a lower actual interest rate on an airport bond. This beneficial tax treatment enables airports to borrow at lower cost than would be possible if they were issuing taxable bonds. While the cost differential varies from time to time, it is reasonable to assume that the savings associated with tax-exempt financing can often be as great as two full percentage points in interest rate. That is, if an airport could issue taxable bonds bearing an interest rate of 9 percent, for example, that same airport could issue bonds at a tax-exempt rate of approximately 7 percent.

Tax regulations in the United States are extremely complex, and certain airport bonds are treated slightly differently from this illustration. The fact remains, however, that the tax treatment that airports enjoy because of their governmental ownership is favorable.

Because they are publicly owned, airports operate in a business framework that must be responsive to the needs of the enterprise while complying with all the requirements governing publicly owned properties. Airports must strive to satisfy all the economic objectives of a continuing enterprise, but they must do so in an environment that tends to preclude much of the flexibility that would be available for a private business.

In general, airports operate within a business framework defined by the charter of the governmental sponsor, the agreements existing with the major users, and the contracts with their creditors. An airport's ability to finance itself is, therefore, dependent upon all these factors.

An airport is not likely to be able to do anything to alter the terms of the charter of the governmental sponsor, but it does have some latitude in determining the terms and conditions of its agreements with its major users and its creditors.

2.2 AIRLINE AGREEMENTS

In general, airline agreements take one of two forms: *leases,* which govern the occupancy of land and buildings, and *use agreements,* which govern the use of airfield facilities. Often, these agreements are combined into a single document called a *use and lease agreement.* For the purposes of this book, the term *agreement* is used to refer to any of these documents.

From a financial point of view, the airline rate-making philosophy is a key feature of the agreement. The rate-making philosophy assigns the proprietary risk of the airport's operation to either the airport or the airlines. The philosophy that leaves the airport at risk is called the *compensatory* approach to rate-making. The philosophy that leaves the airlines at risk is called the *residual cost* approach. The risk involved is that there will be insufficient revenue available from all airport sources to satisfy all the needs of the airport.

Under the compensatory approach, the airport establishes rates and charges (for the use and occupancy of airport facilities) that are based on the recovery of total cost. For example, with regard to a passenger terminal, a tenant at a compensatory airport will pay a rental rate that will recover the cost of the facilities occupied. The cost associated with "public" space is the responsibility of the airport, to be recovered from revenues from other sources.

Under the residual cost approach, the airport establishes rates and charges that are based on the recovery of the *net requirement* of the airport. Again, using the example of a passenger terminal, a tenant at a residual cost airport will pay a rental rate that will recover the net requirement of the airport. The rental rate is calculated to include all the costs of the terminal (without regard to the users) and to offset the total cost with all relevant revenue from other than rentals.

The two approaches can be combined at a single airport. For example, it would be possible for an airport to establish a compensatory rental rate for terminal facilities and a residual cost landing fee rate.

Under the compensatory approach, the revenue potential of the airport is limited to the amount that might reasonably be expected to be generated from all activities given the volume of passenger traffic using the airport. In years when traffic is strong, the total revenue will reflect that strength. However, in years when traffic is weak, the total revenue will also reflect that weakness.

Under the residual cost approach, the revenue potential of the airport is limited to that amount required to satisfy all the airport's obligations. The total revenue is not dependent upon the volume of traffic at the airport. In years when traffic is strong, the revenue to the airport derived from nonairline sources will be relatively high, and the revenue from airlines will be relatively low. Conversely, in years when traffic is weak, nonairline revenue will be relatively high. The total will not vary, but the distribution between airline and nonairline sources will fluctuate.

Lewis (1) has identified the evolution of two principal methods of residual cost accounting:

1. *Total airport residual method.* Using this approach, the difference between total annual cost and all other anticipated revenues is balanced in the airport's budget by the landing fee charges. Depending on the extent to which airline terminal rentals and concessions (restaurants, bars, shops, parking, etc.) make up the revenue structure, landing fees will vary greatly. Landing fees will be low in years when nonairline revenues are high. In a buoyant commercial climate, several facilities in the United States have approached the declaration of a negative landing fee.

2. *Cost-center residual method.* Rather than the overall aggregating approach that was identified in the previous method, this approach disaggregates costs and revenues to cost centers. For the individual cost center, the total annual cost in terms of capital, depreciation, operation, maintenance and administration is computed or anticipated. Against these the concessionary and nonairline-related revenues are offset, and a residual is computed from the costs and revenues for each cost center. The rates charged to the airlines for their facilities are determined from these residuals. Surplus

revenues and deficits from any cost center are charged to the airlines' aggregate account, which is used for computing airline landing fees and other charges for the following year. Using this approach, the risk and possible profits of the nonaeronautical cost centers are preserved for the airport operator, whereas a break-even approach to the operation of terminals and the airside operational area is used. In this way, the commercial opportunities of nonairline-related facilities, buildings, grounds, parking, and the like can be reserved for the airport.

The difference between the compensatory and residual approaches is best illustrated by a simple example. Table 2–1 shows how applying the two methods would result in two different landing and terminal rental rates with the same inputs.

The approach to rate-making is important in financing airport improvements because it has such a major effect on the revenue generation at the airport. In effect, the airport's debt capacity is determined by its ability to generate revenue consistently over the years in an amount sufficient to satisfy all the airport's obligations.

Agreements are not necessary to enable an airport to finance improvements. In the absence of an agreement, an airport can demonstrate revenue-generating potential based on its historic operating results. For airports where agreements are in effect, they are important because they help to identify the airport's revenue-generating potential from the context of the documents. Further, they can incorporate other provisions that either facilitate or inhibit the financing process.

2.3 BASIC FINANCING APPROACH

The financing of airport-improvement programs can be viewed as a systematic stream of events that begins with the perceived need for a particular capital project and ends with the acquisition of the funds required to complete the project and place it in service. To a certain extent, the approach is an iterative process, in that the results of one step can cause the airport to revisit the results of previous steps and make revisions in the program.

In a simplified sense, the following steps define the process for a typical airport capital improvement program. Steps may vary from airport to airport and from program to program, but to some extent, each is required before financing can be obtained for a capital project.

1. Determination that a need exists
2. Development of a *pro forma* capital plan
3. Preliminary design work

TABLE 2–1. Illustrative Calculation of Terminal Rental Rates and Landing Fees for Airlines under Residual Cost and Compensatory Approaches (In Dollars Except as Specified)[a]

Requirement	Residual Cost		Compensatory	
	Terminal	Airfield	Terminal	Airfield
Maintenance, operations, and administration	40,000	40,000	40,000	40,000
Debt service	40,000	20,000	40,000	20,000
Debt service coverage	10,000	5,000	10,000	5,000
Deposits to special funds	5,000	20,000	5,000	20,000
Other	5,000	15,000	5,000	15,000
Total requirement	100,000	100,000	100,000	100,000
Cost center revenue from nonairline sources (−)	−50,000	−50,000	N/A	N/A
Airline share (in percent)	N/A	N/A	65	75
Residual cost	50,000	50,000	N/A	N/A
Activity level	6,500 square feet	100,000 pounds gross landing weight	6,500 square feet	100,000 pounds gross landing weight
Rental rate (per square foot)	7.69	N/A	10.00	N/A
Landing fee rate (per 1,000 lb gross landing weight)	N/A	0.50	N/A	0.75

[a] This is not a comparison of actual rate calculations but a simplified illustration. Rates are not necessarily higher under either approach but differ according to the volume of traffic, amount of debt, and other factors. N/A = not applicable.

Source: From (1), which is adapted from Kluckhohn, "Security for Tax-Exempt Airport Revenue Bonds" (2).

4. Preparation of initial cost estimates
5. Assessment of the availability of fund sources:
   a. Airport surplus funds
   b. Governmental grants-in-aid
6. Derivation of the requirements for borrowed funds
7. Estimation of the cost of borrowed funds
8. Analysis of the impact of the program on the rates and charges of the tenants
9. Assessment of overall financial feasibility
10. Commencement of the financing process

Depending upon the nature of the relationship among the airlines and the airport, the airlines will become involved in the review of the capital improvement program as it proceeds. This involvement can range from the truly minimal (in the case where the airlines are only notified that the airport is undertaking the improvement program) to a substantial role, in which the approval of the airlines must be obtained in order to proceed with the program.

The circumstances that call for the approval of the airlines prior to the commencement of the program arise when the agreement with the airlines includes a provision called a *majority-in-interest,* or MII, clause. Strictly speaking, this clause provides that an airport may include the costs associated with capital improvement projects in the calculation of rates and charges (enabling the airport to recover the costs of the program through airline rentals and landing fees) only if the improvement projects have been approved by a majority-in-interest of the airlines that are a party to the agreement. If the projects have not received MII approval, then the airport may not, pursuant to the terms of the agreement, charge the airlines for any of the costs. In essence, this type of provision precludes an airport from proceeding with a project without approval, because the airport may not have funds available to pay for the project without the support of the airlines.

2.4 SOURCES OF FUNDS

In general, airports have access to several sources of capital: airport surplus (retained earnings generated in prior periods), governmental grants-in-aid, borrowed funds, third-party development, or private sources.

Airport Surplus

Airports can accumulate retained earnings over the course of time. From year to year, the excess of revenues over expenses can be set aside and reserved for any number of purposes, including the financing of capital improvements. In general, the amount of money that can be generated from retained earnings will be relatively small in relation to the overall requirements of an airport capital improvement program. Either because the level of traffic at the airport is insufficient to generate substantial surplus revenues (as might be in the case of a compensatory airport) or because the amount or the application of surplus revenues is limited by the terms of an agreement (as might be in the case of a residual cost airport), surplus revenue tends to fund a somewhat limited share of the capital requirements at most airports.

Grants-in-Aid

Governmental grants-in-aid can fund a major portion of an airport's capital improvement program. The funds are made available from the proceeds of a tax that passengers pay when purchasing a ticket. This money is accumulated in a fund known as the *Airport and Airway Trust Fund*. Depending on the specifics of the legislation governing the grant program at a given point in time, grant funding can provide for as much as 90 percent of the capital cost of certain projects. The ultimate share of project cost eligible for grant funding is related to the nature of the project and the size of the airport applying for the grant. See Table 2–2.

Generally, grant funding is restricted to projects that are undertaken for safety, operational efficiency, environmental reasons, or other public purposes. Grant funding for projects that can generate revenue directly or that benefit "private" users is generally not available.

TABLE 2–2. Federal Share (Percentage of Project Costs)

Type of Project	Type of Airport	
	Large Primary Airports[a]	All Other Airports[b]
Individual airport planning[c]	75	90
Airport development[c]	75	90
Noise compatibility programs[c]	80	90
Terminal development	75	75[d]

[a] Large primary airports are primary airports that enplane 0.25 percent or more of the total annual U.S. enplanements. Approximately seventy airports qualify as large primary airports.

[b] This column includes all public-use airports not included in the first column.

[c] There may be an upward adjustment to these rates in Alaska, Arizona, California, Nevada, New Mexico, Oregon, Utah, and Washington due to the high percentage of federally owned lands in those states.

[d] This rate is applicable only to commercial service airports. The remaining airports are not eligible for terminal development.

Currently, grant funding can take a number of forms. Each year, an airport is entitled to an amount of money that is based on its level of enplanements. This amount is the airport's *enplanement entitlement,* and, if the airport is undertaking eligible projects, this enplanement entitlement will be available to fund a portion of the projects. In addition to its enplanement entitlement, an airport may apply for *discretionary* grants to fund portions of the costs of eligible projects. These funds are available for application at the discretion of the federal government, based on the relative priorities of the projects in question.

Different grant programs exist for special purposes, such as for studies related to environmental matters or the purchase of land. The amount of funds available for an airport under these programs will depend on a number of factors, all of which will be outlined in the specific legislation that enables the particular special grant program. Grants-in-aid often have limitations on use. For example, under the Airport Improvement Program, runways and taxiways are eligible for grants-in-aid but parking garages and cargo terminals are not.

Debt

Airport debt generally takes the form of a bond. A bond is a contract between two parties that specifies the manner for the repayment of obligations. Typically, the repayment is made through periodic scheduled interest payments (usually semiannually) over the life of the bond, with the principal amount due at maturity. The life of the bond is often tied to the length of the most important airport-use agreements. Airport bonds can be categorized by the type of underlying security that provides for the repayment of the debt.

A bond is generally considered to be long-term, or *permanent,* financing in that the term of the bond (the time from the issuance to the final maturity) tends to match the economic life of the facilities being financed. Additionally, bond issues are designed to provide that a portion of the principal amount of the debt is amortized systematically in each year that the bonds are outstanding.

General Obligation Bonds

A bond that is secured by the full faith and credit (and taxing power) of the entity issuing the bond is a *general obligation bond.* The issuing entity pledges that it will pay interest and principal as scheduled over the life of the bond, and this pledge is unconditional. It is the responsibility of the issuer to provide this payment from whatever sources of money are available. The purchaser of the bond (the bondholder) is at risk to the extent that the issuer will be unable to provide sufficient funds, from all sources, to make the scheduled payments.

General obligation bonds are typically issued for smaller airports because the security provided by the pledge of the full faith and credit of the issuer is regarded as being most appropriate in view of the revenue base of a smaller airport. It must be recognized that if general obligation bonds are to be used for airport development, the airport must compete with other community interests (e.g., sewers, lighting, etc.) for the limited amount of funding available within community debt limits.

Airport Revenue Bonds

A bond that is secured by a pledge of airport revenues and not by the full faith and credit (and taxing power) of the issuer is a *revenue bond*. If the bond is secured by a pledge of all airport revenue, the bond is called a *general airport revenue bond*. The issuing entity pledges that it will pay interest and principal as scheduled over the life of the bond, to the extent that sufficient airport revenue is available to make such payments. The issuer is not obliged to provide any other source of money to make the scheduled payments, and in this sense, the obligation is a *limited* obligation—i.e., it is limited to the availability of sufficient airport revenue. The bondholder is at risk to the extent that airport revenue will be insufficient to satisfy the obligations.

Airport revenue bonds are issued to finance improvement programs at medium and larger airports. The revenue base of such airports is sufficiently large and broad-based to render the pledge of airport revenue as adequate in terms of security. The pledge of the full faith and credit of the issuer is, therefore, not required as an additional inducement for bondholders to purchase.

Special-Facility Revenue Bonds

A bond that is secured by a single or limited source of revenue from a special facility and neither by the full faith and credit (and taxing power) of the issuer nor by a pledge of all airport revenue is called a *special-facility revenue bond*. The issuing entity pledges that it will pay interest and principal as scheduled over the life of the bond, to the extent that sufficient revenue from that single or limited source is available. This is another type of limited-obligation bond. The bondholder is therefore at risk to the extent that "special revenue" will be insufficient to satisfy the obligations.

This type of bond is most often issued to finance a single-purpose facility, such as an aircraft maintenance facility or a unit terminal building, on behalf of a single airline tenant. The security for the bond is the stream of lease payments to be made by the airline for the use of the facility being financed.

"Double-Barrel" Bonds

There is a hybrid type of bond that historically appeared in airport financing for a period of time in the late 1960s and the early 1970s, but that no longer really plays a part in the financing of airport improvements. Such a bond is secured by a pledge of airport revenue and further backed by a pledge of the full faith and credit of the issuer. This pledge of the full faith and credit may apply directly to the payment of debt, or it may be restricted to the payment of maintenance and operating expenses. In essence, this type of bond is issued when the pledge of revenue is perceived to be insufficient security for the program. Some issuers, while fully intending that airport bonds be repaid from airport revenues, have issued general obligation bonds for airport purposes because, at the time of issuance, the public was willing to support the airport from their taxes (if the need should arise), and borrowing costs were thought to be lower if the bonds were secured by a general obligation pledge.

For a variety of reasons, principally because the pledge of airport revenue bonds has come to be recognized as a strong source of security and because the taxing power of many issuers has become a truly scarce resource, this type of bond is generally no longer issued for airport improvements. It bears mention here only because some airports have, in the past, financed major programs with this type of bond, and these bonds are still outstanding.

Other Debt

Airport capital improvement programs can be financed with other forms of debt. Notes, for example, are very similar to bonds, in that they pay interest over the life of the note and repay principal at maturity. Notes, however, are considered to be *temporary* financing, in that they tend to be of a relatively short maturity (in the order of one to five years), and they are typically issued contemplating redemption from the proceeds of a bond issue in the future.

Bonds and notes are typically issued to the general public, which comprises a number of market investor segments (discussed in Chapter 4) that actively purchase this type of investment. These segments are typically considered to constitute the public *bond market.*

Airports may also borrow from commercial lenders at terms that are set by the lender. This type of borrowing is relatively rare for airport capital improvement programs, however, because commercial loans are not typically available in amounts sufficient to fund entire improvement programs. This is partly because the maximum term to maturity available tends to be much shorter than that available in the bond market and partly because the interest cost of a bank loan is generally higher than that which would be available in the bond market.

Third-Party Development

In certain circumstances, it may be beneficial for an airport to employ third-party development in its capital improvement programs. Third-party development implies that some party, not related to the airport or to the users of the facility being developed, will create a facility on airport property. Once the facility is completed, the airport will assume the responsibilities of ownership and operation of the facility through some type of business transaction, probably a form of an installment sale or lease, often by a simple title reversion at an agreed date. The airport will then make periodic payments to the third-party developer from payments made by tenants or users of the facility to the airport.

This concept is worthy of note because it enables an airport to undertake a capital improvement project without providing any of the financing prior to the completion and beneficial occupancy of the facility. In cases where the economics of the circumstances demonstrate that third-party development is a cost-effective method of providing funds, it is likely that this form of financing for airport projects will become more prevalent.

Private Funds

Although not typically used for major airport improvement programs currently, it is possible that airports could avail themselves of private capital. This concept of using private capital for public enterprises is part of a concept that has come to be known as *privatization,* and it is likely to become more commonplace for improvement programs at certain airports.

Private funds differ from third-party development in that the private investor assumes an equity interest in the project being financed, where the third-party developer's interest in the project is fully assumed by the airport through the business transaction (e.g., the installment sale or the lease) when the facility is completed. The private investor remains involved in the business of operating the facility and extracts a return on its investment from the financial operations of the facility.

Currently there are significant obstacles in the United States in the path of privatization for airport projects. As airports are public enterprises, the responsibility for their operations rests with public entities and public officials. As such, governmental restrictions apply that make privatization an extremely cumbersome undertaking. Further, the economics of an airport dictate that the return on investment that a private third party might seek could be prohibitively expensive from the standpoint of the tenants and users of the airport and from the standpoint of the traveling public.

In any event, it can be expected that the experience of privatized airports in the United Kingdom will be under close scrutiny and that, to the extent that it can be demonstrated that privatized airports in the United States can be effectively controlled and economically operated, private funds will become a more prevalent source of capital for airport-improvement programs. The question of privatization and its potential for application to U.S. airports are discussed at length in Chapter 5.

Interest Income

Interest income (on unexpended fund balances) can be a major contributor of capital for airport-improvement programs. Interest income has the ultimate effect of reducing the amount of funds that will be required to be borrowed to support a construction program.

Prior to the mid-1980s, airports were able to invest unexpended funds at yields that were substantially greater than the cost of the funds invested. An airport, for example, might issue tax-exempt bonds at an interest cost of 7 percent and reinvest the proceeds of the issue in federal government securities, which, because of their taxable status, would be yielding as much as 9 percent or more. This interest rate differential (tax-exempt in comparison with taxable rates) is referred to as interest rate *arbitrage.* When the reinvestment yield exceeds the cost of the funds being reinvested, the arbitrage is said to be *positive,* and this was virtually always the prevailing circumstance in airport-improvement programs. The magnitude of the arbitrage (the rate differential) would vary over time, but the absolute effect was that airports would benefit from this positive arbitrage.

The positive arbitrage effect provided a strong incentive for airports to borrow in larger amounts and sooner than they might otherwise borrow for a capital improvement program, because arbitrage earnings were greater, the requirement for borrowed funds would be lower, and the overall cost of the program would be less.

In the mid-1980s, the U.S. federal tax code was amended to restrict the allowable reinvestment rate to the effective yield of the bonds in most circumstances. In short, after this change in the law, airports lost the advantage of positive arbitrage because the earnings rate on the reinvestment of funds was limited to the cost of the funds. Even though the contribution available from positive, or *excess,* arbitrage is no longer available, the interest earnings, limited to their cost, are still a major element of capital funds for airport-improvement programs.

2.5 USES OF FUNDS

In an airport-improvement program, financing can be obtained to cover all costs associated with the program. It is clear that capital can be raised for design, architectural, and engineering work and for construction costs. There are additional elements of capital improvement programs, however, and these may also be financed, the cost being amortized over the life of the facilities.

Interest During Construction

Funds must be available at the start of a construction program in order for work to proceed. The facility will be unable to produce revenue, however, until it is completed and occupied. Because the typical method for financing involves the issuance of bonds for at least a portion of the project, some provision must be made for the payment of interest on the bonds during the construction period.

The typical approach in the financing of airport-improvement programs involves the borrowing of the funds that will be needed for periodic interest payments throughout the construction period. This practice is called *capitalizing interest,* and it has the effect of increasing the total amount of funds that would be required to be borrowed. If, for a simplistic example, bonds were to be issued with an average interest rate of 7 percent and if the airport project in question were to require a two-year construction period, then the airport would be required to borrow sufficient funds to make interest payments for two years, in addition to the amount required to fund construction. Simplistically, the airport would be required to borrow approximately 14 percent more than if interest payments were not required. The costs associated with the additional borrowing are amortized, along with the construction costs, over the life of the bonds.

At first glance, it may appear that capitalizing interest is an expensive feature of airport-financing programs. It is true that longer construction periods can add substantially to the cost of a project, but it must be acknowledged that if there is no other way to provide for the payment of interest during the construction period, capitalizing interest is a cost-effective feature. If it is possible for an airport to provide for the payment of interest during a construction period from some other source of revenue (other than the revenue to be derived from the project under construction), the concept of capitalizing interest should be reviewed to determine if it is still a cost-effective approach.

Reserve Requirements

It is a convention in the issuance of airport revenue bonds that certain funds be set aside and held in reserve to provide for the payment of interest and principal on the bonds in the event that there should be a temporary shortfall in airport revenues. Most typically, the amount of this reserve is equal to the approximate debt service (the sum of interest and principal) requirements for one year. The establishment of a *debt service reserve* fund has come to be a standard security feature in the issuance of general airport revenue bonds, and it serves as an additional inducement to investors to purchase the bonds.

Although airports may provide for this reserve in any of a number of ways, it is common for the airports to fund the reserve from the proceeds of the bonds themselves. In the issuance of the bonds, the airport would include an amount that would be sufficient to satisfy this requirement as of the date that the bonds are sold. It is expected that the reserve will not be used for the payment of bonds, but that it will be maintained on deposit until the final maturity date— at which time it will be applied to the payment of the final debt service installment. In essence, it may be viewed as if the airport is borrowing the funds that will be required to make the final debt service installment.

As in the case of capitalized interest, it may appear that the borrowing of funds to establish a reserve fund is an expensive feature in airport revenue bond financing. For planning purposes, it may be considered that the provision of the reserve from the proceeds of the bonds will require the borrowing of an additional 10 percent over the amount that would otherwise be required to finance the program. But again, if the reserve is required and if the airport is unable to make other provisions for it, then the bond funding of the reserve is a cost-effective approach. With appropriate reinvestment of these funds, the cost of capitalized interest is largely self-financing.

It should be noted that some insurance companies offer a policy that can satisfy the reserve requirement for a number of airports. In deciding the appropriate approach to the reserve funding for these airports, the cost of the insurance policy should be compared to the cost of borrowing the amount required in order to determine which is the most economical approach to providing for the reserve.

Financing Costs

During the cost of the financing process, costs are incurred by both the issuer and the initial purchaser (the underwriters). It is normal practice that these costs are also funded from the proceeds of the bond issue, so these costs are also considered to be a "use of funds" in the process. As a general rule, the sum of all of these costs is approximately equal to 2 percent of the total proceeds of the issue.

Perhaps coincidentally, current U.S. federal tax legislation limits the amount of these costs that can be funded from the proceeds of the bonds to 2 percent of the issue. In order to maintain the tax-exempt status of the bonds, any financing costs in excess of 2 percent of the issue must be funded from some source other than bond proceeds. It is generally the responsibility of the issuer to provide for these costs (in excess of 2 percent of the proceeds) from airport operating funds.

Issuer's Costs

The issuer retains a number of outside experts to assist in the preparation of a bond issue. These experts and their roles in the process are discussed subsequently, but all the costs associated with their services are the responsibility of the issuer. In addition, the issuer incurs additional expenses in the course of the transaction, and to the extent that these costs can clearly be allocated to the financing transaction, they can be financed from the proceeds of the bonds.

Because these costs are associated with the issuance of bonds, they are generically referred to as *issuance costs,* and they are separate from the costs that are incurred by the underwriters in the transaction. In reviewing documentation for an airport financing, issuance costs are typically disclosed as a separate element of the transaction.

Underwriter's Costs

In the course of underwriting and distributing the bonds to the ultimate investors, underwriters incur costs that are also typically funded from the proceeds of the bonds. These costs include the commissions that are paid to the securities' sales personnel who are involved in the marketing of the bonds, the fees of legal counsel retained by the underwriters to assist in the process, and various other costs. As these costs are directly related to the issuance of the bonds, underwriters recover them in the determination of the price to be paid for the face value of the bonds.

Underwriters, as the initial purchasers of the bonds, pay a price to the issuer for the bonds. This price is *discounted* from the face value of the bonds. The underwriters calculate the sum of the costs incurred and express that sum as a percentage of the face value of the issue. This percentage is referred to as the *underwriting discount,* and it is deducted from the face value in determining the price to be paid for the issue. For example, if the sum of the costs were equivalent to 1.25 percent of the issue, then the underwriters would pay a price to the issuer of 98.75 percent of the face value of the issue.

The effect would be the same if the underwriters were to pay a price of 100 percent of the face value of the issue and charge the issuer an amount equal to 1.25 percent of that amount to cover the costs. Convention and practicality dictate, however, that the underwriters retain an amount sufficient to cover their costs and pay the net amount to the issuer. The amount actually paid to the issuer is thus referred to as the *net proceeds* of the issue.

Refunding

One other use of funds can occur in an airport financing. Airport bonds can be issued to refund prior airport obligations. In a refunding issue, new bonds are issued to repay outstanding bonds or notes for one of three reasons:

1. The prior issue is maturing, and at its initial issuance it was contemplated that the prior issue would be redeemed from the proceeds of a refunding issue. This is a common circumstance when notes are issued to finance a construction program.

2. The prior issue bears a high rate of interest, and interest rates prevailing in the market at the present indicate that savings could be achieved if the outstanding bonds were refunded with bonds bearing a lower interest rate. This circumstance is very similar to the refinancing of a home mortgage loan.

3. The prior bonds were issued pursuant to some form of authorization that poses restrictions that have become unduly onerous in the view of the current business environment of the airport. As long as the prior bonds are outstanding, the airport must conform to the restrictions imposed by the authorization. Refunding the bonds under a new and revised authorization eliminates these restrictions. This circumstance can generally occur when a novel financing instrument is developed and the existing authorization cannot accommodate this new instrument.

Regardless of the purpose involved, subject to certain provisions in the tax code, bonds may be issued for the purposes of refunding outstanding notes or bonds. Refunding bonds are issued separately or in combination with bonds that are being issued to finance new construction or acquisition.

2.6 PRIMARY OBJECTIVE OF FINANCING

The primary objective of the airport-financing process is to provide sufficient funds to satisfy the requirements of the capital improvement program without borrowing in excess of the amount required. Approaching the financing process in this way will enable the airport to accomplish the following:

1. Allow the construction program to proceed, without interruption attributable to cash flow shortfalls, so that the project can be completed and placed in service in an expeditious manner
2. Avoid the additional amortization burden associated with borrowing in excess of the amount required to complete the program
3. Conform with the provision of federal tax law that limit the amount of tax-exempt borrowing to that amount that can reasonably be expected to complete the program

Ideally, for an airport-improvement program the balance available for construction purposes would be completely expended when the project is completed. For several reasons, however, this is not possible in a practical sense. In airport programs, grants-in-aid are received as reimbursements for funds expended, and their receipt can lag the expenditure by as much as one year. Further, the final installments of interest income are often received after the completion of the program.

The major reason that funds remain after the completion of a capital improvement program is that airports cannot accurately foresee the precise requirements of any given program. Prudent planning dictates that airports include a reasonable contingency allowance for unanticipated costs. In most cases, the contingency is not fully expended, and upon program completion, the airport tends to have remaining funds available. The practice in the airport industry is to apply this surplus (regardless of the source of the surplus) to the retirement of debt if possible, or to reserve the surplus for application in future capital improvement programs.

2.7 PARTICIPANTS IN THE FINANCING PROCESS

The preparation of an offering of bonds requires the specific knowledge and skills of a number of professionals. The following specialists are typically involved in the process.

Airport Staff

Representatives from the finance and administrative departments of the airport staff are required to provide all the relevant financial and operational information that is incorporated in the offering documents. These individuals are among the people most knowledgeable about the airport, and their participation ensures the accurate presentation of materials related to the ownership, control, and management of the airport, the historic results of operation, the description of existing facilities, and the explanation of the facilities being financed.

Airport Counsel

Airport counsel may be either a staff attorney or an outside law firm retained by the airport to represent its interests in matters such as the offering of securities. The airport counsel monitors the process and verifies that the terms of the transaction make no demands on the airport that would conflict with the airport's legal capabilities. Further, the airport counsel attempts to secure the most favorable business terms possible for the airport in the process.

Airport Consultant

The scope of services of the airport consultant can be exceptionally broad in some cases. At a minimum, in the offering of general revenue bonds, the consultant submits a report rendering an independent judgement as to the financial feasibility of the projects being financed. This report, which is sometimes referred to as a *feasibility study,* comprises the review of all relevant information, the preparation of financial forecasts, and the conclusion that (upon completion of the projects being financed) the airport will be able to satisfy all its obligations. In essence, the feasibility study presents an unbiased view that the project will be able to sustain itself—i.e., that there will be sufficient revenue available to pay debt service and provide for all other financial obligations of the airport.

Architects and Engineers

The airport's architects and engineers are responsible for preparing the basic design work that is required for the derivation of project cost estimates. These estimates, arrayed in the form of a construction *draw-down* schedule identifying the amount and timing of the requirements for funds, are the basis of the calculation of the financing requirement.

Bond Counsel

Bond counsel is retained by the airport to render an opinion that the bonds, when issued, are legally valid and binding obligations of the airport and that, under current legislation, the interest on the bonds will be given the tax treatment that is described in the offering documents. Generally, the opinion of bond counsel is referred to as the *legal opinion,* and this opinion is critical in the marketing of the bonds. Consequently, investors have come to expect that the legal opinion should be rendered by a large law firm with a favorable reputation for its expertise in this area of law practice.

Bond Insurer

In some offerings, the airport will decide that interest cost savings can be obtained by insuring the bonds. In these cases, the airport purchases an insurance policy that provides coverage of all interest and principal payments in the event that the airport is unable to make such payments. These insurance companies are large, well-capitalized firms that insure many types of bonds. The value of the insurance policy is that the rating agencies (discussed subsequently) assign the highest-quality credit rating to bonds that are insured. The airport can make an estimate of the savings available through the purchase of an insurance policy and compare this saving with the insurance premium. If the savings exceed the cost, then the policy can be economically justified, and insurance would be a prudent course of action for the airport.

The insurance premium is a one-time cost, which is due and payable when the bonds are issued. As this cost is clearly attributable to the issuance of the bonds, the custom is that the premium is paid from the proceeds of the bond issue as an item of the issuer's cost.

Financial Adviser

The airport's financial adviser is an individual or a firm with special expertise in the offering of securities to finance airport capital improvement programs. Because most airports are infrequent issuers of bonds, it is extremely unlikely that the requisite expertise would be available among any of the airport staff. The financial adviser assists the airport in every step of the preparation of the issue for airport sale. In a *competitive* sale, where the bonds are offered for sale to the general market and competitive bids are solicited from any interested underwriters, the financial adviser evaluates the bids and makes a recommendation to the issuer as to the advisability of accepting the best bid or rejecting all bids. In a *negotiated* sale, where the airport appoints a group of underwriters in advance of the sale, the financial adviser reviews the purchase proposal of the underwriters and makes a recommendation to the issuer regarding the fairness of the proposal.

Rating Agencies

The rating agencies are independent organizations that review the economic circumstances and the operating characteristics of the airport and the terms of proposed bond issues. Then, based on their independent view of the transaction, they assign a credit rating for the bonds. The rating is a critical factor in the determination of the interest cost of a bond issue. Bonds with higher credit ratings will bear lower interest rates than lower-rated bonds.

The rating agencies that are generally regarded to be the most widely accepted in the market are Moody's Investors Service, Inc., and Standard and Poor's Corporation. For each of these, the top four categories of ratings (*best* grade through *medium* grade) are considered to be *investment grade* ratings—implying that interest and principal can be expected to be paid, as scheduled, over the life of the bonds. A rating below investment grade implies that there are some speculative elements to the bonds, and such a rating would be a major disincentive for investors who typically invest in tax-exempt bonds (including airport bonds).

Table 2–3 illustrates the investment grade rating categories of Moody's Investors Service and Standard and Poor's Corporation. Credit ratings are assigned when bonds are issued, and they are maintained throughout the life of the bonds. If bonds are *upgraded* subsequent to the assignment of the original ratings, the value of the bonds will increase. Conversely, if bonds are *downgraded* or if the ratings are withdrawn or suspended, the value of the bonds will decrease.

TABLE 2–3. Investment Grade Rating Categories

Grade	Moody's Investor's Service	Standard & Poor's Corporation
Best grade	Aaa	AAA
High grade	Aa1	AA+
	Aa	AA
		AA−
Upper medium grade	A1	A+
	A	A
		A−
Medium grade	Baa1	BBB+
	Baa	BBB
		BBB−

Underwriter

In the offering of bonds, the underwriter is the party that purchases the bonds initially from the issuer. Once the underwriter has purchased the bonds, the issuer is effectively removed from the transaction. It is the responsibility of the underwriter to reoffer (sell) the bonds to the ultimate investor. To the extent that the underwriter is able to sell the bonds to investors at a price greater than the price paid to the issuer, there is an *underwriting profit.* If the underwriter is unable to sell the bonds at a price equal to or greater than the price paid to the issuer, there is an *underwriting loss;* this loss is the responsibility of the underwriter.

Typically, airport bonds are underwritten by a group of securities firms, which, for the purpose of a particular issue of bonds, form a business affiliation known as a *syndicate.* The managing underwriter is the lead underwriter in the syndicate and, in that capacity, acts on behalf of all of the firms in the syndicate. It is the responsibility of the managing underwriter to allocate bonds to the other firms in the syndicate and to keep records of the sales results for the issue.

The existence of a syndicate implies that there is a sharing of the underwriting profits or losses associated with the issue. This sharing is in proportion to each underwriter's *participation* in the offering. If a single firm has a large participation in an issue, it has a large potential for profit and a large liability in the event of a loss.

In recent years, it has become customary for a syndicate to incorporate a *selling group* (a group of firms whose assistance is enlisted for purposes of selling bonds to investors but who do not share in the underwriting profit or loss) for some of the larger issues. If a selling group is employed, the entire risk associated with the underwriting is borne by the firms that comprise the traditional syndicate.

For the most part, underwriters of airport bonds have traditionally been major securities firms. Until recently, commercial banks had been precluded by law from underwriting revenue bonds. A change in securities law has enabled commercial banks, subject to certain restrictions, to underwrite revenue bonds by removing the statutory prohibition.

Underwriter's Counsel

In a negotiated sale, when underwriters are appointed by the airport prior to the issuance of the bonds, the underwriters retain an independent counsel with specific knowledge and experience in the issuance of revenue bonds. Throughout the financing process, underwriters' counsel is responsible for monitoring the process to assure that securities law is observed. At the conclusion of the transaction, the underwriters' counsel renders an opinion to that effect.

Other Parties

The financing process can involve a number of other parties in roles that become effective following the issuance of the bonds. A *trustee* may be formally designated to act on behalf of the bondholders collectively upon the occurrence of certain events. A *registrar* may be appointed to keep records regarding the registered ownership of the bonds. For bond issues involving payments to bondholders (through means other than a check mailed to the owner of a record), one or more paying agents may be appointed.

Although these parties play an important role in the overall administration of the bond issue, their involvement in the process is ancillary in that they have little role in determining the terms of the transactions as they affect the airport.

2.8 BOND MARKET

As in any other market, the bond market is composed of sellers and buyers. From the "new-issue" point of view, the sellers are the underwriters, the securities firms that initially purchase the bonds from the issuer. The buyers are the investors who purchase the bonds from the underwriters.

There are two broad investor market segments: institutional investors— i.e., investors that purchase bonds for the portfolios of their employers—and the individual investors—i.e., those that purchase bonds for their own personal portfolios. Each market segment has its own distinct characteristics.

Institutional Investors

Institutional investors are market professionals. In the long term, they tend to account for a major portion of the volume of new issue purchases. In some years, because their preference for tax-exempt income varies from time to time, the volume purchased by such investors will be exceptionally high; in other years, they may be virtually absent from the market. On balance, however, they constitute the driving force in the tax-exempt market.

Commercial Banks

Historically, commercial banks accounted for a substantial volume of new-issue purchases. Investing for their own accounts or through trust departments for the accounts of others, bank purchases were substantial. In the late 1980s, changes in tax law altered the favorable treatment of interest on bonds that banks held in their own portfolios. Consequently, most of the current volume of bank purchases is made through their trust departments, and the total volume of bank purchases is somewhat less than it once was. Although not necessarily true for trust department purchases, the traditional *bank range* in the overall term and maturity structure of a tax-exempt bond issue was in the area from one to five years. Banks do purchase outside of this range, but the maturities in which the banks have tended to be the most active are those with shorter terms.

Fire and Casualty Insurance Companies

Fire and casualty insurers constitute another major market subsegment. Although their appetite for tax-exempt income also varies from year to year (depending on general market conditions and the insurance industry's prevailing claims experience), they generally account for a major share of the new-issue volume of tax-exempt bonds. They constitute a particularly important subsegment of the market because their term preferences tend to be in the middle of the maturity spectrum: arguably, between seven and twenty years, depending on market conditions. Fire and casualty companies do purchase shorter and longer maturities, but traditionally, they have been most active in the midrange of the spectrum.

Bond Funds and Money Market Funds

Fund managers purchase securities from a variety of issuers, repackage the securities in different portfolios, and sell participations in the portfolios to other investors—principally to individual investors. The funds offer the individual investors the advantage of investment diversification, which might otherwise be unavailable for individuals given the relatively large unit price ($5,000) of a tax-exempt bond.

Funds are designed for a variety of purposes: safety (funds that include only insured bonds); high-yield (funds that include an accumulation of lower-quality but still investment grade bonds); state tax advantage (funds that include a variety of bonds issued in a single state, where the interest on "in-state" bonds is exempt from state tax); or the preservation of principal (funds that include bonds of very short maturities, thereby protecting the portfolio from price fluctuations due to changing market conditions). Any of these funds could include airport revenue bonds.

Fund managers are active in the very short end of the maturity spectrum for their money market funds and in the very long end of the maturity spectrum for their bond funds. They are absent from the market only on rare occasions and seldom for more than a brief period of time.

Individual Investors

Individual investors purchase and sell securities for their own personal portfolios. Their preferences vary from time to time, but they vary more for personal reasons than they do for reasons related to underlying bond market conditions. For this reason, individual investors, as a market segment, are virtually always "in the market" for new-issue tax-exempt bonds.

Individual investors are active throughout the maturity spectrum of tax-exempt bonds. Assuming that the general level of interest rates is attractive, individual investors will purchase in the bank range, the midrange, and the long-term maturities. Individual investors tend to prefer the higher yields that are associated with the longer maturities, however, and for this reason, they tend to be the most active in the long-term maturity range.

Table 2–4 summarizes the characteristics of the institutional investor and the individual investor segments of the tax-exempt bond market. Investors do

TABLE 2–4. Characteristics of Investors

	Institutional Investors	Individual Investors
Size of purchase	Relatively large	Relatively small
Yield sensitivity	High	Low
Benchmarks	All new issues	Existing and holdings and taxable alternatives
Credit review	Rigorous	Varies
Effectiveness sales effort	Relatively low	Relatively high
Cost of sales effort	Relatively high	Relatively low
Absence from market	Periodic	Extremely rare

not always exhibit these characteristics, but, in general, the table reflects the characteristics of the two segments as they are most typically observed in the market. With specific regard to airport bonds, neither segment has demonstrated an aversion or a particular affinity. Investment decisions tend to be made in view of the circumstances prevailing at the time the bonds are offered for sale.

2.9 INVESTOR RISKS AND SAFEGUARDS

In an airport revenue bond issue, the risks that investors bear can be categorized as being airport-related or nonairport-related. The airport can do nothing to affect the general level of interest rates, so the risk that the market value of the bond will decline because of rising interest rates is a *nonairport* risk, for example.

The principal airport-related risk is that, for any of a number of reasons, there is insufficient revenue available to make debt service payments as scheduled. The market has come to expect airports to make use of several generally accepted safeguards to help mitigate this risk.

Insufficient Construction Funds

During the course of an airport construction program, it is possible that cost overruns may result in a shortage of funds, jeopardizing the completion of the project. If the project is not completed, it is highly unlikely that there will be revenue forthcoming to make debt service payments. The market has come to expect that the airport will make provision to issue *completion bonds* in the event that the initial issue or issues fail to provide for all the construction requirements. Completion bonds are bonds that are issued without regard to many of the restrictions that might apply to the issuance of additional bonds for an additional project. Simply stated, if and when the airport determines that there will be insufficient funds to complete construction, it has the authority to issue an additional series of bonds to complete the project that had been financed with the initial issue.

Revenue Shortfall During Construction

During any construction period, it is likely that the facility under construction will not be a revenue-producing entity. Because the terms of airport bonds generally require that interest be paid semiannually from the date of issuance through the final maturity, the airport must make some other provision for the payment of interest until the project is completed. The standard approach to dealing with this circumstance is the financing of interest payments during construction through bond proceeds. This technique is called *capitalized interest*. In effect, the airport borrows money to provide for these interest payments, adds the cost to the value of the facilities, and amortizes the cost over the life of the bonds.

Temporary Revenue Shortage After Completion

For a variety of reasons, it is possible that there might be a shortage of revenue at some time during the life of the bonds.

Airport rates and charges are established based on estimates of activity, for example, so it is possible that the actual results may fall short of these estimates. As an initial safety feature, the market has come to expect that the airport base its calculations of rates and charges on an artificially higher level than that which would otherwise be required. The industry standard is that the airport agree to set rates and charges to recover 1.25 times the amount required to make debt service payments (in addition to amounts required to satisfy all other requirements). This "agreement" on the part of the airport is part of the contract that constitutes the airport revenue bond. It is called the *rate covenant*, and the amount in excess of "1.00 times" the debt service requirement is called *debt service coverage*. Once the debt service payments have been made, the coverage can be applied each year for other airport purposes, or it can be *rolled over* to satisfy the coverage requirements for the following year. The rate covenant gives the bondholder an additional level of comfort that minor forecasting problems will not affect the timely payment of debt service.

It is also possible that a more serious problem might occur that could lead to a prolonged shortage of revenue at an airport. The market relies on reserve funds to mitigate this element of risk.

Debt Service Reserve Fund

The terms of each airport revenue bond generally include the provision for a debt service reserve fund. The airport is required to maintain a balance in this fund approximately equal to one year's debt service reserve payment. The fund is usually funded initially from the proceeds of the bonds and replenished, to the extent it is expended, from airport revenues. This fund is specifically restricted to the payment of debt service when other funds are insufficient to make the payment. It provides a second level of safety—after the initial level provided by the rate covenant.

Traditionally, airports have been required to maintain this balance in cash or liquid investments. More recently, however, insurance companies have offered a surety policy that can effectively satisfy the reserve requirement, thereby enabling the airport to avoid borrowing for this purpose if the payment of the insurance premium is the more cost-effective option.

Maintenance and Operating Reserve Fund

Airports can be subject to labor disputes (either airport- or airline-related labor disputes) that can be financially disruptive. Similarly, it is possible that certain airport facilities could be damaged and rendered unusable for a period of time. In each of these cases, it is possible that there might be insufficient revenue available to pay maintenance and operating expenses for a period of time. Failure to pay maintenance and operating expenses can be a substantial problem for bondholders, so the market has come to expect that airports provide for such circumstances. The typical method of addressing this circumstance is the establishment of a *maintenance and operating reserve fund*. Like the debt service reserve fund, this fund is required pursuant to the terms in the initial issuance of the bonds. Generally, the amount required to be on deposit in the fund will vary from airport to airport, but an amount approximately equal to three month's expenses (25 percent of the annual operating budget) would satisfy the requirement for most airports. Amounts in this fund are typically accumulated from cash flow over the course of time rather than being funded from bond proceeds. The market tends to view this reserve as a type of *business-interruption* insurance.

Emergency Capital Requirements

Periodically, an airport can have a need for emergency capital funds. Although airports can generally borrow funds for any emergency purpose, it is sometimes costly or time consuming to borrow. Consequently, the market expects that airports will establish a separate fund for this purpose. This fund is generally called a *renewal and replacement fund*. As the name implies, the amounts on deposit in this fund may be expended for emergency purposes or for purposes of replacing assets that have been worn out. The amount of the requirement varies widely among airports. A representative amount in the early 1990s might be considered to be in the range of $1 million to $3 million, depending on the size of the airport. Funding approaches for this reserve vary. It is common to fund a portion of the requirement from bond proceeds and to accumulate the balance from annual cash flow.

Overall Credit Enhancement

The market can be resistant when it comes to accepting lower-rated offerings, because these offerings are perceived to be riskier than the stronger credits. Although investors may purchase lower-rated bonds, they expect additional compensation for the additional risk they bear, and this compensation takes the form of a higher return on their investment. This higher return for the investor equates to a higher cost of borrowing for the airport issuer.

As discussed previously, a number of insurance companies will write policies insuring municipal bonds, thus covering the risk that interest and principal will not be paid as scheduled. These companies are paid a single premium at the date of the issuance of the bonds. The premium is calculated as a percentage of the total debt service covered by the policy, and this percentage varies, depending on general market conditions and on the "uninsured" credit quality of the bonds. Generally, the premium is less than 1 percent of the total debt service, but for certain issues in unfavorable markets, the premium can exceed this amount.

Bonds that are insured are awarded a credit rating of Aaa by Moody's Investors Service and AAA by Standard and Poor's Corporation. When the bonds are offered for sale, the value of the insured ratings is demonstrated in the lower interest cost achieved by the issuer. Consequently, the issuer can make an economic judgment as to the appropriateness of bond insurance. The premium will be known, and the interest rate differential can be accurately estimated. The airport can compare the cost of the premium with the savings in interest cost, and, if the savings exceed the cost, the airport can elect to purchase the insurance.

Bond insurance is typically applicable for long-term offerings, because these offerings provide the most meaningful interest cost–saving opportunity.

For airports issuing short-term or variable-rate bonds, an additional form of credit enhancement is sometimes employed to make the offering more marketable. This credit enhancement is a *letter of credit,* typically provided by a major commercial lender. It differs from a policy of bond insurance in that the letter of credit provider will make payments in the event that the airport is unable to do so, but in such case, the letter establishes a schedule of payments by which the proceeds of the letter of credit must be repaid to the provider. Letters of credit typically provide *liquidity* for an offering of adjustable-rate bonds that give bondholders the option of tendering their bonds back to the airport on an interest rate adjustment date in the event that the interest rate adjustment offered by the airport is not acceptable to the bondholder.

Bonds backed with a letter of credit are generally offered with the credit rating of the letter-of-credit provider. Generally, the providers carry the highest short-term ratings—ratings that are analogous to the Aaa/AAA ratings that characterize the best-quality long-term offerings. Consequently, the airport could make a similar economic evaluation of the cost of the letter of credit. Often, however, cost is not at issue in the short-term or variable-rate market. Generally, these offerings are not marketable without credit enhancement. Investors perceive the risk (associated with the lack of liquidity on the part of the airport) as being too great.

2.10 FEDERAL-STATE AID TO AVIATION

In the United States, the federal and state governments contribute substantially toward the capital construction of airports through grant-in-aid programs. The federal contributions are financed through the Airport and Airway Trust Fund, which was originally established in 1954. Recent major legislation affecting the level of financing for airports includes the Airport and Airways Development Act (1970), the Airport Development Acceleration Act (1973), the Airport and Airway Improvement Act (1982), the Airport Safety and Capacity Expansion Act (1987) and the Airport Safety and Capacity Expansion Act (1990). The federal share of project costs depends on the type of project, and these shares are shown in Table 2–2. The scale of federal and state involvement in capital financing is extensive on a nationwide basis. In the financial year 1988, federal grants-in-aid to airports amounted to $825.2 million. This federal money attracted $70.8 million in matching state funds. The states also expended a further $285 million in monies not matched by federal grants, giving total state spending of $355.8 million in that year. By 1990, the balance of the Airport and Airway Trust Fund had reached $14.6 billion, accumulated largely from the 8 percent federal ticket tax. Table 2–5 shows breakdowns of federal and state airport expenditures for the year 1988 (3).

To be eligible for grants-in-aid in the federal program, an airport must be a public-use airport and must be included in the National Plan of Integrated Airport System (NPIAS), which acts as a guide to appropriate funding levels and priorities in the U.S. national context (4). During the latter part of the 1980s and the early 1990s, the trust fund built up a balance of unspent monies, largely due to the cutbacks on all federal spending associated with deficit

TABLE 2–5. State and Federal Contributions to U.S. Airports in 1988 (in dollars)[a]

State	Amount Used to Match Federal Grants	State Expenditures Not Used to Match Federal Grants	Total of State Expenditures	Federal Expenditures
Hawaii	5,000,000	124,000,000	129,000,000	16,061,000
Alaska	3,300,000	67,940,800	71,240,800	36,676,000
Florida	6,566,500	36,879,500	43,466,000	57,421,000
Illinois	11,590,000	4,500,000	16,090,000	30,849,000
Virginia	10,000,000	700,000	10,700,000	14,846,000
Tennessee	125,000	8,600,000	8,725,000	23,141,000
Minnesota	0	8,041,800	8,041,800	9,683,000
Maryland	7,306,482	165,201	7,471,683	14,895,000
Arizona	300,000	4,900,000	5,200,000	17,671,000
North Carolina	1,976,522	3,132,304	5,108,826	19,915,000

(continued)

TABLE 2–5. *(Continued)*

State	Amount Used to Match Federal Grants	State Expenditures not used to Match Federal Grants	Total of State Expenditures	Federal Expenditures
Pennsylvania	2,626,000	2,421,000	5,047,000	36,178,000
South Carolina	3,500,000	350,000	3,850,000	6,945,000
Wisconsin	1,393,000	2,367,700	3,760,700	13,942,000
New York	3,700,000	0	3,700,000	42,926,000
Rhode Island	3,227,000	0	3,227,000	4,949,000
Georgia	484,014	2,104,185	2,588,199	26,641,000
California	0	2,539,000	2,539,000	59,696,000
Arkansas	200,000	2,200,000	2,400,000	9,936,000
New Mexico	639,324	1,552,834	2,192,158	10,338,000
Utah	400,000	1,400,000	1,800,000	11,976,000
Michigan	1,136,957	652,684	1,789,641	18,260,000
Iowa	0	1,750,000	1,750,000	5,496,000
Washington	180,000	1,558,420	1,738,420	17,565,000
Missouri	345,531	1,257,404	1,602,935	25,213,000
Ohio	221,079	1,267,081	1,488,160	20,124,000
Massachusetts	550,918	914,490	1,465,408	10,426,000
Indiana	1,125,000	0	1,125,000	20,035,000
Oklahoma	225,974	733,824	959,798	12,025,000
New Jersey	378,800	530,900	909,700	11,433,000
Wyoming	412,025	458,805	870,830	2,340,000
Connecticut	800,000	0	800,000	2,263,000
North Dakota	400,000	260,000	660,000	3,486,000
Nebraska	257,921	381,122	639,043	7,822,000
Delaware	400,000	161,000	561,000	126,000
Montana	519,680	2,000	521,680	6,716,000
South Dakota	420,000	100,000	520,000	6,312,000
Maine	318,267	189,706	507,973	4,794,000
Alabama	48,149	425,351	473,500	6,360,000
New Hampshire	120,000	315,092	435,092	1,359,000
Kentucky	161,000	225,000	386,000	8,815,000
Vermont	200,000	0	200,000	2,200,000
Idaho	118,000	55,250	173,250	6,088,000
Oregon	89,984	0	89,984	10,963,000
Texas	14,120	0	14,120	65,749,000
Kansas	13,300	0	13,300	15,087,000
Nevada	3,000	0	3,000	4,692,000
West Virginia	0	0	0	3,263,000
Colorado	0	0	0	18,400,000
Louisiana	0	0	0	23,556,000
Mississippi	0	0	0	4,299,000
Totals:	$70,793,547	$285,032,453	$355,826,000	$809,952,000

[a] State agency figures are based on year ending June 30. Federal figures are based on year ending September 30.

Source: National Association of State Aviation Organizations.

reduction. Passenger facility charges were seen as offering U.S. airports an important and unencumbered solution to the problem of attracting money for capital improvements. Consequently, the larger airports generally lobbied for and supported the change in U.S. law in 1990 that permitted the introduction of passenger facility charges.

REFERENCES

1. Lewis, D. "Airport Ownership and Financial Management: An International Review." *International Atlantic Economic Conference*. London: James F. Hickling, Ottawa, April 1988.
2. Kluckhohn, H. "Security for Tax-Exempt Airport Revenue Bonds," summary of remarks presented at the *New York Law Journal*'s Seminar on Tax-Exempt Financing for Airports, 1980.
3. *The States and Air Transportation*. Cooperative Study of the National Governors' Association and the National Association of State Aviation Officials. Silver Spring, Md.: NASAO Center for Aviation Research and Education, 1989.
4. Ashford, N., and P.H. Wright. *Airport Engineering*. 3d ed. New York: Wiley Interscience, 1992.

BIBLIOGRAPHY

Financing U.S. Airports in the 1980s. Washington, D.C.: Congressional Budget Office, April 1984.
Airport System Development. Washington, D.C.: Congressional Office of Technology Assessment.

3

Financing Airports in Various Countries Other than the United States

3.1 GOVERNMENTAL OWNERSHIP

As was stated in Chapter 1, the most widely adopted airport ownership involves some form of governmental or quasi-governmental body. This ownership structure dates from the infancy of civil aviation, when the provision of civil air transport was considered an essential service function and, consequently, a suitable area for governmental ownership and involvement. In a number of countries, governmental primacy was further ensured by military activity at all but the smallest airfields during World War II (1939–1945). In Western Europe, Australasia, South America, and many parts of Asia, the airfields built and owned by the military during this conflict were given over to civilian authorities at the end of the war for the purposes of civil aviation. These facilities, initially built entirely for the operation of heavy military aircraft at some distance from the centers of urban areas, became the commercial transport airports of the second half of the twentieth century, the early close-in airports having to be abandoned because of inadequate field lengths and insufficient facilities for expansion.

The actual form of ownership varies among individual sovereign states. In some countries, all air transport airports belong to and are the responsibility of central government. In others, facilities are run by state, provincial, regional, or local governments. In all cases such facilities are managed and operated by civil servants employed by the appropriate level of government. Even where quasi-governmental authorities operate the airports, the background experience and ethos of management is drawn from the civil service.

Outside the United States, the financing of government- and authority-owned airports has traditionally reflected public-sector borrowing:

1. Government grants
2. Low-cost government loans
3. To a lesser degree, loans from banks and other lending institutions secured by the full faith and credit of the appropriate level of government

With the scale of operation of the civil airports greatly increasing in the 1980s, pressures arose for a more commercial style of operation of the larger facilities, as did some doubt about the efficiency of operation in the absence of competition of what were in fact governmental monopolies.

3.2 THE MOVE TOWARD PRIVATIZATION

The dramatic deregulation of the U.S. airline industry in 1978 set into motion a worldwide reappraisal of the civil aviation industry, which engendered a broad thrust toward bringing the "market" and overt competition into the operation of civil air transport. In some countries, the airports—rather than the airlines—have been in the forefront of this move toward market competition and deregulation. In the United States, where the initial leap towards the deregulation of civil air transport began, airports on the whole have remained firmly in the public sector. Partly because of the innovative financing procedures that have been practiced for many years, there has been little political will to divest government of this responsibility. The very high level of government grants-in-aid, through the FAA–administered Airports and Airways Development Fund, has worked against a widespread privatization of airports. Even so, within the United States the scale of capital development projects required over the next ten years has meant that even more innovative financing techniques have had to be found to provide the scale of funding required for projects only marginally funded by the FAA. The $5 billion JFK 2000 development is an example of such a project.

Elsewhere in the world, user-funded trust funds are remarkably absent from the scene. Airports are, therefore, generally directly dependent for capital financing on central government in the form of grants and loans or from loans that are subject to the approval and control of the treasury of central government. It has been estimated that the capital requirement for airport development in Europe alone over the period 1990–2000 is between $30 and $40 billion (1). If governments continue to maintain a monopoly on airport ownership, they face the prospect of huge public-sector borrowing. This would occur at a time when, worldwide, central governments face problems of holding public-sector spending under control; consequently, there has been a desire to remove from the public sector those facilities and services that are revenue generating. Airports have widely been seen to come within this ambit. A number of countries therefore moved rapidly in the late 1980s toward a radical change in the structure of airport ownership and in the form of capital financing used for developing the airport system. In some states, the form of privatization or denationalization is relatively limited, with the involvement of the market economy in only a limited number of airport activities. In other cases, the government has elected to remove itself entirely from the airport-related aspects of the provision of civil aviation.

3.3 FORMS OF PRIVATIZATION

Depending on the economic circumstances of governments and the political views of those in power, a variety of options have been chosen in the worldwide drive to more widespread adoption of privatization measures (2). These include six basic options:

1. Management contracts
2. Third-party facility development
3. Public incorporation, with share ownership retained in the public sector (i.e., central state, regional, provincial, or local governments)
4. Public incorporation with shares available to public
5. Management buyout
6. Outright sale

Management contracts are a method of introducing competition into the airport economic environment with a minimum level of administrative upheaval. Private contractors bid and are awarded contracts to perform services that were previously carried out entirely by airport staff. Contracts that typically fall into this category are engineering and architectural design services, cleaning, maintenance of buildings and grounds, security services, and the operation of heating and air-conditioning plants. The use of the management contract permits competition within the airport operation without a change in ownership. As such, this technique can be seen to be a minimum step toward privatization and is extremely widely used. A more radical form of management contract, as envisaged by firms such as Lockheed and Pan Am, involves the total management of the entire airport facility.

Third-party facility development is a financial concept that has been used in the United States since the late 1960s; it is now being picked up and adopted widely throughout the world. A developer who is neither the airport authority nor the airlines provides turnkey arrangements of finance, design, construction, operation and ownership of an aviation facility on the airport. A variation of this is a *joint venture development,* such as that used to provide a second British Airways hub terminal at Birmingham, England, where a joint company of the airport, British Airways, and other partners have provided the capital and participated in the design and construction of a terminal specially designed for a new British Airways hubbing operation.

Public incorporation with share ownership retained by the public sector was the method of privatization chosen by all the British airports except those owned by BAA at the time of denationalization of transport airports in the United Kingdom in 1987. These regional airports became private companies (PLCs), but all shares were retained by the originally owning local authorities. Their representatives became nonexecutive directors on the airport company boards. The British regional airports therefore have structures and financing methods very similar to other major European airports, such as those at Munich, Amsterdam, and Frankfurt. This form of structure can meet only some of the aims of privatization. Because the airport operates as a private company, it operates under many of the same financial restrictions, such as requirements for depreciating its assets, the liability to corporate tax, and the obligations of the directors to act in the interests of shareholders. In the United Kingdom, however, because the shareholders are public authorities, capital borrowing is subject to central government treasury control and thus is severely constrained.

The option of *public incorporation with market flotation of shares* enables the airport to be sold to individual shareholders of the general public, initially through an underwriting of the whole issue by a syndicate of share underwriters. On initial flotation, the entire issue is offered at a fixed price by the underwriters to the general public; thereafter, when trading commences, shares are bought and sold in the usual manner at market prices on the stock exchange. As in the case of bond underwriting described in Chapter 2, the share underwriters make a profit if the issue is taken up by buyers at flotation. If the issue is not taken up, the underwriters stand to take a loss on unwanted shares when trading starts at what will inevitably be a price lower than the flotation price. A public flotation of this nature removes the airport entirely from the public sector. The company must conform to all regulations that control the manner in which companies operate and is subject to corporate tax as a private company. Accounting procedures must conform to the laws that govern companies and cannot continue in the public-sector format previously used. However, management is no longer subject to the financial constraints of the public sector. As such, the management can borrow from the general financial markets at market rates and is not subject to limits that apply to private investment appraisal rather than governmentally imposed limits.

Management buyouts can occur, where the workers and management offer to purchase a facility at a negotiated price. Part of the price is raised in capital from workers and management and part comes from a loan from some investment source such as a bank. Individual equity in the airport is owned in proportion to the amount of capital contributed to the nonloan portion of the total capital.

Management buyouts have a mixed history. They potentially offer the possibility of introducing great vitality and initiative into the restructured operation, because higher profitability can bring large rewards to the participants. In a buoyant industry, with a history and potential of growth, a profitable airport operation that grows over time can, because of the leverage on investment, give substantial profits on equity to those participating in the buyout. There have been instances, particularly in the United Kingdom, where management buyouts have spectacularly improved an operation's performance. In practice, in many cases management buyouts have occurred only in operations where more conventional forms of equity holding cannot be attracted. Airports are peculiar in their requirement of large periodic infusions of investment for long-term profitability. As such they can be seen as unattractive investments by many potential funding sources, which are likely to want short-term returns on large capital investment. A great social problem associated with a failed management buyout is that the investors are likely to lose both their jobs and their savings. Before arranging a management buyout, the long-term capital position must be very carefully examined.

Outright sale has been described by Peters (2) as the most Draconian form of ownership transfer. There is an implication that if a large publicly owned hub airport were to be sold to a privately owned corporation, thousands of jobs could be lost in the restructuring. This is at the moment unlikely, but it is not inconceivable that in the future industrial conglomerates might view airports as a suitable diversification of activities.

3.4 THE BRITISH EXPERIENCE

The British experience with airports is an interesting case study of how changes in the form of ownership and management have affected the form of financing in a national airport system. After World War II, the British civil airports were almost entirely in the hands of either central or local governments. In 1965, the British Airports Authority (BAA) was created to run three London airports (Heathrow, Gatwick, and Stansted) and four Scottish airports (Glasgow, Edinburgh, Prestwick, and Aberdeen). The autonomous board of the BAA reported through its chairperson directly to the Minister of Trade in central government. A handful of airports that either were private or were operated by the Civil Aviation Authority for social purposes (i.e., to provide service to islands off the British mainland) were excepted.

On grounds that were strongly founded on political belief, in 1986 the Conservative government of Margaret Thatcher moved to denationalize or privatize the civil air transport airports of the United Kingdom with two main reasons in mind:

1. To decrease the proportion of the economy in the public sector. This was a political decision aimed at switching revenue-generating activities as much as possible into the private sector.
2. To help control inflation by the mechanism of reducing public borrowing. Long-term and high-capital borrowing requirements for airports were perceived to be a potential strain on public borrowing requirements.

The denationalization of the BAA portion of the British airport system was, therefore, politically popular within the Conservative government of the day. A potentially profitable government holding could be sold off, generating income for the Treasury and relieving the public sector of the large capital spending requirements that airports generate. Of the $30 to $50 billion capital spending requirements on airports in Europe between 1990 and 2000, up to $7 billion can be expected in the United Kingdom. The 1986 Airports Act also required local-authority airports to be formed into private companies by 1987. These companies were formed, but in all cases, the local authorities retained the entire share issue. It was felt by central government that, although the commercial disciplines would be better observed if the regional airports were privatized, it was unwise to force the local authorities to sell their interests in the airports.

British Airports Authority and BAA plc

Prior to 1987, the British Airports Authority was entirely in the public sector and for capital borrowing requirements was under the control of the Treasury Department of central government. Since its creation in 1965, the BAA had always been a profit-making organization.

Because it was a public-sector activity and controlled by the Treasury in its borrowing, access to the national and international financial markets was strictly controlled. The structure of the former British Airports Authority is shown in Figure 3–1.

In 1987, the British Airports Authority (BAA) was converted into a private company, BAA plc. All shares in this company were initially owned by the British government. Using the mechanism of share underwriters, the entire shareholding was floated on the London Stock Exchange. This was achieved by an offer of shares by the underwriters at a set price; the shares were shortly after traded openly on the Exchange. Central government retained one "golden share," which was designed to be used to veto undesirable events (such as a hostile takeover for asset-stripping purposes or a buyout by an airline or airline combine that would present monopoly conflicts). Since 1987 the organizational structure of BAA plc has changed a number of times. At the end of 1989, the structure of the company was as shown in Figure 3–2. The operating

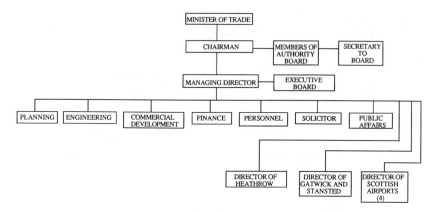

FIGURE 3–1. Structure of BAA (1984)

airports formed an Airports Division. Additionally, the company comprised Lynton plc, a development company for on-and-off-airport properties, and British Airport Services Limited, a consultancy-advisory company.

As a private company, BAA plc is free of governmental restrictions on capital financing. Consequently, the company is able to access any of the commercial financial markets, both nationally and internationally. There is no restriction on the type or number of financial instruments to be used or on the location

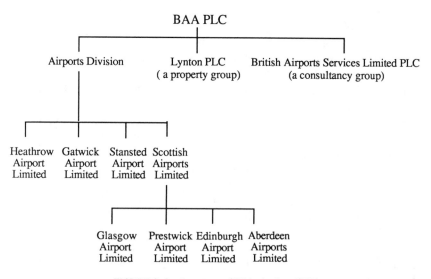

FIGURE 3–2. Structure of BAA plc (late 1989)

and number of financial sources that can be combined to achieve desired ends. Typically, BAA uses the following financial instruments (3). (For a discussion of the nature of these instruments the reader is referred to Sections 4.3 through 4.5.)

Short term	Sterling commercial paper
Medium term	Transferable multioption facility
Medium/long term	Fixed-rate loan—European Investment Bank
Long term	Fixed-rate loan
	Equity funding (ordinary shares)
	Preference share issue
	Long-dated sterling bond

The transferable multi-option facility referred to is a specially designed instrument of fourteen underwriting banks and twelve tender panel banks that backs up the Sterling Commercial Programme. If a request for funds does not yield the required amount, the fourteen underwriting banks are obliged to meet the BAA's requirements.

The reorganization after privatization has affected the manner in which the finances of the group have been handled in the short term (3). To maximize financial efficiency, day-to-day finances are controlled through a centralized Treasury function. BAA now has a number of subsidiary companies; all these companies have accounts with a single British clearing bank and all company accounts are linked with the central BAA Treasury account. At the end of each working day the balances of the individual company accounts are netted down to zero. All surplus funds are transferred to the central account and transfers are made out of the central account to cover overdrafts. This is achieved by a direct computer linkage to the bank's computer, giving the Treasury direct access to subsidiary accounts. Without this type of arrangement, the accounts of the larger airports would show a permanent surplus, whereas the smaller group airports' accounts would be almost constantly in overdraft, causing unnecessary interest charges. The overall profitability of the group would also be seriously distorted. Careful planning of the short-term use of Treasury funds ensures that the funds remain in slight surplus, with arrangements for over-night interest on those monies. The balances are removed for short-term investment.

British Airports (Non-BAA)

Under the terms of the 1986 Airports Act, all British airports with an annual turnover in excess of £1 million were required to become private companies. These airports included a number of major regional airports owned not by BAA

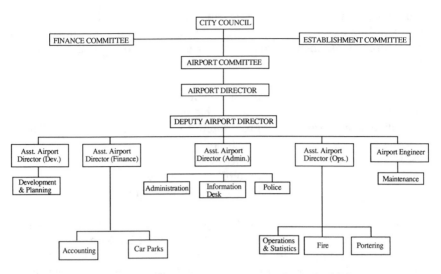

FIGURE 3–3. Manchester airport—municipal organization

but rather by local-authority governments—e.g., Manchester, Birmingham, Newcastle, and East Midlands. Unlike the central-government-owned BAA group, which was required to float shares publicly, these airports became private companies whose shares remained in total ownership of the local governments that had previously directly owned and operated them. The reorganization of an airport typical in size of many of the airports affected by this act is shown in Figures 3–3 and 3–4, which show the organogram of the administrative structure before and after privatization. The act was intended to bring commercial disciplines to the airport sector by requiring these organizations to conform to the requirements of commercial accounting and normal company procedures and reporting. Because the shareholdings remained entirely with the local authorities and were not available for public participation, the airports remain for economic purposes in the public sector and are, therefore, required to obtain central government Treasury approval of all borrowings. Free access to the capital markets is not open to these airports. Currently, local-authority airports typically borrow from the following sources:

Short term	Clearing bank loan
Medium term	Clearing bank loan
Long term	Local-government-authority funds covered by general obligation borrowings

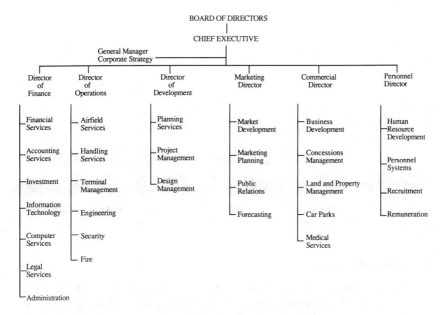

FIGURE 3–4. Manchester airport—private company

In the financially strict public-sector borrowing climate of the early 1990s, severe pressure to move out of the public sector has been felt by those airports where there is an urgent need for capital spending for development. Such a move is likely to occur either by public flotation of shares or by management buyouts.

3.5 OTHER EXPERIENCES

The pressure to move airports out of the public sector is widespread throughout the world. The concept that major airports are revenue generators and, as such, can be moved out of the public sector, permitting them access to the commercial financial markets and subjecting management to commercial discipline, has strong political attraction. By 1989, moves toward various degrees of privatization had taken place in areas as far apart as Canada, Australia, New Zealand, Belgium, Singapore, Hong Kong, Chile, and Algeria. Given that financing methods tend to follow current preference, or "fashion," the move toward privatization can be expected to continue at least in the next twenty years, and the international financial markets will become even more important in the development of airport financing.

3.6 WORLDWIDE DEVELOPMENT AGENCIES

Many countries find it extremely difficult to finance airport equipment or infrastructure from normal commercial institutions. The noncommercial basis on which most airports are organized and operated make them unattractive customers to such tenders. Therefore, a number of development agencies have been established to provide funds for priority needs to countries that find it difficult to raise loans through normal commercial sources (4). These funds are normally provided on a relatively untied basis subject to a demonstrated need and an adequate economic rate of return. There is normally a five-year grace period free of payments, followed by payback terms of up to fifty years. Interest rates vary. For very poor countries, very low rates are granted. Normal bank rates are set for most countries. A description of some of the more important development agencies follows.

The World Bank

The World Bank, or World Bank Group, as it is more correctly called, is composed of the International Finance Corporation (IFC) and the International Development Association (IDA). In terms of lending volume, the group is the largest agency in the world, providing financial and technical assistance to developing countries. The various agencies within the group operate in different ways. Loans through IDA are aimed at the poorest countries. They carry no interest but have a ¾ percent commitment charge. Payback periods range up to fifty years. Loans granted by the International Bank for Reconstruction and Development, on the other hand, have interest rates close to the generally prevailing borrowing rate. Only private-sector development can be aided by IFC. This is generally done in conjunction with participation on an equity basis.

World Bank Funding typically aids a fairly small number of large projects. In the late 1980s the average loan was approximately $50 million toward a total project cost of $140 million. In all loan and credit transactions, major emphasis is placed on project appraisal. The procedures used are designed to ensure a satisfactory rate of return on investment and a high priority of the project in a general development program.

The European Investment Bank

In 1958 the EEC member states founded the European Investment Bank (EIB) to support and integrate, at the international level, the banking systems of individual countries when they are operating in the area of community development. Loans are made principally for the development of infrastructure, energy, and industry. In addition to aiding in community development, the bank now plays a role in the provision of finance to countries outside the European community. Nearly one hundred Mediterranean, Caribbean, African, and Pacific countries have signed association and cooperation agreements that link them to the European community through the EIB for the purposes of participating in the development program. Interest rates are low, within 5 to 8 percent range. Funding is conditional upon obtaining financing from other sources and is limited to one-half of fixed asset costs.

European Bank for Reconstruction and Development

In 1991, a new financing institution appeared on the scene. With an initial capitalization of $10 billion ECU (approximately $10 billion U.S.), the European Bank for Reconstruction and Development was founded as an institution with wide-ranging areas of potential activity, but with a special initial interest in the reconstruction of the previously socialist economies of the former Eastern European bloc.

3.7 REGIONAL DEVELOPMENT BANKS

In addition to the worldwide agencies already discussed, there are a number of regional agencies that also provide financial and technical assistance sources for airport and aviation finance. Many of these agencies were initiated to serve only member countries in the regions but have subsequently expanded their coverage to extraregional states.

Inter American Development Bank

Founded in 1960 and originally operating as an agency for countries in the Americas, by 1990 the Inter American Development Bank accepted membership of sixteen extraregional countries, for a total membership of forty-three states.

Caribbean Development Bank

In 1990 there were twenty regional and three nonregional member states in the Caribbean Development Bank. Used as a source of project funding, the bank, which was founded in 1970, has a technical assistance fund, which provides preproject and postproject assistance. Such assistance includes advisory services, preinvestment studies, training for project preparation, and implementation.

African Development Bank

When the African Development Bank initially started operating in 1966, only African nations were allowed membership. By 1990 membership had increased to fifty regional member countries and twenty-five nonregional states. The aims of the bank are to finance projects of member states only and to select projects that make the economies of these states increasingly complementary and expand foreign trade. The bank "selects, studies and prepares projects, mobilizes resources for financing projects, promotes the investment of public and private capital and provides technical assistance" (4). In 1973 an associated African Development Fund was established to enable the provision of low-cost loans to African countries. Such loans have a grace period of ten years, followed by a payback period of forty years.

Asian Development Bank

Established in 1966, the Asian Development Bank's aims are to promote development in Asia and the Pacific region by the investment of public and private capital in projects that, although of high economic priority, are of a nature that it would be difficult to attract financing from conventional sources. In 1990 there were thirty-one regional member states and fourteen nonregional members. To aid poorer countries, the Asian Development Fund was established, with the object of making available low-cost loans. These typically have a 1 percent service charge, a ten-year grace period, and by a thirty-year payback period. The bank gives technical assistance for project preparation and implementation, technical and policy studies, and creating new institutions.

Islamic Development Bank

The Islamic Development Bank was founded in 1975 to finance the social and economic development of member states and Islamic communities. By 1990 it had thirty member countries. The bank provides technical assistance, gives loans to both the public and private sector, and provides equity capital for infrastructural projects. Typically loans carry a 2.5 to 3 percent service charge, a ten-year grace period, and a forty-year payback period.

Arab Bank for Economic Development in Africa

The Arab Bank for Economic Development in Africa was established in 1975 with the objectives of "fostering technical, economic and financial cooperation between African and Arab nations through assistance in financing development in African countries, stimulating the contribution of Arab capital to African development, and the provision of technical assistance."

Other Sources

In addition to these banks, a number of funds that have provided financial assistance in the development of airports and aviation are as follows:

• The Arab Fund for Economic and Social Development
• The Kuwait Fund for Arab Economic Development
• The Abu Dhabi Fund for Arab Development
• The OPEC Fund for International Development
• The Saudi Fund for Development

3.8 FINANCING AIRPORTS IN DEVELOPING COUNTRIES

In developing countries, airports are almost always owned directly by governmental or quasi-governmental organizations. However, the degree of autonomy varies considerably. The financing of airport development is achieved in a variety of ways: government loans; equity financing; bank loans, either from commercial or government development banks; export credits; tied aid or loans; and credits from the international and regional development agencies. In some ways, airports are more fortunate than other entities in the economy in that they may be able to generate some of their revenues in hard currency, which can appropriately be used for maintenance purposes and even to provide some of the necessary funds for capital investment. The preponderence of funds for capital development, however, is often provided by agencies described in Sections 3.6 and 3.7.

Before any major construction or equipment purchase can be envisaged, considerable effort and expense is required for project preparation. Preparation includes such elements as feasibility analysis, economic studies, design and engineering, and financial studies. Because the services of specialist consultants are needed, these preparatory studies require hard currency. It is normal for funding bodies such as the World Bank and the European Development Fund to provide such funds. Finance for these activities is also often available from the UNDP cooperative program and bilateral aid sources.

The financing of equipment and major works can be assisted by the worldwide and regional development agencies. The World Bank will provide funds when a suitable investment project has been identified that cannot be implemented due to a shortage of foreign exchange or domestic capital. Bank procedures are designed to help strengthen the capability of the agency receiving the funding by requiring the adoption of procedures and working practices, which include the following (5):

1. Recruiting contractors under international or local bidding procedures
2. Designing and supervising by competent consultants

3. Strengthening of the capability of the local executing agency to prepare and implement projects by training domestic staff and supplying expatriate help where required
4. Promoting the development of the funded agency to ensure it has the mandate, structure, and staff to discharge its necessary responsibilities, particularly with respect to project maintenance
5. Analyzing the need for a technical labor force and developing necessary staff-training programs
6. Improving accounting procedures and financial discipline and ensuring that prices are related to underlying costs

Since the 1970s, the World Bank has shown increasing interest in supporting sectorwide and subsector development programs rather than individual (standard) investment projects. This policy has been adopted on the basis that individual projects have a better chance of long-term viability if they stand within an evenly developed sector or subsector. In practice, this has meant that there is continued support for individual infrastructural investments but that the bank places great emphasis on the improvement of the management and operation of the sector. Consequently, there has been a shift toward increased technical assistance and advice in strengthening sectoral policies in the following areas (5):

1. Revision of pricing and taxation policies to strengthen the mobilization of domestic resources
2. Development of a labor policy to control the hiring of excessive labor and to improve productivity
3. Relaxation of regulatory policies to improve the performance of industry, to strengthen market discipline, and to encourage better-quality services
4. Removal of subsidies or adoption of procedures to make subsidies less covert, in order to control costs
5. Improvement of safety
6. Provision of adequate and sufficient attention to environmental consideration through improved formulation and design of projects

World Bank funding is also available in the area of policy reform through a program entitled *Adjustment Operations,* designed to quicken the pace of policy reform in the face of unfavorable externally driven shocks. Such funding has been made available in Guinea to support major reform in roads, ports, and airports. Other transport-related projects have been funded in Colombia and Indonesia, for example.

Assistance for projects to developing countries may also be obtained in the forms of *tied aid* or *bilateral aid*. It is common for the more developed countries to make financial assistance available to the less developed countries through aid programs that are related to the supply of goods and services directly from the aiding country. This is achieved by a variety of mechanisms: export and supplier credits, low-interest, long-term loans, and grants. In 1976, the OECD countries reached an agreement that laid down ground rules governing export credits. These rules include minimum interest rates, maturity periods, minimum down payments, and local cost-financing allowances. Financing through export credits is usually very attractive to airport authorities where long construction periods and long economic project lives are concerned. As compared with conventional commercial loans, export credits often have the following advantages (5):

1. Fixed and concessional interest rates
2. Assured disbursement of funds
3. Attractive grace periods after delivery or commissioning
4. Long repayment periods
5. Bank guarantees to the value of the contract outside the airport's normal requirements for financial coverage (The airport's ability to borrow in the normal commercial market is therefore unaffected by the contract.)
6. The ability to pay off export credit loans without penalty should other more attractive interest rates become available
7. Loan documentation that is usually much simpler than with conventional commercial loans

Supplier credit is the most common form of export credit. In this form of assistance, the supplier, through an export agency, offers deferred payment terms at attractive interest rates when tendering. Payments are made to a commercial bank appointed by the supplier. The bank obtains a guarantee from the export credit agency to cover the supplier's need for funds.

A less common form of export credit is known as *buyer credit*. The supplier is paid through a commercial bank from the proceeds of a loan agreed between the buyer and the bank. The transaction is guaranteed by the export credit agency. The supplier is, in this case, not involved with the financing arrangements.

Cofinancing of development projects is now frequent. Even large development agencies such as the World Bank and the EDF have limited resources. It is, therefore, common for large development projects to be funded jointly from a number of sources. In practice, cofinancing is arranged in such a way that the funding is achieved by *parallel financing* or *joint financing*. Where parallel financing is used, the project is broken into components and individual elements are financed from single identifiable sources. Joint financing occurs when the entire project is funded from joint resources; with this type of finance, individual elements cannot be identified as being funded by a particular source. Because many sources of cofinance put strict limitations on the ways in which their funds may be used, parallel financing arrangements are more commonly found in cofinanced projects. This applies particularly to projects cofinanced by export credit agencies, national aid organizations, regional development banks, and special regional funds.

Finally, a discussion of the need for provision of financing for recurrent costs as opposed to capital development costs is needed. It has become apparent that many projects fail to live up to original investment appraisals due to inadequate operation and maintenance. Equipment maintenance, especially of high-technology equipment, frequently requires continual use of hard currency. Even though an airport development may be capable of generating hard-currency revenues, these may be diverted for political purposes to nonairport uses. Access to foreign resource credits for the operational period of the project can and should be provided in the initial financing agreement where this seems appropriate.

3.9 EXAMPLES OF DEVELOPMENT PROGRAMS AT TWO AFRICAN AIRPORTS

The ways in which airport development programs for Third World countries can be financed are very varied. Two rather different methods are illustrated by projects at Lilongwe and Gaborone, respectively (6). The differences between the two approaches indicate that there is no unique way of structuring the financial package under conditions of limited available hard currency.

Sir Seretse Khama International Airport (SSKIA) was built in the early 1980s to serve the new capital of Botswana. Constructed at an elevation of just over 1,000 m, the 3,000-m runway was designed to accommodate Boeing 747 wide-bodied aircraft. The other principal features of the project were a terminal building and apron with connecting taxiways, a control tower, and an operational block. Project design and construction of the financial package lasted two years, with an invitation for tenders of the contracts in 1981; construction itself started in 1981. The new airport became operational in 1984.

In many aspects, the management and the financing of the SSKIA project were conventional. Project management was undertaken by a central government ministry, the Ministry of Works, Transport, and Communications, with the Department of Civil Aviation playing the principal role. A liaison committee was set up to ensure coordination among all interested parties. With respect to financial control, the government recognized that special care was needed to ensure compliance with the terms of the loans. Therefore, control of the financial aspects of the project was assigned to a special section of the Ministry of Finance. The expected costs at the planning stage were anticipated to be approximately £14.3 million at 1979 prices. In that no single source of funding could be arranged, a "packaging" of funding from a variety of sources was necessary. In the case of this project, the whole loan package was negotiated and obtained before tenders were invited. The package, which is illustrated in Table 3–1, contained provisions for the rescheduling of loans to accommodate differences between planned, tendered, and actual cost of works due to changes in the scope of work and variations in the local currency value of the loan in comparison with foreign currencies. There was full liaison between the lending agencies prior to the award of contracts and during the progress of project construction. A donor's conference was held in 1980. At this meeting, the lending agencies pledged loans to cover the majority of the foreign currency expenditure.

The arrangement of the borrowing agreements was such that the government of Botswana was held to be responsible for all local costs and also for a contribution toward other costs incurred in the construction. The balance was obtained from the six different funding agencies identified in Table 3–1. It is reported that the arrangements proved to be complex, requiring constant monitoring throughout the course of the project (6). Under the terms of the agreements, the contracts were let on the basis of proportional payment in terms of a nominated foreign currency at fixed rates of exchange and payment in Botswana pula. The nominated foreign currency was not necessarily that of the funding agency involved in the particular contract. Furthermore, it had been agreed that the funds to be drawn from the various donors would be scaled to the total commitment. Throughout the course of the project, world currencies were subject to severe relative fluctuations. As a result, progress payments required very careful monitoring, and to ensure a balance of borrowing, drawings were made on each loan. In order to maintain regular contact between the government of Botswana and each donor, there was a general circulation of quarterly reports of financial status.

The government of Botswana raised sufficient funds for the first stage of this project and a surplus that enabled it to finance additional contracts for an aircraft maintenance area apron and an additional taxiway. Table 3–1 reflects these additional works and the escalations in cost in the first stage of the project.

Contracts for civil works and building works were priced principally in local currency (93 percent and 75 percent, respectively), which depreciated significantly against the loan currencies during the progress of construction. As a result, the lending organizations were required to finance a greater proportion of the project than anticipated, even though there was a general increase in local currency (pula) costs (6).

Kamuzu International Airport was constructed at Lilongwe in the late 1970s with a runway length of 3,540 m. Built at an elevation of just over

TABLE 3–1. Contract Allocation and Funding, SSKIA Gaborone

Contract	Costs: Pula × 10⁶		Funding	
	Tender	Actual	Agency	Amount: Pula ($\times 10^6$)
1. Civil works: earthworks; surface water drainage; graded strip; aircraft pavements; markings, roadworks, fencing and fire main[a]	20·12[g]	25·33	KF SF BADEA GRB	5·18 12·19 7·72 0·24
2. Building works: passenger terminal, control tower and technical block, crash, fire and rescue station, all ancilliary buildings and houses; water supply and sewerage systems; roadworks adjacent to buildings[b]	7·73	12·50	KFW GRB	5·04 7·46
3. Electrical works: main electrical distribution system, external lighting, AGL installation, control cabling; pump house equipment/booster pump and associated pipework[c]	6·95	5·80	ADB OPEC[f]	2·77 3·03
4. Navigation aids and telecommunications: air traffic control, telecommunications and navigation aid installations, meteorological equipment[d]	4·97	6·38	KFW GRB	2·10 4·28
5. Fire vehicles: Fire appliances and ambulance[e]	1·33	1·41	ADB	1·41
Total	41·10 (£24 × 10⁶)[h]	51·42 (£30 × 10⁶)[i]	Outside agencies GRB	39·44 11·98

[a] Main contractor: Sir Alfred McAlpine and Son (Botswana) (Pty) Limited.

[b] Main contractor: Kier Botswana (Pty) Limited.

[c] Main contractor: Spie Batignolles.

[d] Main contractor: Standard Elektrik Lorenz A.G.

[e] Main contractor: Chubb Fire Security Services Limited.

[f] Financing agencies were: Kuwait Fund for Economic Development in Africa (KF); Saudi Fund for Development (SF); Arab Bank for Economic Development in Africa (BADEA); Kreditanstalt fur Wideraulbau, West Germany (KFW); African Development Bank (ADB); OPEC Fund (OPECF); Government of Republic of Botswana (GRB).

[g] Excludes costs of aircraft maintenance apron and associated works.

[h] Sterling equivalent, 1981 exchange rates.

[i] Sterling equivalent, 1984 exchange rates.

Source: Reference 6, with permission

TABLE 3–2. Contract Allocation and Funding, Kamuzu International Airport, Lilongwe, Malawi

Contract	Costs: KW × 10^6		Funding	
	Tender	Actual	Agency[f]	Amount: KW × 10^6
1/76. Earthworks, drainage for airfield; ducts[a]	6·71	8·66	ADB GRM	5·00 3·66
1/77. Flexible aircraft pavements and airfield lighting civil works[a]	7·18	10·61	ADB GRM	5·00 5·61
1/78. Passenger terminal, operations building and control tower[b]	7·81	8·83	OECF GRM	6·26 2·57
2/78. Main electrical distribution services and airfield lighting[c]	5·37	6·28	OECF GRM	5·98 0·30
3/78. Telecommunications, navigation aids and meteorological services[c]	4·48	7·35	OECF GRM	7·07 0·28
4/78. Rigid aircraft pavements; markings; roads; water supplies; soil drainage and fencing[a]	10·78	13·49	ESL GRM	5·39 8·10
5/78. Freight building; fire station; substation and minor buildings[d]	2·85	3·43	GRM	3·43
1/79. Flight catering buildings[e]	2·66	3·15	GRM	3·15
1/80. Air Malawi operations block, cabin services building and cafeteria[e]	0·83	0·87	GRM	0·87
16/80. Motor transport maintenance depot[e]	0·65	0·67	GRM	0·67
Total	49·32 (£30 × 10^6)[g]	63·34 (£35 × 10^6)[h]	Outside agencies GRM	34·70 28·64

[a] Prime contractor: Nello L. Teer Company
[b] Prime contractor: Mitsubishi Corporation; main contractor: Tachwa Corporation.
[c] Prime contractor: Mitsubishi Corporation; main contractor: Toshiba Corporation.
[d] Prime contractor: Tachwa Construction Co. Ltd.
[e] Prime contractor: W.C. French (Malawi) Ltd.
[f] Financing agencies were: African Development Bank (ADB); Overseas Economic Cooperation Fund of Japan (OECF); Eurodollar syndicated loan (ESL); Government of Republic of Malawi (GRM).
[g] Sterling equivalent, 1977–1978 exchange rates.
[h] Sterling equivalent, 1981–1982 exchange rates.

Source: Reference 6, with permission

1,000 m, the airport was designed for wide-bodied Boeing 747 aircraft. The design included a partial parallel taxiway, a passenger terminal–apron complex, a control tower, and operations blocks. Financing and design of the project took approximately two years, culminating in invitations for contract tenders in 1977. Construction commenced in late 1977, with operations at the new airport beginning in 1982.

The government of Malawi took the somewhat unusual step of setting up a separate corporate body (Airport Developments Ltd.) for the development of the airport project. Although owned entirely by the government and managed by senior government executives, it had its own financial structure, through which all development funds could be channeled. In 1976 prices, these costs were initially expected to be in the region of £22 million. As in the case of SSKIA in Botswana, a single source of financing for the entire project could not be found. It was, therefore, necessary for the government, in conjunction with the consultant engineers, Scott Wilson and Kirkpatrick, to assemble a financial package of loans from multiple sources to meet the needs of the total project. In putting such a package together, it was decided that the loans would be associated with individual contracts and that each contract should comprise work of a similar nature, the total value of which would be likely to be acceptable to individual lending agencies. The role of the engineering consultant was to provide technical backup and advice and to assist in project presentations to the various loan institutions to secure funds.

A very tight financial regime was established. It was decided that no contract was to be let until sufficient funds had been secured to meet the estimated cost of that contract, although the early stages of work could be started prior to firm commitment of the financing of the later stages. The loans were regarded as entirely separate and were for fixed amounts. Overruns due to currency exchange rate changes or increased works were to be met entirely by the government of Malawi from its own resources. Table 3–2 shows the amounts loaned with respect to the individual projects, the sources of the loans, and the amount ultimately financed by the government of the Republic of Malawi.

REFERENCES

1. Unpublished report to Hickling Association of Canada. N.J. Ashford (Consultant Engineers) Ltd., July 1990.
2. Peters, S. "Promises and Pitfalls of Privatization," *Airport Forum* 1 (1989).
3. Goldin, F. "Financing Airport Operations Day to Day." In *Financing Airport Developments in the 90s in Europe and the USA*. Joint AOCI/ICAA Seminar, Zurich, 28–29 March 1990.
4. Lethbridge, J.R. "Financing Airport Development." *Airport Forum* 1 (1989).

5. Lethbridge, J.R. "Airport Financing." *IAMTI Management Course,* Montreal, April 1988.
6. Powter, J.R., D.J. Farthing, and S.W. Logan. "Development of International Airports in Southern Africa at Lilongwe Malawi and Gaborone Botswana: Management and Construction." *Proceedings of the Institution of Civil Engineers Part 1* 88 (February 1990): 47–80.

4

Types of Financing

4.1 INTRODUCTION

Many managers at individual airports will find that the forms of financial instruments used for financing capital debt or for providing short-term credit are limited to very few types of funding. However, as the airport sector outside the United States seems more prone to move from the public to the private sector, a more comprehensive grasp of the various forms of financial instruments becomes more important. The limited range of financing permitted by current public-sector ownership patterns is likely to be significantly broadened as the commercialization of airports permits a more diversified approach to capital and operational finance. Similarly, as more sovereign states use negotiable hard currencies, especially within Europe, the likelihood that debt will cross international borders becomes more likely. In a text written for the community of airport management at large rather than for managers in any one country, the authors are convinced that an overall treatment of the types of financing instruments, however summary, is unavoidable. Therefore, this short chapter attempts to explain the financial terminology used and to indicate how the various financial instruments relate one to another.

4.2 OVERALL STRUCTURE OF FINANCING

The financial markets can be divided into three principal categories:

1. Credit agreements
2. Equity markets
3. Capital markets

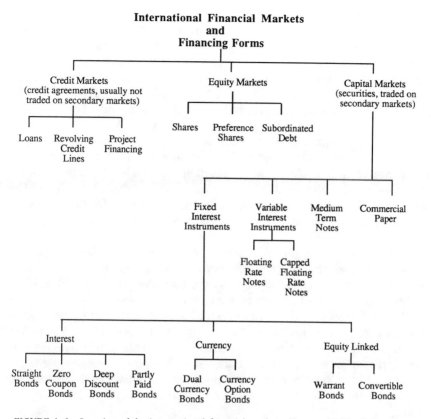

FIGURE 4–1. Overview of the international financial markets (Source: M. Wood, Dresdener Bank AG, Frankfurt.)

The interrelationship between these markets, and the subcategories of financial instruments that make up these main categories, is shown in Figure 4–1 (1).

4.3 CREDIT MARKETS

Credit markets are constituted of credit agreements between lender and borrower. In spite of general use of the term market, this word is somewhat of a misnomer. Credit agreements are not normally traded, even on secondary markets. There are three categories of credit agreement: loans, revolving credit lines, and project financing.

A straight *loan* can be made between a lender and a borrower. The lender may be a person or other single entity or, more commonly, in the case of airports, an institution. In certain circumstances, the lender may be in the form of a syndicate comprising several institutions. Loans may be secured or unsecured by some form of asset. Unsecured loans normally incur considerably higher rates of interest, which may be either fixed or variable. Fixed-rate loans have been most common in the past, but in the last twenty years, rapidly fluctuating bank rates engendered by high inflation have induced many lenders to insist on variable-rate loans, often in the form of a fixed percentage rate above that bank rate prevailing at any time throughout the life of the loan.

Revolving credit lines are established to ensure that there is sufficient working capital at all times. In some organizations, expenditures greatly outweigh revenues at particular points of the business cycle or the calendar year. The assurance of adequate working capital in the face of such fluctuation means that cash is available as and when needed. Such credit agreements permit flexibility in both drawing and repayment. Because revolving credit lines require financial institutions to retain reserves to cover possible drawings on these credit lines, the lenders commonly require a commitment fee in return for a firm commitment of liquidity to the borrower. This fee is charged in addition to the interest payable on actual credits granted.

Project financing covers credit extended with little or even no recourse to the assets of the borrower other than the income generated from the project under finance. In return for agreeing to provide credit where repayment is dependent to some extent on the success of the project, lenders inevitably require a higher success rate. For obvious reasons, credits of this nature are extended only to projects where income returns appear to be absolutely assured.

4.4 EQUITY MARKETS

Financing via *equity markets* is a form of financial instrument where there is a potential for trading the instrument on the primary or secondary market. Equity financing is not uncommon in airports, such as Frankfurt, Amsterdam, Munich, Birmingham, and Manchester. As has already been explained, however, the shares of these airports are held by public authorities and are not publicly traded. The BAA plc was the only major airport in 1990 with shares openly traded on a major stock exchange. The term *equity financing* implies that those providing the finance participate in the fortunes of the organization being financed. There are three categories of equity markets: shares, preference shares, and subordinated debt.

With *shares*, the shareholder receives a portion of profits via dividends or capital appreciation of the share value. Should losses occur, the shareholder fully participates in these. It is normal practice that the shareholder, in return for taking a full risk on the profitability of the venture, retains voting rights in the conduct and management of the enterprise at its general meetings by means of an equity share.

Preference shares are a limited form of equity holding. The preference shareholder participates fully in all losses, but if profitability ensures that funds are available, this shareholder receives a guaranteed fixed dividend income prior to the declaration of any dividend to the ordinary shareholder. It is not usual for preference shares to convey the same voting rights as ordinary shares, and in many ventures, preference shareholders have no voting rights at all.

Unlike ordinary and preference shares, *subordinated debt* is not usually traded on the markets. However, it is treated as part of the equity market in that lenders accept terms of debt repayment that place liability after ordinated debt but before shareholder interests. Lenders of subordinated debt require a high rate of interest as recompense for the higher risk involved.

4.5 CAPITAL MARKETS

Capital markets, otherwise known as *bonds* or *securities,* come in many forms, which are traded on the secondary markets. Four principal subcategories of securities can be identified:

1. Fixed-interest instruments (linked to interest, currency, or equity)
2. Variable-interest instruments
3. Medium-term notes
4. Commercial paper

Fixed-Interest Instruments: Interest

The bond markets trade in four kinds of bonds, which differ mainly in the type of interest paid or the manner in which payment is made for the bond itself.

Straight bonds are issued with a fixed rate of interest, either to a few investors by negotiation (private placement) or to the public by offerings to broad groups of investors. Interest is paid on an annual or semiannual basis. As the term *securities* implies, bonds of this nature have traditionally been issued by institutions with a sound record of financial stability and a strong asset base. In recent years, straight bonds guaranteed only by a promise of future income have been issued by institutions with a less proven record. Such "junk bonds" carried a correspondingly higher rate of interest, but it was generally recognized that the investor was at greater risk.

Zero coupon bonds are also issued at a fixed rate of interest. However, no interest payments are made until maturity. The interest is said to be "rolled up" until the maturity date, when repayment is made of the original capital, the interest accrued, and all interest on the rolled-up interest. Zero coupon bonds can be less attractive than straight bonds in periods when interest rates may rise over the life of the bond, because the capital and interim interest are locked in during the life of the bond. The market-traded price of the bonds reflects this fact.

Deep-discount bonds are securities issued with lower-than-market interest payments, at a correspondingly lower-than-market price (the so-called discount) to make them attractive to the buyer. Such bonds may be attractive in tax jurisdictions where capital gains tax is low or nonexistent.

Partly paid bonds can, in their original issue, be bought with staged initial payments in up to three installments. This permits bond purchase at a fixed interest rate, but the investor has the right to opt out after the initial payment if interest rates change, making subsequent bond issues more attractive. On the other hand, if interest rates fall, the bonds become very attractive, since the investor can continue to purchase the security at the original interest rate.

Fixed-Interest Instruments: Currency

Two bond types are linked to their ability to provide a security related to two currencies.

Dual-currency bonds are instruments in which the issue price and interest payments are in one currency, but the capital repayment on maturity is in a second currency. Exchange rates are usually fixed at the time of issue and are not those that pertain at maturity.

Currency option bonds provide the investor or the issuer with the option of payments of interest or capital at maturity to be made in one or two predetermined currencies. The rate of exchange is set at the time of issue. It is usual that the currency option is written either by the issuer or investor at that time.

Fixed-Interest Instruments: Equity Linked

Two types of bonds are linked to the equity of the issuing company itself.

Warrant bonds are securities with attached warrants. Warrants give the purchaser the opportunity to buy equity shares at some predetermined price at some predetermined time or within a predetermined period. After the issue of the warrant bond, the bond and the warrant are normally traded separately. Therefore, the imputed value of the warrant itself is reflected in the issuing price and the interest rate of the bond.

Convertible bonds offer the purchaser the right to convert the bonds into equity shares of the issuing company at some predetermined conversion rate. Securities of this nature can be very attractive to the investor. Should the issuing company not be successful, the investor is given the full guarantee of the bond. On the other hand, there is the possibility of gaining a share of the equity of what proves to be a successful company. For the issuer, the convertible bond can bring investment in a company that might otherwise find it difficult to attract finance; this, however, carries the penalty that at a later time a successful company may find its equity diluted with bondholders converting their securities for shares that have greatly increased in value. The benefits of the convertible bond to the purchaser are reflected by the ability of the issuer to offer lower-than-market interest rates.

Variable-Interest Instruments

Variable interest instruments may be divided into two categories:

1. Floating-rate notes
2. Capped floating-rate notes

Floating-rate notes are generally regarded as long-term financial instruments. They are, in fact, bonds, the interest rate of which varies to reflect prevailing market rates. The resetting of interest rates may be quarterly, semiannually, annually, or any period agreed upon at time of issue. The formula for the change in the floating rate is also specified at that time.

Capped floating-rate notes are variations of floating-rate notes in that the maximum floating interest rate is set at some predetermined level. These bonds pay a higher interest rate at issue than the ordinary floating-rate note; in return, the borrower foregoes possible higher interest rates in the future.

Medium-Term Notes

Medium-term notes (MTNs) are a relatively new market in securities. This market has been developed for investors who are looking for assets with specific medium-term maturities and currencies. It may be also useful for borrowers with specific medium-term borrowing requirements. These notes may be regarded as an extension of the more usual commercial paper market into the medium term of one to five years.

Commercial Paper

Commercial paper (CP) is a method of providing short-term finance to corporations (usually for up to six months) by investors through a dealer system. European Commercial Paper (ECP) is a relatively recent development of the original U.S. commercial paper system. It is common for standby lines of credit to be arranged for issuers so that short-term paper can be rolled over at maturity in order to provide for ongoing short-term financial commitments to be met. Commercial paper is an important element in short-term liquidity of enterprises that have highly fluctuating revenues.

REFERENCES

1. Wood, M. "Airport Development and International Financial Markets." In *Financing Airport Development in the 90s in Europe and the USA*. Joint AOCI/ICAA Seminar, Zurich, 28–29 March 1990.

5

Privatization: The Record to Date

Robert W. Poole, Jr.

President, Reason Foundation[1]

5.1 INTRODUCTION

During the late 1980s, the aviation world was swept up in the rush toward privatization or denationalization, as nations everywhere sought to sustain economic growth via increased use of the market economy. By 1991, however, only one nation had taken the major step of privatizing all its significant air transport airports. Consequently, there has been much interest in evaluating how this economic experiment has worked.

Much of the debate over airport privatization has consisted of unsupported claims by both sides. This chapter reviews the record of privatization in practice to shed some light on the questions most often raised by proponents and opponents. The discussion will be set within the context of the U.S. airport system and will examine the question of privatization in the United States by stating the contrary argument and then drawing on available evidence from longstanding or newly privatized facilities to test the validity of that argument.

Because national systems are intrinsically unique, the reader is left to apply the reasoning here to facilities and systems outside the United States, where environmental and tax legislation, labor laws and practices, capital financing options, and airport planning and operational procedures are different. The issues examined relate to

1. Stimulation to create new airports
2. Increasing capital investment in airports
3. Achieving operational cost savings

---

[1] Reason Foundation, Santa Monica, CA 90405

4. Shifting to market pricing of services
5. Reducing capital costs
6. Sustaining noise-abatement procedures
7. Improving passenger service

It is largely with respect to these issues that the privatization of U.S. airports has been discussed. The issue of monopoly power and its control, which has dominated discussions in Europe and elsewhere, has not, as yet, been seen to be important in the U.S. context.

5.2 CRITICISMS OF PROPOSED U.S. AIRPORT PRIVATIZATION

In response to the controversy over the 1989 proposal by Albany, New York, to sell or lease its airport to a private consortium, U.S. Transportation Secretary Samuel K. Skinner directed the Federal Aviation Administration to have the issue addressed by the Aviation System Capacity Task Force, headed by J. Donald Reilly. The Reilly task force's Privatization Working Group split into two factions on the issue and was unable to reach an overall consensus.

The antiprivatizers, led by certain airline and general aviation interests, argued that privatization of airports would increase costs to users and possibly restrict access to general aviation. The other group, led by companies interested in being in the airport business, argued that privatization would lead to efficiencies and to increased investment in capacity additions.

Some degree of consensus was achieved, acknowledging that private firms can and do legally manage and operate airports already, but it was felt that the federal government should continue to ensure airport safety and access in the event of privatization and that each proposed privatization should be evaluated on its own merits, with extensive consultation with user groups.

In terms of the forms that privatization might take, there was general support for the idea that private firms might continue to manage airports under contract and to build and operate new airports that increase existing capacity and do not eliminate existing airports. But there appeared to be significant concern with respect to the possible sale or long-term lease of existing airports and creation of major new privately owned terminal facilities (1). This type of privatization raised two key issues: the taking of profits off the airport and the protection of the public interest in the airports.

Several submissions to the working group advanced the position that privatization (generally meaning the sale or long-term lease of existing airports) should be considered only if it can be "proven to result in improved safety, greater efficiency, and lower costs for the shipping and traveling public" (2) or "where it can be demonstrated that privatization will add capacity and lower use cost" (3). Opponents also raised concerns over whether private firms would be able to deal as well as government with such issues as noise and other environmental impacts. And much concern was raised over the monopoly aspects of airports in many cities.

Although many of these points have been elaborated in various ways, the following list covers the major questions that were raised during the 1989–1990 debates on this issue:

1. Would privatization lead to capacity-increasing investment in airports?
2. What evidence is there for lower operating costs and greater efficiency with private ownership and operation?
3. What impact would there be on the prices charged to airport users?
4. Would capital costs be higher, given the lack of access to tax exempt bond funding?
5. How would private airports deal with noise mitigation?
6. Would private operators provide better or worse service to airline passengers using their airport facilities?
7. What kind of regulations would be needed to deal with potential monopoly problems?

The study on which this chapter is based examined evidence in the form of available data of the performance of public and privatized airports.

5.3 AIRPORT PRIVATIZATION TO DATE

Five different forms of airport privatization had taken place by 1991: the sale of existing airports, long-term leases of airports to private firms, contract operation of airports, creation of new terminal facilities by build-operate-transfer consortia, and the creation of new airports as private business ventures. Each offers lessons for policymakers making decisions on whether or not privatization is to be allowed and how it should be carried out.

Sale of Existing Airports

The best-known privatization to date is undoubtedly the British government's 1987 conversion of the British Airports Authority into a private company, BAA plc. Initially all stock was owned by the British government, but in 1987 the company was floated by a public stock offering on the London Stock Exchange. The company owned and operated the three large London airports (Heathrow, Gatwick, and Stansted) and the four main Scottish airports (Aberdeen, Edinburgh, Glasgow, and Prestwick). The initial offering valued the company at $2.5 billion, and by spring of 1990, the market valuation had grown to $4 billion.

Less well-known is a second British privatization, the recent purchase of a 76 percent interest in Liverpool's Speke airport by British Aerospace for $21 million. While the airport currently has only a small degree of airline service (it is only 20 m from Manchester airport), BAe developed plans to turn the airport into a $2 billion wayport and industrial airport to handle the expected continued growth that cannot be accommodated at Heathrow, Gatwick, and Manchester. Its plans call for new terminals and runways designed to handle 200,000 air transport movements (ATMs) per year, with the early development of a business park on 450 acres of the 4,000 available acres (4).

By 1991 several other planned airport sales had been announced. The Danish government planned to sell Copenhagen's Kastrup airport, with the first 25 percent of the shares to be offered during 1991. The New Zealand government planned to sell its three (already corporatized) international airports at Auckland, Christchurch, and Wellington.

Belgium partially privatized the Brussels airport by setting up the Brussels Airport Terminal company. BATC's ownership is 52 percent by private investors (mostly banks) and 48 percent by the government's airport and airways agency. The agency contributed the old terminals and land at the airport, whereas the private parties provided the capital for a new, larger terminal. The government is empowered to sell some of its 48 percent to the public but may never own less than 30 percent.

By 1991, a number of other governments were considering selling major commercial airports. Among those studying the issue were France, Germany, Jamaica, Malaysia, Singapore, and South Africa.

Long-Term Leases

Although no commercial airport in the United States has yet been sold to private enterprise, several sizable airports have been leased to private firms.

Rickenbacker field in Ohio is a former Air Force base that has been converted to civilian use. The land and facilities have been leased for seventy years to Turner Construction Company. Turner and Diversified Investors created Rickenbacker Development Corporation to attract business investment for an industrial airport concept. Its first major project was a $70 million hub facility for Flying Tigers (subsequently mothballed following that airline's merger into Federal Express). Airport operations are managed by Lockheed Air Terminal under a several-year management contract.

A second example of a long-term lease is the Morristown, New Jersey, airport. In 1982, the municipality leased the airport for ninety-nine years to D.M. Airport Developers, Inc. The company took over the airport's debt, agreed to refurbish the rundown facility, and contracted to pay rent plus a percentage of certain sales in exchange for the right to develop office facilities on the property. As a condition of the lease, the city required D.M. to provide professional airport management; consequently, the airport is operated by Avco Services. The airport today is solidly profitable, with some 250,000 general aviation operations per year.

Another major general-aviation airport operated under lease is Teterboro, New Jersey. Its owner, the Port Authority of New York and New Jersey, leased it to Pan Am World Services for thirty years in 1970. As is the case with Morristown, the lessee (in this case, Pan Am) makes the relevant grant applications to the Federal Aviation Administration (FAA), and both airports routinely receive federal grants, despite being operated by private enterprise under long-term lease agreements. World Services pays the Port Authority an annual fixed fee plus a percentage of the gross revenues. To the extent that it keeps costs under control, therefore, World Services keeps a percentage of each year's revenues as profit.

Two airports with commercial airline service are also operated by the private sector under lease-management contracts. In 1986 the city of Atlantic City signed ten-year lease agreements (with the option for a fifteen-year extension in each case) with Pan Am World Services for the operation of its two airports, Bader Field and Atlantic City International. The former has commuter airline operations in addition to general aviation, whereas the latter has both commuter and larger jet airliner operations (USAir Fokker 100s). At Atlantic City International, World Services is leasing some 83 acres, encompassing the terminal, commercial aircraft apron, parking lots, and other civilian activities, whereas the FAA (which has a substantial facility at this airport) owns and operates the actual runways and the tower. Under both lease agreements, Atlantic City receives either a base amount or a percentage of the airports' gross revenue, whichever is greater.

Contract Operation

The best-known U.S. example of a large airport being operated by a private firm is the Burbank Airport in California. Owned by an airport authority of the cities of Burbank, Glendale, and Pasadena, the airport has been operated since the authority's creation in 1978 by Lockheed Air Terminal. Burbank ranks 59th in size among U.S. airports, as measured by annual passenger enplanements. It receives federal grant funds on the same basis as other air carrier airports, despite being operated by a private contractor.

Several other air carrier airports are operated by private firms. Lockheed also operates Stewart International, a former Air Force base in upstate New York (which owns Stewart), and the FAA is encouraging other airlines to begin service there. In addition, the Westchester County/White Plains (New York)

Airport is operated under contract by Pan Am World Services. It is served by several airlines and also handles extensive general aviation traffic.

Contract operation is also well known in Britain. BAA (through its Airports U.K. subsidiary) has at various times operated the Biggin Hill, Exeter, and Southend airports under contract.

Build-Operate-Transfer

The *build-operate-transfer* (B-O-T) concept involves government contracting with a private consortium to finance, design, build, own, and operate a major facility, with title eventually reverting to the government once the investment has been paid for. Well known in the highway, bridge, and power-plant fields for several decades, B-O-T has recently begun to be used to create new airport facilities.

Toronto's terminal 3 was the first major project of this type. The team of Huang and Danczkay and Lockheed Air Terminal developed this $300 million, 24-gate terminal at the Lester B. Pearson International Airport, which Lockheed then operated. The project included freeway access roads and runway improvements, with a total cost of nearly $500 million.

In 1989, BAA joined Canadian Airports Ltd., a joint venture with Toronto Dominion Bank, the Ontario State Pension Board, and a real estate group. In July 1990 they announced an unsolicited proposal to Transport Canada to finance, expand, and operate the existing terminals 1 and 2 at Pearson International.

In Turkey, a Lockheed-led team (including several Turkish firms) developed a $200 million 18-gate terminal at Ataturk International Airport in Istanbul. Upon its 1992 completion, Lockheed is expected to operate both the terminal and the airport itself.

In England, a public-private consortium, Euro-Hub, has been formed to develop and operate a large new terminal at the Birmingham airport. Similar consortia are expected to develop the new airports in Hong Kong and Macao.

Creating New Airports

One of the basic premises of airport privatization as a national policy is that putting *existing* airports on a commercial basis will attract investment into the airport business, ultimately leading to the creation of entirely new airports. That premise appears to be being borne out in Britain.

The first such airport to be created opened its doors in 1987. London City Airport (LCA) was created specifically to serve short-take-off-and-landing (STOL) aircraft, such as the Dash 7. The $52 million facility is located in the Docklands area of London, the center of a $7 billion office and residential development area just 6 mi from the City of London. Not yet a commercial success, the airport's fortunes depend on attracting additional airline service and obtaining permission for operations by the BAe 146 jetliner in addition to the turboprop Dash 7. Although the LCA facility was planned and constructed prior to the privatization of airports in Britain, it can be construed as an example of private interest in investment in the increasingly deregulated airport sector.

By 1991, a second new airport project was under development in Britain at Sheffield. Budge Mining went forward with plans to develop the $170 million airport and to begin construction in 1992. It included a major business park adjoining the M1 motorway. Budge announced that the airport will be managed by Airports U.K., a subsidiary of BAA.

Private firms also planned major property expansions of two other British airports. At Newcastle, European Land revealed plans for a $1.275 billion business park and residential complex. Furthermore, BAA, having not long previously purchased the privately owned Southampton Airport, planned to add a $500 million business park and hotel, as well as building a new terminal and upgrading other facilities.

In the entire United States, to date there has been only one new commercial service airport created as a quasi-private project. Alliance Airport, which opened in December 1989, was developed by the Perot Group and the City of Forth Worth. The Perot Group assembled the 3,400 acres of land and dedicated 418 acres to the city for runway/taxiway use, and the FAA provided a $31 million grant for construction and additionally funded the control tower and landing aids. The remaining property is all privately owned and offers direct aircraft access to the airport's taxiways, if desired. As an Industrial Airport, Alliance serves business and private aviation, relieving congestion at DFW and Love Field.

5.4 CAPACITY ADDITIONS AND INVESTMENT

Investment at BAA Airports

The most important evidence on the question of capital investment comes from BAA, the only case thus far of large air carrier airports being sold to private investors.

Although BAA is privately owned, additions to landside (terminal) and airside (runway) capacity in Britain require government approval. In particular, airport capacity in the southeast of England (London area) is governed by the government's Traffic Distribution Rules (TDRs), established by the 1986 Airports Act. Under these rules, there can be no further addition of international passenger service at Heathrow, no charter flights at all, and no general aviation

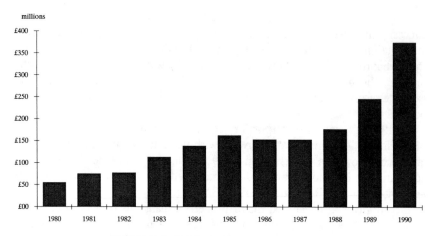

FIGURE 5-1. BAA capital investment, 1980-1990

or cargo operations during peak hours. The intent was to direct growth to Gatwick and, later, to Stansted. While the government is considering changing or abolishing the TDRs, to date they have been a major factor in directing BAA's investment decisions.

Overall, the TDRs constrain the addition of any new runway in the southeast until sometime after 2003; instead, capacity increases are being made on the landside. BAA opened its new terminal 4 at Heathrow in 1986, after which it refurbished and expanded Terminal 3. A second (north) terminal at Gatwick was opened in 1988, which will be expanded in a second phase. A new terminal was developed in Stansted, opening in 1991. If the Stansted facility is expanded, as BAA plans, the London airports are expected to have sufficient capacity through the late 1990s.

Figure 5-1 shows total BAA capital investment for the financial (fiscal) years ending March 30, 1980, through 1990. Capital spending more than doubled in the three years following privatization (5). However, much of this capital spending was visualized and planned for prior to privatization.

It is perhaps relevant to note that the first major investment after privatization was the approval of £55 million (approximately $94 million) for the expansion of Glasgow. This demonstrated the company's continued interest in its smaller facilities.

In addition to the terminal expansion projects noted previously, BAA is also investing in improved service to passengers. One of the most dramatic of these projects is the Heathrow Express Rail Link. This $440 million project will serve an estimated six million people per year. Linking all four terminals with downtown London's Paddington Station, the line will supplement the congested Piccadilly Line (part of the London Underground), which now serves Heathrow. The new line will cut the current journey time of nearly one hour to central London to just sixteen minutes.

The project is a joint venture between BAA and British Rail. BAA is investing 80 percent of the cost and will operate the trains itself, using an existing BR main line from Paddington to Hayes, near the airport. The trains and station platforms are being designed to accommodate people with luggage as well as wheelchairs. Onboard display screens will provide departing flight information on outbound trains. The line is scheduled to be in operation by 1994.

BAA has also diversified into the hotel business. BAA Hotels Ltd. planned to develop thirty hotels over the period 1991–1996. Two four-star Sterling Hotels opened in 1990, one at Heathrow and one at Gatwick. Each is connected by walkway to a terminal (terminal 4 at Heathrow, north terminal at Gatwick). Also, a medium-priced Harlequin Hotel opened at Stansted in 1991.

Investment at Lease-Managed Airports

The prominent examples of airports leased to private owners are the busy general aviation airports of Morristown and Teterboro, New Jersey.

Morristown has leased its airport to D.M. Airport Developers, Inc. since May 1982 (for a ninety-nine-year term). Under municipal operation, the airport had consistently operated at a loss and was in a run-down condition at the time of the agreement. During the first three years, D.M.'s contract manager, AVCO, carried out an extensive renovation of the airport, investing some $350,000 in rebuilding and replacing the inoperative airport lighting system, resurfacing and grooving the main runway, and refurbishing the snow-removal and maintenance vehicles. (The airport won the AAAE's Balchen Certificate in Snow and Ice Removal in 1985.) In 1984–1985, with the aid of a federal grant, the airport added a new holding apron to relieve runway congestion, installed a visual approach slope indicator system, and installed new signage. Today, the airport is considered a model operation.

The Teterboro airport was leased in 1970 by its owner, the Port Authority of New York and New Jersey, to Pan Am World Services, Inc. for thirty years. Since the lease was signed in 1970, some $29.2 million has been invested in the airport. World Services invested $13.7 million of that total, comprising $9.6 million in new hangars and improved facilities and $4.1 million as the sponsor's share of federal grant-supported airside improvements. Another $15.5 million has been invested by tenants, primarily in hangar facilities. Under Port Authority operation, Teterboro had been losing up to $400,000 per year. The airport has operated profitably since 1973, with World Services paying the Port Authority an annual fee plus a percentage of the gross revenues.

Proposed Private Investment at Albany Airport

The proposal by Lockheed Air Terminal and British American, Ltd., to buy or lease the Albany Airport involved a substantial investment in increasing that airport's capacity. A two-phase expansion of the small and inadequate terminal was proposed, bringing enclosed passenger loading bridges (jetways) to the airport for the first time. The initial twenty-seven-gate addition (thirteen jetway gates and fourteen commuter gates) would add 233,000 ft² to the existing terminal, as well as double-decking the arrival and departure roadway and adding a multilevel parking facility. The terminal expansion (phase 1) alone would be a $106 million project and would be completed within three and one-half years.

LAT/BA also proposed spending another $69 million to construct a 250-room hotel plus office, warehouse, and service-center facilities on airport property. In addition, BA proposed to invest $75 million in office and retail facilities in its British American Plaza, adjacent to the airport.

5.5 OPERATING COSTS AND PRODUCTIVITY

Does the private sector's need to earn a profit lead to lower operating costs and increased productivity? Data are available from BAA's experience as an airport owner/operator and also from Lockheed Air Terminal's experience as a contract operator.

One basic measure of productivity is output per employee; output is often measured by revenue generated. Figure 5–2 shows BAA's labor productivity by this measure, both in nominal and in real (corrected for inflation) terms. By

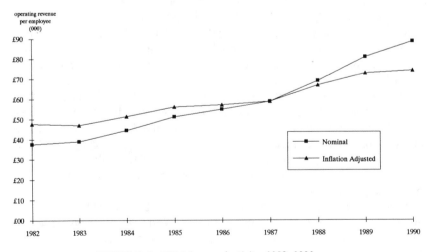

FIGURE 5–2. BAA labor productivity, 1982–1990

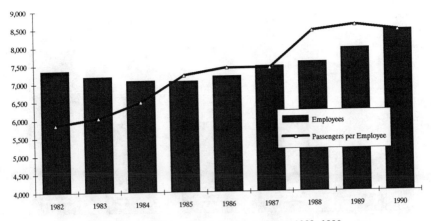

FIGURE 5-3. BAA workforce and productivity, 1982–1990

either measure, productivity increased sharply upon privatization in 1987, though it had been trending upward for the previous four years as BAA was getting ready to be privatized. Figure 5–3 shows another measure of productivity: the number of passengers handled per employee each year. That measure, too, has trended steadily upward, whereas total employment has grown very slightly since 1985. Care, however, must be taken in interpreting this measure over time. By contracting out services previously performed by airport staff, the productivity per employee can be artificially inflated.

How well is BAA keeping its costs under control? Figure 5–4 shows the

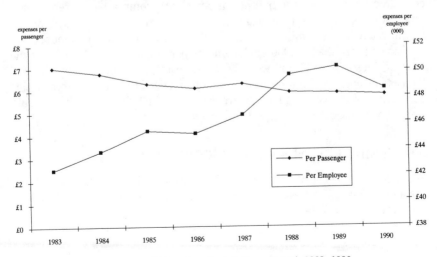

FIGURE 5-4. BAA unit costs, inflation-adjusted, 1983–1990

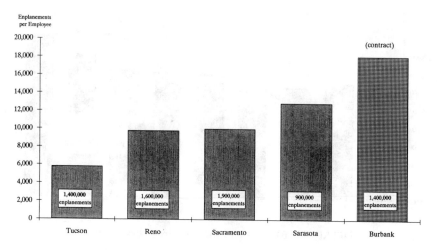

FIGURE 5–5. U.S. airport productivity comparison (Nonhubs)

trends in inflation-adjusted operating expenses. On a per-employee basis, these costs have gone up by 16.4 percent over the past seven years, an annual average real cost increase of just 2 percent. On a per-passenger basis, however, operating expenses have trended steadily downward, declining by 18 percent in real terms since 1983.

In the United States, figures for contractor-operated Burbank Airport were compared with those of four other airports with comparable passenger volumes. All five have annual enplanements of between 900,000 and 1.9 million (compared with 1.4 million for Burbank). As can be seen in Figure 5–5, Burbank's more than 18,000 enplanements per employee are three times the level of Tucson's 5,833 and well above the levels of Reno, Sacramento, and Sarasota airports. Again, however, it must be realized that such a cross-airport comparison may overstate true differences in productivity where there is substantial subcontracting of airport functions.

5.6 AIRSIDE REVENUES AND PRICING POLICY

Much concern has been raised in the U.S. airport privatization debate that a privately owned airport would drastically raise prices to airlines, thereby harming either (or both) the airlines and their passengers. Antiprivatizers generally cite BAA's London airports, especially Heathrow, as a prime example of how bad privatization would be.

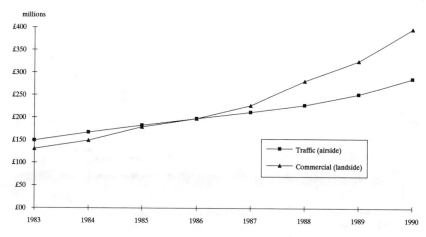

FIGURE 5-6. BAA revenue sources, 1983–1990

BAA's Pricing Policies

Despite the common perception that BAA derives a majority of its revenue from airline charges, since 1987 an increasing majority of its revenues have come from landside ("commercial") sources. Figure 5–6 shows the relative growth in two types of revenue since 1983; as of financial year 1990, airside revenue was down to 42 percent of the total. Clearly, there was significant untapped potential for deriving increased revenue from concessions, rents, and services, and BAA began tapping into that potential after privatization.

On an overall basis, BAA's revenue per passenger and revenue per air transport movement (ATM) have trended upward during both pre- and postprivatization, with a faster rate of growth (as expected) since privatization, as seen in Figure 5–7.

Some U.S. airlines have contended that airside charges at Heathrow and Gatwick are excessive. Indeed, Pan American and TWA have had a long-standing lawsuit against BAA and the British government over pricing at Heathrow. That action has focused considerable attention on the relative cost to airlines and passengers of using Heathrow. BAA has compared landing fees, passenger charges, and aircraft parking charges at Heathrow with those at other large European airports. Holding traffic constant at Heathrow's level, the results are shown in Table 5–1, based on 1988 fee schedules (6).

How do Heathrow's charges compare with those of other major U.S. international airports? The most accurate and complete data are provided by Avmark Aviation Economist's annual index of airport charges. Table 5–2 shows

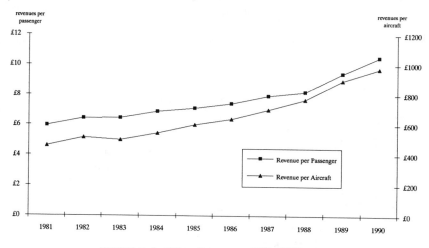

FIGURE 5–7. BAA unit revenues, 1981–1990

the actual amounts for landing, aircraft parking, and passenger charges for three types of aircraft at major U.S. airports compared with Heathrow, for international flights. The Heathrow charges are based on a weighted average of peak and off-peak charges; the U.S. charges include the $3 ticket tax paid by departing passengers on international flights. Kennedy is seen to be more costly than Heathrow, with Chicago's O'Hare coming in very close behind.

Underlying the charges made concerning BAA's "excessive" rates is some airlines' opposition to the fundamentally different basis on which BAA charges

TABLE 5–1. Comparative Total Airport Charges for Five European Airports

Airport	Total International Charges (pounds sterling)
Heathrow	119,300
Amsterdam	128,600
Copenhagen	146,100 (high est.) 141,100 (low est.)
Frankfurt	158,500 (high est.) 152,600 (low est.)
Paris (CDG)	121,200 (high est.) 110,600 (low est.)

TABLE 5–2. Comparison of Airport Charges for Three Aircraft Types Handled at Seven Airports

Airport	DC-9-30	A-300B2	747-200B	Index[a]
Heathrow	$1,022	$2,339	$3,480	111
Kennedy	1,134	2,763	4,451	130
O'Hare	786	2,200	3,433	98
LaGuardia	599	1,523	—	77
Miami	599	1,594	2,559	73
Newark	543	1,443	2,820	70
Los Angeles	257	722	1,155	32

[a] Index based on twenty major airports; 100 is average of all airport charges. Data are for 1988.

Source: Avmark Aviation Economist, with permission

airlines and passengers for its services. BAA uses a modified form of marginal-cost pricing. In the late 1970s BAA changed its depreciation policies from historic cost accounting to a current-cost basis (which increased the value of its assets more than threefold). By the mid-1980s, well before privatization, it had in place a policy of charging for landing weight of the aircraft. These pricing policies include peak and off-peak values for landing charges, aircraft parking charges, and passenger facility charges in the form of the passenger load supplement; peak values are based on both time of day and season of the year. Since 1985, there have also been noise-related surcharges for noisy (Stage I) aircraft and rebates for quiet (Stage III) aircraft (7).

In sharp contrast, many U.S. airports still follow what is called a *residual cost* approach. As explained in Chapter 1, airlines agree to pay only the residual of each year's airport expenses not recovered from all other sources—primarily from concession revenues. The other approach, called *compensatory,* negotiates in advance a set of airline fees and charges according to rules related to costs. Under both approaches, however, landing fees are based on aircraft weight, which typically means that smaller planes pay far less than the value of the service being provided. In addition, virtually no U.S. airport charges higher prices at peak hours or seasons, and very few charge differential fees based on noise.

Economists are virtually unanimous in endorsing marginal cost pricing of the kind employed by BAA and most other investor-owned companies with public-utility characteristics. This kind of pricing promotes the most efficient use of airport resources—e.g., by providing incentives to shift some operations out of congested peak periods or to lower-priced reliever airports. This kind of price also generates additional revenues precisely at those points in the aviation system that most need new capacity investment.

Protesting U.S. airlines fear that private airport operators would price their services in a businesslike way, meaning "similar to the way BAA does business." However, their claim that a switch to market pricing would have a large negative impact on consumers is highly questionable.

5.7 CAPITAL COSTS

Another concern is that the capital costs of privately owned and operated airports will be higher than those of municipal airports. Because the latter have access to tax-exempt municipal bonds in the United States, it is assumed that their interest expenses will be less and, therefore, that their capital costs will be lower.

It seems obvious that the exact same facility financed on a taxable-debt basis will cost more over its life than if it were financed on a nontaxable-debt basis. However, there are other factors to be considered.

Lower Construction Cost

The first consideration is what capital costs will have to be financed in the first place. In other words, does private ownership make any difference in the construction costs of an airport terminal or other facility?

The old adage that "time is money" is nowhere more true than in the field of construction. In this respect, privatization is already well known for producing substantial savings. Numerous case studies in such areas as wastewater treatment plants, highways, and correctional facilities developed under B-O-T privatization plans have documented savings in development time of up to one-half what would have been required under traditional public-sector procurement methods.

The proof of this method's cost effectiveness is its successful track record in numerous B-O-T projects around the world. In the airport area, the Terminal 3 project in Toronto is a good example. Transport Canada has estimated that conventional government procurement of this project would have required seven years, from the go-ahead decision to opening day. The Lockheed/Huan and Danczkay team's schedule, by contrast, calls for just under three and one-half years from start to finish. With one year less in the actual construction cycle, this time saving saves a full year's interest on the construction funding. Similar savings are expected on the Istanbul airport terminal project.

Another example of time savings is the Perot Group's public-private partnership to develop Alliance Airport. From groundbreaking to opening, the airport took just over eighteen and one-half months to build—the shortest time on record. Factoring in the previous eighteen months from original concept to groundbreaking, the airport's total development time was just over three years, considerably less than for typical public sector airport projects.

A key element in both time and cost savings is a technique known as *design-build*. The private firm heading the project assembles in advance a team of firms to design and build the facility, often using fast-track scheduling, in which certain phases of design overlap with the start of construction. The major time saving is due to the elimination of the conventional competitive bidding process. This process, which is usually necessary in the public sector to prevent under-the-table deals (which presumably would lead to higher costs than the competitive process), adds large amounts of time and paperwork to the process.

The private firm that owns and will operate the project has every incentive to obtain the best price deal (otherwise it will inherit an overly costly and, hence, less profitable project). But it is free to do this by a process of negotiation, generally involving guarantees of cost and schedule by the construction contractors. In addition, because the contractors are involved in negotiation during the design process, the designers and the builders can interact to develop lower-cost solutions to various design problems, reducing the number of costly change-orders that would otherwise occur during construction. The owner can and does influence both the designers and the builders to cooperate in this fashion, in order to hold down total project costs.

Taxable versus Tax-Exempt Financing

Because the private sector has strong incentives to lower the cost of construction as well as to develop the project in considerably less time, the total amount that must be financed will generally be lower with a privatized project. But what about the financing costs?

Financial analysts have pointed out that, with all things considered, the cost of money for public and private infrastructure projects is approximately the same (8). McDonough points out, first of all, that the after-tax cost of debt to the private borrower is generally less expensive than tax-exempt debt to the municipal borrower (typically 6.69 percent for the former compared with 8.05 percent for the latter). The reason for this is that interest costs are deductible to the private taxable borrower.

On the other hand, the equity component of private projects is expensive, since private investors of risk capital require a substantial rate of return on that kind of investment. Even though equity is usually only a small fraction (5 to 20 percent) of the total financing of a privatized project, the higher cost of this component raises the total financing costs.

McDonough points out that public-sector projects also include what amounts to an equity component in their financing package—the debt service reserve fund. He argues that the true cost of this component (which ultimately comes from either customers or general taxpayers) is comparable to the cost of private equity. Hence, overall, private-sector financing is inherently less costly than public-sector financing.

There is, nonetheless, a widespread perception that public-sector financing is less costly. To compensate for this perceived advantage, McDonough recommends modifying the tax code to provide for accelerated depreciation for private infrastructure projects and/or permitting transportation projects to be eligible for private-activity bonds in the tax-exempt market.

5.8 NOISE MITIGATION

Is the private sector less able to cope with the problem of noise impact on surrounding communities? Noise is both a nuisance at common law and the frequent object of specific governmental laws and regulations. The evidence to date suggests that private sector airports cope with noise at least as well as public sector airports.

In Britain, government regulation of airport noise predates privatization. Under the Aviation Security Act of 1982, the Secretary of State has the power to require airport operators to limit noise or to mitigate its effect. Britain's southeast airports have been designated for regulation under the act. Hence, regulations designate approach and departure paths and impose limits on night operations. In addition, maximum takeoff noise limits have been set for Heathrow and Gatwick and are planned for introduction at Stansted as that airport develops. Heathrow and Gatwick were also required to make noise-insulation grants to certain nearby residences during the 1980s. In addition, under the Land Compensation Act of 1973, each BAA airport is liable to pay compensation for loss of value of nearby properties due to certain additions to the airports.

How has BAA responded to these regulations? Prior to privatization, as part of its commercialization, BAA adopted noise-related surcharges and rebates as part of its landing charges. Specifically, since 1985 the older, noisier Stage I aircraft have been required to pay a 25 percent surcharge on all landing fees, whereas the quieter Stage III aircraft enjoy modest rebates on those fees. In addition, since January 1987, BAA has offered to purchase a limited number of properties near Heathrow and Gatwick that are severely affected by noise but that predate the qualifying dates for payments under the Land Compensation Act.

Figure 5–8 shows that during 1975–1988, the noise impact of Heathrow steadily diminished, despite the continued growth of air traffic. The figure shows the area, in square kilometers, affected by noise of a certain magnitude

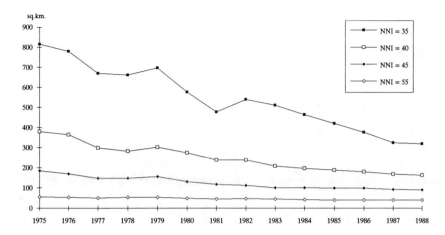

FIGURE 5–8. Heathrow noise impact reduction, 1975–1988

[using the British Noise and Number Impact (NNI) system]. In addition, the number of "noncompliance" incidents at Heathrow has declined sharply. In 1979, such incidents constituted 1.7 percent of takeoffs; this number fell to 0.5 percent in 1984, 0.18 percent in 1986, 0.14 percent in 1987, and 0.11 percent in 1988.

Similar progress has been shown by contractor-operated Burbank airport. The grant agreement by which the FAA helped fund the purchase of the airport in 1978 specified that its noise impact area could not increase in the future. In fact, that impact area has shrunk dramatically over the subsequent twelve years, as shown in Figure 5–9. The 403 acres of land impacted by noise levels of 70 decibels or higher in 1978 had declined to just over 25.1 acres in 1989—a 93.8 percent reduction.

The airline agreed to a unique noise-control program, under which non–Stage III aircraft were phased out by April 1987. In exchange, the airport has declined to impose slot restrictions like those in effect at John Wayne airport in Orange County and the Long Beach airport—both of which, like Burbank, are surrounded by residential areas. Thus, at Burbank from 1978 to 1989, annual air transport movements have increased from 34,395 to 43,828, despite the ban on non–Stage III aircraft. On the basis of this program's success, the FAA has awarded the airport a $2.5 million grant to begin sound insulation of nearby schools.

Although the Burbank Airport Authority and Lockheed Air terminal did not use noise-related fees to accomplish the substantial noise reduction (cf. BAA), they did use an economic incentive, no slot controls, to win the airlines'

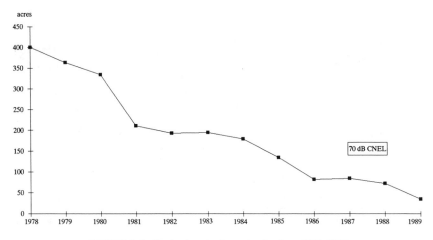

FIGURE 5–9. Burbank noise impact reduction, 1978–1989

approval of phasing out noisy aircraft. Several other U.S. airports are moving in the direction of economic incentives.

The Washington state legislature has considered a noise-fee ordinance for the Seattle-Tacoma International Airport and Boeing Field. It would charge $25 for each daytime landing or takeoff and $50 for each such operation at night (after 11 P.M.). Stage III aircraft would pay only 20 percent of these amounts. All revenues from the fees would go into a noise-mitigation account in the state treasury and be used only for that purpose.

In November 1989 Palm Beach County adopted a noise fee ordinance for Palm Beach International. Stage I aircraft are already banned from the airport, so the main targets of the fees are Stage II planes. Daytime operations by these aircraft are charged $13, whereas night landings must pay $130 and night takeoffs, $1,300. Night operations by Stage III planes pay only $10, whereas daytime Stage III operations receive a credit. The proceeds from the noise fees can be used for noise mitigation and to pay for credits to Stage III operators.

It seems quite clear, based on the foregoing, that private operators of airports can operate aggressive noise-control programs. Noise-related fees are already in operation in the United States and would be readily available as a tool for use by private airport owner-operators. The private sector's exposure to liability actions for noise impacts provides a strong motivation for it to act aggressively on noise mitigation. Furthermore, noise fees provide a powerful means of both (1) giving aircraft operators economic incentives to alter their operations toward quieter aircraft and (2) providing the airport company with revenue needed for noise-mitigation activities.

Indeed, the ability of a privatized airport to charge noise fees and fund compensation to those near the airport who are impacted by noise may, over time, reduce community opposition to the airport's presence and thereby make it easier for capacity expansions to occur. In addition, as (9) suggests, a city that depends on a regular stream of revenue from the airport (e.g., from property taxes) may be overreceptive to requests for zoning changes and other permissions required for expansion. Privatized airports, in short, are no more likely to be regarded as bad neighbors than their municipally owned counterparts. In some cases, they are less likely to be so regarded (10).

5.9 CUSTOMER SATISFACTION

How do passengers fare in a privatized airport? Are they taken for granted and herded about like cattle? Are they pampered and fussed over, as valuable customers? We have already seen that BAA is managing to derive increasing revenue from each passenger, on average (Figure 5–7). But how do the customers feel about using a for-profit airport?

BAA began quarterly passenger opinion surveys in June 1983, in the years when it operated as a governmental authority and was expected to be self-supporting. In 1989, two years after privatization, the frequency was changed to monthly. Approximately 20 different aspects of airport service are covered, with an emphasis on those areas over which BAA (as opposed to airlines or customers/immigration staff) have direct control. Reports of the survey results are circulated to airport management, and targets are set for service levels in terms of customer satisfaction levels, as revealed by the surveys. The surveys are conducted by BAA's in-house market research group. Such measurements are further discussed in Chapter 9.

Figure 5–10 shows the results on an annualized basis for the four principal services that are monitored (11). The figure reports the percentage of departing passengers expressing satisfaction with the given service. First, note that all the results show a slight upward trend over the five-year period, with no significant difference before and after privatization. Assuming no changes in the survey methodology before and after, it seems as if privatization has not interrupted the steady improvement in the level of passenger satisfaction. Second, it can be seen that BAA does a much better job with some services than with others. Although passengers are highly satisfied with their interactions with uniformed staff and with the terminals' cleanliness, some 15 percent are not happy with the catering service. Clearly, there is still room for improvement in these areas.

No comparative study data are available for major U.S. airports, so it is not possible to say whether passengers using JFK and LAX are more or less satisfied than those using Heathrow and Gatwick. However, the fact that BAA is devot-

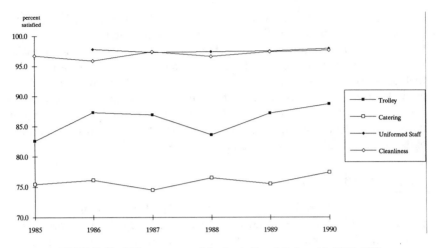

FIGURE 5–10. BAA customer satisfaction indices (all airports), 1985–1990

ing considerable attention to surveying upward of 65,000 customers each month indicates BAA's seriousness, as the airport owner, about pleasing the customer.

Will private enterprise design airports for greater customer convenience and satisfaction? BAA's development of a high-speed rail link to central London is one indication that this can be so. The design of Toronto's privately developed Terminal 3 is another case in point. Lockheed Air Terminal and Huang and Danczkay planned it from the outset to be user-friendly. Already named Trillium, after the provincial flower of Ontario, the terminal features a great hall "totally dedicated to the traveller's convenience and pleasure," to quote the marketing literature. Planned amenities include shopping (including a branch of London's famed Harrods department store), dining and hospitality outlets, art and cultural exhibits, an attached business complex, and an international hotel.

While many U.S. airports include advertising signs in certain areas, others do not. As a commercial enterprise, Trillium is being designed from the outset for advertising displays, including the purchase of time on the terminal's own video network and the opportunity to sponsor events and activities within the great hall. Given the upmarket social status of most air travelers, these advertising opportunities are being marketed at premium prices to select advertisers. While some may object to such commercialization, advertising can relieve the boredom of passenger time spent in terminals, as well as generating revenue that, other things being equal, will mean less pressure for increased passenger fees.

A preview of what would be likely to happen under privatization is appearing at certain U.S. airports. Those hub airports that are in competition with others, especially gateway hubs competing for international business, have begun changing their concession policies, opening up the business to a number of firms, both local operators and affiliates of national chains. Among the pacesetters have been Boston, Miami, Seattle-Tacoma, and San Francisco. One of the key findings has been that brand-name firms attract higher volume, permitting the airport to reduce the percentage of gross revenue it takes while still maintaining revenue levels. The result is lower prices to consumers as well as increased revenue to the airport (12).

These limited experiments, both in Britain and the United States, indicate that airports present huge commercial opportunities for the retailing of both goods and services. Some 40 percent for all caviar sold in Western Europe is purchased at Heathrow, which is also home to the world's highest-volume Burger King. Recreational services, such as at Denver and Pittsburgh's new Tee-Off and Take-Off golf-playing shops, are an almost totally untapped market. Other services, such as fully equipped business centers, conference facilities, and short-term hotel accommodations, are sorely lacking at most airports. There is significant scope for entrepreneurship in this field, discerning additional human wants and filling them, at a profit.

There is considerable evidence that U.S. airports are, in many cases, far from fully exploiting the commercial landside revenue potential. The opportunity to sell goods and services to an audience that is virtually captive, has time available for shopping, and is of above-average income is something that is commercially salable to many merchandizing and service companies.

5.10 PRICE/PROFIT REGULATION

The British Model

In the 1986 Airports Act, which authorized airport privatization in the U.K., a regulatory framework was set forth. It provides that any airport with an annual turnover of £1 million[2] or more is subject to economic regulation of its airside charges, specifically aircraft landing, takeoff, parking, servicing and passenger/cargo handling charges. Exempted are groundside activities, including car parking and all concessions.

In addition, the act provides for a quinquennial review of airport practices and regulation. Every five years, the CAA is to ask the Monopolies and Mergers Commission (MMC) to review the rates charged by airports and to examine

---

[2] Approximately $1.6 million at that time

whether there have been discriminatory or predatory prices with respect to airlines, other airports, or air travelers.

Besides these two major features, there are several other regulatory constraints. First, privately owned airports are subject to the United Kingdom's general antimonopoly legislation. At any time (not just at five-year intervals), the MMC may review any potentially abusive practice. In addition, although there is no private right of action in antitrust in Britain, private parties may make complaints to the CAA, which may investigate them. Finally, private airport companies are also subject (like any other business) to the general antimonopoly provisions of the European Community (EC), specifically Article 86 of the Treaty of Rome, which prohibits "any abuse . . . of a dominant position" by a firm.

As in the case of other privatized utilities in Britain, the regulators of BAA have rejected conventional U.S.–type public-utility regulation, which limits the allowable rate of return. Instead, the CAA subjects airports' airside charges to price regulation, under the RPI-minus-X formula (the retail price index minus some factor). This regulation applies only to the three London airports. Significantly, as already stated, landside charges were not covered by this legislation. Whereas conventional rate-of-return regulation provides incentives for overinvestment (in order to earn the allowable return on a higher rate base), inflation-adjusted price regulation provides incentives for more efficient operation, since cost reduction under a price ceiling translates directly into higher profits. The British are using RPI-minus-X-type regulation in the privatized telephone, gas, water and electricity industries, in addition to the airport industry. During the past five years, a number of state public utility commissions have begun switching to this type of price regulation for telephone service in the United States, and the Federal Communications Commission has used it selectively as well.

Criticisms of the British Model

Many transportation economists have criticized the British government's decision to privatize BAA as a single company rather than breaking it up and selling the London airports as separate, competing airports. Independent studies by the Centre for Policy Studies (13), the Adam Smith Institute (14), and the Institute for Fiscal Studies (15) all recommended competitive divestiture of the London airports. But the British government, realizing that it would probably obtain a higher sales price by selling BAA as a single company, opted for the latter course. To some extent, then, the need for economic regulation of London's airports is the result of an explicit government decision to forego putting the airports into competition with one another.

The British government has also been criticized for the way in which it implemented the RPI-minus-X formula in the case of BAA's London airports. Although this type of price regulation does promote efficiency in operations, its overall value depends critically on the initial pricing structure making sense, prior to the start of annual regulation of the permitted increases. In the BAA case, it was decided to use the prices that were in effect at the London airports at the time of privatization as the base prices. As the Gellman report notes, "This decision was taken despite the fact that there was substantial evidence that the landing fee charges at both Heathrow and Gatwick were substantially below long run marginal costs" (9). More specifically, according to an analysis by Starkie and Thompson, landing fees were too high at Heathrow and about right at Gatwick, but passenger fees and aircraft parking charges at both airports were far too low (16).

Gellman concludes that the British erred both in failing to readjust airside prices before implementing RPI-minus-X price regulation and in failing to sell the airports separately (9). Both decisions represent "missed opportunities" to improve the allocation of resources for greater economic efficiency. It is important that the United States should, prior to any move toward privatization, learn from the British example.

The Gellman report raises an additional criticism of the RPI-minus-X approach as applied to airports. It points out that BAA's airside and landside services are complements of one another (i.e., demand for aircraft seats is closely linked to demands for passenger services in the terminals). When a price cap is applied to one set of services but not the other, a firm will raise prices in the unregulated sector (the landside, in this case) as a way of also limiting demand in the regulated sector. Hence, "the price cap may cause the airport operator to produce even less output than a monopolist; such an outcome would be inconsistent with improving economic efficiency" (9).

When is Regulation Needed?

Traditional public utility theory argues that certain types of infrastructure (water, gas, electricity) are inherently monopolistic in the following sense. Since the larger they are, the lower their average cost of serving each customer (economies of scale), it is better to have one large utility serving a given locality than two smaller (each higher-cost) ones. Economists refer to this characteristic as exhibiting *declining long-run average costs* as size increases. If this if the case, however, and the utility is operated for profit, its profit margin will increase without limit as it gets larger. Hence, the historic trade-off has been government regulation, to limit monopolistic prices in exchange for obtaining the lower inherent costs of a large, single utility.

But do airports actually meet these conditions for utility monopoly status? There is growing economic evidence that they do not. Gellman summarizes research that indicates that airports exhibit *increasing* long-run average costs (9). Particularly where there are capacity limits, either in terms of land-use constraints or ATC constraints, it can be far more expensive to add a runway at a La Guardia or a Lambert Field (St. Louis) or a DFW than to start up a new airport on low-cost land at the limits of the metro area.

Why then do competitive entries not emerge? Disregarding the problems associated with regional planning and environmental impact, Gellman points out that today's below-cost airport pricing policies distort economic decision making. Current prices charged to airlines are very low; they do not reflect the very real delay costs at many airports. In addition, they generally do not reflect current-value asset costs (which the builder of a new airport would have to take into account). If current airport prices reflected these costs, it would be far more feasible for entrepreneurs to invest in starting up new airports to relieve today's capacity shortfall.

Citing the work of the Brookings Institution economist Steven A. Morrison (17) and others, Gellman concludes that at large airports, airside operations exhibit increasing costs due to congestion. As a result, they deduce that the traditional public utility reason for regulation, in order to capture the benefits of decreasing costs, is absent in the airport industry.

Are there other reasons to regulate airports? The main temptation of a monopolist is to limit its output, thereby driving up its prices, which customers have no choice but to pay. How serious a danger would that be in the absence of some form of direct regulation?

Gellman concludes that if airports are allowed to price their services in accordance with supply and demand—i.e., to charge different prices at different times of the day and to different classes of users, as the airlines do now under deregulation—then the airport company will have no incentive to restrict its output. It will maximize its profit via yield maximization, just as the airlines do now by fine-tuning their pricing to different categories of user: tourists willing to accept restrictions in exchange for low prices, business travelers needing to make reservations at the last minute (and therefore willing or needing to pay higher prices, and so on).

If, on the other hand, airports are forced to charge the same price to every user (i.e., no peak-hour differentials or off-peak discounts, not charging what the market will bear), then they will have an incentive to restrict output, drive up prices and revenues, and earn monopoly profits. Paradoxically, pricing freedom leads to ordinary (competitive) profits, giving rise to a case for regulation.

Gellman also points out a secondary problem: the distribution of the airport's profits. Under today's system, airports' "profits" are unseen but are essentially passed along to the airlines in the form of below-market prices (since the airport itself is not supposed to be showing a net profit, under municipal ownership and FAA grant assurances). Under a privatized system, airport profits would be explicitly seen. Government could seek to limit those profits via regulations, essentially redistributing a portion of the profits to one or more categories of users. But it would be economically more efficient simply to tax the profits. The federal government (and most state governments) would share in these profits via corporate income taxes, and local governments would also enjoy a new revenue stream from the annual property tax payments. The public sector goal of limiting excess profits could be met via the tax system, rather than by explicit price or profit regulation.

Promoting Competition: Indirect Regulation

In their study of British airport privatization, Starkie and Thompson review the disadvantages of both rate-of-return and RPI-minus-X regulation, pointing out that both types of regulation introduce distortions into the market place and both carry high costs of administration. They conclude that "if regulation is used only to supplement, as necessary, competitive forces, it is more likely that the final outcome will be efficient." They also note that "regulation that supplements competition has the advantage of drawing upon competing sources of information and opinion," rather than being essentially dependent on information produced by the regulated company (16).

Among the most powerful forms of indirect regulation are the antitrust laws. As noted earlier, in Britain there is no right of private action in antitrust; all such complaints must be brought by the government. By contrast, in the United States any airline, competing airport, car-rental company, or passenger who believes that a privatized airport's pricing or other policies are predatory, discriminatory, or otherwise anticompetitive is free to seek redress in court under federal and state antitrust laws.

There is a tendency to forget that the anticompetitive practices that have grown up in today's government-owned airports are exempt from antitrust laws, because of the governmental status of these airports. Current case law, based on municipal ownership, exempts airports from the essential facility doctrine, which would otherwise make it the duty of an airport to provide reasonable opportunities for new airlines to enter. Likewise, majority-in-interest clauses in airline-use agreements, which can cut off entry to newcomer airlines by giving incumbent airlines a veto power over building new gates, would be actionable as restraints of trade if the airports were ordinary private businesses.

Enlightened government policy can impose other conditions aimed at fostering and maintaining competitive behavior in the airport business. The explicit objectives should be to: (1) facilitate new entry by airlines into airports, (2) promote competition between airports, and (3) maintain pricing freedom for airport charges. Besides the application of antitrust law, the following additional policies would serve these objectives:

- *Prohibit airline purchase of airports.* The conflict of interest between an airline owner and other airlines, both existing tenants and would-be entrants, is too great to permit airlines to purchase existing airports. The federal government should make this prohibition a condition of approving the sale of any existing air carrier airport. On the other hand, airlines should not necessarily be barred from taking part in the creation of wholly new airports (as Hawaiian Airlines has done at Kapalua, Maui).
- *Prohibit multiairport ownership in a single metro area.* Many major metro areas already have more than one air carrier airport, including New York, Baltimore-Washington, Miami–Fort Lauderdale, Houston, Dallas, Chicago, Detroit, Los Angeles, and San Francisco. Federal law could prohibit the ownership of more than one of the airports in a single metro area by a single corporate entity. As Gellman notes in connection with the BAA privatization, "It is unclear whether a monopolist owning all three airports will have the same incentives to increase capacity as rapidly as competing airports. A single owner can thrive on the scarcity of airside capacity and need not worry about competitive alternatives. Competing airports do not have this luxury, and so would probably (be) more willing to act."
- *Pre-empt state economic regulation of airports.* As was done regarding airlines in the Airline Deregulation Act of 1978, the federal government could prevent states from engaging in economic regulation of airports (whether private or public). This would preserve competitive conditions on a national basis, in accordance with sound national transportation policy.

These indirect measures could serve to maintain competition, preserve pricing freedom, and maximize economic efficiency in our national airport system, without imposing the economic losses and administrative costs of direct economic regulation.

5.11 CONCLUSIONS

This chapter has attempted to examine the arguments for and against privatization in the context of the U.S. system using material gleaned from United States, British, and other experience. It is recognized that in some cases the history of private-sector operation, from which data are drawn, is necessarily very brief, especially in the United Kingdom. Furthermore, it is realized that privatization as discussed here is seen to be an economic strategy to improve the provision of service by airports; this chapter, therefore, has largely concerned itself with the economic dimension. In truth, this is an oversimplification because the factors that affect the choice of public or private ownership are economic, social, environmental, and political. Indeed, the political dimension may overrule all others, as in the British situation in 1987.

Notwithstanding these reservations, it is apparent from the previous discussions that there would appear to be no insurmountable economic difficulties associated with the privatization of airports within the U.S. system of airports or the National Plan Integrated Airports System (NPIAS). This is not, of course, to say that the system can or should be privatized. Airports have more than an economic dimension, and it is likely that the political, environmental, and social factors will dominate the decisions whether U.S. airports, either as individual facilities or as operating groups, would be privatized.

REFERENCES

1. Reilly, J.D. Aviation System Capacity Task Force. Letter to James B. Busey, IV, March 30, 1990.
2. "Approaches to Airport Management: Privatization." *ATA Issue Brief.* Washington, D.C.: Air Transport Association (undated), January 1990.
3. DePoy, J.L. USAir. Letter to George Howard, AOCI, March 13, 1990.
4. "Liverpool Airport Sold." *PW Financing* (July 1990): 6.
5. Nearly all the BAA operational statistics are derived from "BAA Offer for Sale," County NatWest Limited, 1987, and BAA's annual "Report and Accounts" and "Financial and Operating Information" for 1988, 1989, and 1990.
6. "BAA Charging Structure." Undated BAA manuscript.
7. "Conditions of Use." BAA (April 1, 1989).
8. McDonough, F.J. *Privatization in a New Key.* New York: Goldman, Sachs and Co., November 1989.
9. "Analysis of Airport Cost Allocation and Pricing Options." *Work Element III Report, Part II,* Jenkintown, Pa.: Gellman Research Associates, Inc., April 11, 1990 (prepared for the FAA).
10. Poole, R.W., Jr. "Privatizing Airports." *Policy Study 119,* Santa Monica, Calif.: Reason Foundation, January 1990.
11. "Passenger Opinion Survey: BAA Airports." London: British Airport Services Ltd., March 1990.
12. Chandler, J.G. "Making Concessions." *Frequent Flyer.* (June 1990): 30.
13. Colvin, M.P., et al. *Airports UK: A Policy for the UK's Civil Airports.* London: London Centre for Policy Studies, June 1982.
14. Barrett, S. *Airports for Sale: The Case for Competition.* London: Adam Smith Institute, 1984.
15. Starkie, D., and D. Thompson. *Privatising London's Airports.* London: Institute for Fiscal Studies, 1985.
16. Starkie, D., and D. Thompson. "London's Airports: The Privatisation Options." In *Privatisation and Regulation: The U.K. Experience,* edited by John Kay, Colin Maayer, and David Thompson. Oxford: Clarendon Press, 1986.
17. Morrison, S.A. "Estimation of Long-Run Prices and Investment Levels for Airport Runways." *Research in Transportation Economics* 1 (1983): 103–130.

6

Concessionary Agreements

6.1 FUNCTION OF CONCESSIONS

Concessions at airports serve both primary and secondary functions. The *primary* function of a concessionary agreement is to contract out the operation of a portion of those facilities or services within the area of responsibility of the airport operator to an organization providing specialized operational expertise in that area. *Secondary* functions of concessionary arrangements include broadening the thrust of commercial activities with the airport complex; maximizing the number and types of services and facilities provided; maximizing profit to the airport from commercial activities subject to providing minimum levels of service; confining the function of the commercial section of the airport operator's staff to the management of agreements rather than the operation of diverse enterprises; and limiting the number of staff directly employed by the airport operator.

Concessionary agreements can be considered as satisfactory if both parties to the arrangement, the airport (concessionee) and the concessionaire, are satisfied with the contract and the conditions of service and remuneration of the work force are reasonable when judged in comparison with similar operations outside the airport.

6.2 CLASSIFICATION OF CONCESSION TYPES

The ICAA has classified concessionary arrangements in the following manner (1):

1. Shops within terminals
2. Services within terminals

114

3. Hotels, restaurants, and other catering
4. Activities outside terminals
5. Advertising, filming, sightseeing, and miscellaneous

Some shop and service activities are found in both the public area and the restricted airside area, where public access may be denied either by customs or by security requirements.

Shops within Terminals

With the increased commercialization of airports following the general move toward deregulation in the aviation industry from the mid-1970s, an increasing range of shopping activity can be found within airport terminals. The most commonly found shops include the following items: alcohol, tobacco and smokers' needs, perfumes, women's wear, men's wear, children's wear, leather goods, lighters, fountain pens, glassware, china, antiques, coins, stamps, watches, jewelry, precious stones, gold, books, journals, newspapers, cameras, electrical goods, pharmaceuticals, drugstore materials, art, local or national speciality goods, and craftwork (1).

Services within Terminals

Commercialization of airports has also expanded the range of services provided by concessionaires within the terminal complex. The most commonly provided include the following:

Financial: Banking, foreign exchange, and insurance
Automobile related: Car parking, parking-payment machines, self-drive car rentals, chauffeur-driven car rentals, taxi desk, and sale of duty-free cars
Entertainment: Movie theaters, playrooms, amusement machines, pay television, slot machines, and children's rides
Medical and hygiene: Medical center, toilets, showers, baths, restaurants, nursery, and ambulances
Accommodations and other reservations: Hotel reservations, very important person (VIP) and commercially important person (CIP) lounges and facilities, reservations for theaters, ballet, opera, and cinema, business center facilities, including hire of offices, lounges, and secretaries, trade promotion, and travel agencies
Personal: Shoe repair and shoe polishing, cleaning, pressing, laundry, barbers and beauty salons, key cutting, manicurists, photographic studio, tailors
Visitors: Observation terraces, sightseeing, including rental of binoculars, radios, and telescopes

Communications: Post office, telegrams, telex, and telefacsimile

Miscellaneous: Baggage and passenger handling (in some airports), porters, cleaners, baggage trolleys, baggage lockers, lost-luggage room, delivery of luggage to town, photocopying, lotteries, and employment agency

Hotels, Restaurants, and Other Catering

A variety of types of catering is required at any airport. The following gives a comprehensive range of facilities that can be provided. Only at the very largest of airports is it likely that all these facilities will be supplied. At small airports, only a very limited catering function is likely to be present. The full range of facilities includes deluxe restaurant, grill room, brasseries, speciality restaurants (Chinese, pizza, hamburger, or oyster bar, for instance), self-service cafeteria, coffee shop, snack bar, staff canteens and restaurants, bars, drinks and snack dispensers, ice-cream dispensers, flight catering, and outside catering.

Activities Outside Terminals

Concessionary agreements should not be considered as being limited to those highly visible activities that take place in the terminals. Many of the more lucrative concessions are external to the passenger terminal. Such activities can include aircraft fueling, flight catering, other aircraft apron servicing, car parking, service stations and car valeting, ground transport facilities, and coach and bus terminals.

Advertising, Filming, Sightseeing, and Miscellaneous

Activities not covered in the preceding classifications include hiring out display areas for advertising both within and outside the terminal, use of the terminal for filming and sound recording for films, radio, and television, guided tours of the airport, air shows, joy flights, and use of airport materials for profit.

6.3 MARKETING STUDIES

Successful operation of the nonaviation aspects of the airport's activity requires a careful marketing approach and the adoption of commercial principles. A number of market studies should be carried out.

1. *Client structure: air passengers.* Obtain current traffic and planning estimates of future traffic. These figures should be detailed, permitting the following breakdowns:

a. Percentage originating or at destination and percentage transferring or transiting
b. Leisure versus business
c. Scheduled versus charter
d. Domestic or international within a customs union, short-haul international, or long-haul international

For commercial purposes long-term forecasts have little significance. For example, ten- and twenty-year horizons are used only for long-term planning purposes. Accuracy of current figures is, however, important, and the robustness of the forecasts within a five-year time frame is most significant for commercial decisions.

2. *Client structure: airport based.* A number of the concessions will be dependent on the nonpassenger portion of the airport's daily population. Current estimates and a five-year forecast should be made of the numbers of ground personnel at the airport, flight personnel, sightseers, visitors, and people meeting flights or accompanying departing passengers. In the anticipation that some concessionary facilities may generate a clientele within the environs of the airport, estimates of the populations of local communities should be made.

3. *Consumption patterns.* Separate estimates should be made of total purchasing potential for the average passenger, total purchasing potential per passenger within the various passenger categories identified under client structure, and purchasing potential for the various types of concessions under consideration. At an existing airport these consumption patterns can be estimated from past experience. Where no previous experience is available on which to base estimates, use can be made of figures available from other airports in the vicinity. Because many airport administrations regard this information as commercially sensitive and are consequently reluctant to share such data, consultants are frequently employed to develop estimates.

4. *Estimate of potential concessionary turnovers and income to airport.* If consumption patterns and the structure of the air passenger and airport-based clientele are known, it is fairly easy to estimate potential concessionary turnover. When the income to the airport is determined, however, considerable judgment must be exercised with respect to

Pricing policies
Profit margins for the concessionaires
Public service aspects of providing concessions

For example, with respect to *pricing policies,* the airport may be able to generate high commercial income by permitting concessionaires to charge high prices to the "captive" airport market. This, however, may generate ill will in the community in general and severe industrial problems with airport-based staff. Similarly, different policies can be adopted with respect to *profit margins*. Some airports demand little concessionary revenue on low turnovers and increase the airport's share dramatically as turnovers increase. Although this encourages concessionaires to come into the airport, it does little to reward efficiency. A policy that reduces the airport's revenue on marginal increases of turnover can reward an efficient, high-volume concessionaire handsomely but does little to encourage a concessionaire to take on what may be a marginally profitable operation. *Public service aspects* come into play in the decision to include within the concessionary mix activities that are marginally profitable or to require activities to be staffed at unprofitable periods.

5. *Mix of activities, location, and dedicated areas.* From the various turnover estimates, a mix of activities can be chosen, selecting a combination of facilities and services that meets level-of-service standards in addition to providing a good level of profitability. During the completion of any strategy for the provision of concessionary services, considerable attention must also be given to the location of such activities and the areas to be dedicated to them. Location is generally an important factor in the success of any commercial enterprise. This tenet also holds for the positioning of facilities within airports. For terminal concessions, good positioning, for example, presents the facility to the passenger at a point in time when the individual has no incumbrances, has time to consider using the facility, has a need, is not preoccupied with other matters, and finds the facility easily accessible. Care must be taken in locating facilities so that concessions are presented to the user in the course of normal passage through the airport without unnecessarily obtruding into the general flow of operations.

The sizing of facilities is dictated by good commercial practice. Oversizing wastes space and gives the facility an unwanted aspect of unattractiveness. Prospective customers may be deterred by an appearance of inactivity. Under provision of space, while giving the appearance of bustle and great commercial activity, is stressful on both staff and customers, resulting in loss of some discretionary customers due to overcrowding and consequent perceived lack of service.

6.4 CHOICE OF OPERATING METHOD OF COMMERCIAL ACTIVITIES

There are a number of modes in which commercial activities may be carried out.

1. *Direct operation.* Many airports operate commercial activities directly, either by choice or because their legal status requires them to do so (an

unusual condition). Strictly speaking, activities carried out directly by airport staff cannot be termed concessionary, but they are included in this discussion for completeness. Direct operation has the advantages that the airport has complete managerial control and suffers no dilution of profit. its disadvantages lie in the lack of specialized expertise, distraction of airport management into diverse activities, potential staffing and industrial relations problems, and the requirement of capital involved in the operation.

2. *Fully owned subsidiary.* Establishing a fully owned subsidiary is an option open to larger airports or multiple-airport organizations. The subsidiary is entirely operated and staffed by personnel with experience and interest in the commercial activity, leaving airport management free to concentrate on other matters. For large organizations, this is an efficient and practical method of operation that prevents dilution of profits with no significant increase in managerial staffing. It is not practical for small-airport operation because administrative costs are likely to be high.

3. *Associated company.* In this type of arrangement, the airport forms an association with a company specializing in the field of the concession in question. The advantages to the airport accrue from the expertise of the associating company and divesting airport management of the problems of the commercial operation.

    On the other hand, there is some loss of management control, dilution of potential profits, and frequently the need for some level of capital investment.

4. *Joint airport/airline company.* This is an arrangement that is frequently formed between the airport and the based flag carrier. The latter has a vested interest in the provision of high levels of service for its passengers while they are on the ground. Because of the size of large airlines, they are frequently in a position to have large specialist divisions expert in the operation of ground concessions. In many cases some carrier other than the based flag carrier is chosen for the joint company arrangement. The advantages and disadvantages are similar to those discussed for the associated company.

5. *Separate enterprise.* Under conditions where a separate enterprise is appointed, the arrangement "enables the airport to benefit from the knowledge, know-how, and, if necessary, the purchasing capacity of an enterprise specializing in the activity in question which shall guarantee the provision of a quality service" [1]. Depending on the contract, capital investment may also be minimal. The introduction of a third party into the airport-airline relationship can be difficult. It is, therefore, necessary to set out the concessionary contract in a way that binds the concessionaire by a series of rules related to quality of service and prices that not only promote the airport's own commercial policy but also prevent conflict with the commercial poli-

cies of the airport and the airline. Separate enterprises include operators, airlines and their wholly owned subsidiaries, and other airports and their wholly owned subsidiaries.

6.5 SELECTION OF A CONCESSIONAIRE

The method of selecting concessionaires at any given airport is inevitably linked to the political ethos within which the airport operates. Given that the facility is functioning in an open-market economy, the procedure for selecting the concessionaire should reflect the aims of any policy statement for the management of the airport. These are likely to be more complex than simple profit maximization and possibly may have inherently contradictory goals. In the selection procedure, some or all of the following aims should be considered:

- Maximizing the airport's profit position from concessional operations
- Providing the highest attainable levels of service
- Ensuring that the concessionaire has significant experience in the field and can supply a range and depth of applicable expertise
- Ensuring that the concessionaire is able to sustain cyclical periods of adverse business conditions
- Ensuring that management of the enterprise is innovative and open to market changes

The generally recommended selection procedure (1) is normally initiated by developing commercial interest in participation by a mix of *advertising* and *invitation*. Advertising, which may be a legal requirement at a publically owned airport, is normally carried out in the public press and in the specialist trade press. Invitations requesting expressions of interest can also be sent to individuals and organizations with which contacts have been generated through trade associations, trade unions, agencies, chambers of commerce, and so on. The aim of publicizing the letting of a concession is to provide the opportunity of selecting from the widest possible range of suitable applicants. Where the airport already has experience with commercial concessionary operations, the special conditions of operation are familiar and obvious. In the case of initiating commercial activities, applicants must be made aware of the extraordinary nature of concessionary facilities at airports. The special conditions include extended working hours, operation during holiday periods, very limited space, the peaking of airport traffic both through the day and throughout the year, and the limitations on commercial freedom due to exclusive rights of sale.

The selection procedure itself can be made in a number of ways:

Open or closed tender
Selection of the highest bidder

Performance tender
Negotiation by private treaty

The *open-tender* system is perhaps the simplest concept. Under the structure of an open tender, the conditions of contract are stated and bids can be made by any individual or organization wishing to undertake such a contract. Whereas the concept of open competition may lend credence to this form of tender, it offers little protection to the contractee (in this case the airport) against incompetent or dishonest contractors. A more usual arrangement is, therefore, the *closed-tender* system whereby bids are invited from a selected list of potential contractors, who may or may not have indicated interest. Provided that the list of invitees provides a true level of competition and does not unfairly discriminate against small but competent and growing companies, the closed-tender system works well. Often the tender list is compiled using a *prequalification* procedure, which requires putative contractors to demonstrate financial and business competence. A number of legal jurisdictions, especially in the United States, require that contracts in the public domain be awarded to the lowest-cost bidder. In the case of an airport concessionaire, this would be interpreted as the contractor offering the highest bid. To protect the airport against capricious, incompetent, or dishonest bidders, *performance tenders* may be useful, whereby all contractors must satisfy conditions relating to financial, organizational, and operational abilities.

Another very common arrangement for concessions is contract negotiation by *private treaty*. In this arrangement, the airport is satisfied that the contractor is capable of providing and operating the service or facility required. The contract is granted subject to being able to negotiate financial and operational conditions satisfactory to both parties.

6.6 CONTRACTS

It is common practice for concessionary contracts to have clauses that cover both *general* and *special conditions*. General conditions are those that apply to all concessionaires and are common to all contracts. Special conditions apply to particular facilities or services.

General conditions specify, for example, the nature of the contract, identify the contracting parties, state requirements for observing the laws and ordinances pertaining at the airport, indicate that the contract is specific to identified persons or organizations, and indicate the procedures for cancellation and for recovery of facilities at the end of the tenant's occupancy.

It is not uncommon for concessionaires to have exclusive rights to the sale of certain items or for the provision of certain services within the terminal. This is in the interest of the concessionaire in that it relieves him or her of the need to compete for commercial advantage; it is also of benefit to the concessionee in that it reduces the chance of providing redundant sales or service space.

6.7 PROVISION OF SPACE OR LOCATION

The space a concession occupies can be provided in a number of ways: bare land, an independent building, space within a building, or fully equipped space.

Where bare land is provided, the location, size, land level at transfer, and type of utilities are stated in the contract. Space of this type is provided normally only for long-term leases, because the concessionaire is required to construct his or her own building. As the location becomes more intensely equipped or furnished, the length of lease can become much shorter, because the capital commitment by the concessionaire is much less. A number of airports that seek to keep very close control over their concessionaires' commercial activities provide fully equipped space with short-term leases. In the case of inadequate commercial performance by the contractor, the lease is rapidly terminated. However, a policy of this nature requires available capital for investment in furnishings and equipment. Where utilities or services are required, the tariffs to be charged should be stated (for example, water, gas, air conditioning, electricity, and sewerage).

6.8 DURATION OF CONTRACT

There is a tendency toward the use of short-term contracts for concession operations whenever feasible. Long-term contracts can tie a concessionaire to an operation that is chronically unprofitable, involving an inevitable failure to provide a quality product. Equally undesirable from the airport's viewpoint is a contract that provides, over a long period, windfall profits to the concessionaire and an inadequate return to the airport. Where considerable initial concessionaire investment is required, short-term contracts may still be feasible if contractual arrangements can be made to reimburse the contractor for the residual value of invested assets. These assets can be transferred to the new concessionaire or to the airport itself.

6.9 CHARGES

The manner in which charges are to be made for concessional rights is a most important matter for the airport operator, because commercial, or nonaeronautical, revenues represent a substantial proportion of total airport revenue, this proportion tending to increase as passenger throughput grows. There is little need to justify the policy of charging for the use of commercial facilities; they generate overhead and would have no reason to exist if the airport were not there. However, the policy of charging depends partially on whether the airport operates on a compensatory or residual basis in the United States or as a private or public enterprise elsewhere. Three main systems of tariff construction are used: fixed, variable, and fixed plus variable.

Fixed tariffs are usually based on the area or location of the space for the facility or service. With this arrangement both parties know in advance the size of the charge for the concession. However, it is inflexible, taking no account of traffic or usage. Such inflexibility can be to the disadvantage of either party, but it may be severely to the airport's disadvantage in a growth market. It is, therefore, generally accepted that fixed tariffs should be used only for short-term contracts of up to two years, for example.

Variable tariffs can be of several types. The most common include

- Stated sum per product
- Percentage of gross margin
- Percentage of net margin or net profit
- Percentage of turnover

The *stated sum per product* tariff is possible only when the concessionaire sells one or a few products. In this case the airport can establish control over a system that monitors amounts to be paid by the concessionaire. Typically, fueling concessions have used this type of tariff.

Percentage of gross margin is calculated, in the case of a retailer, on the margin between the sale price of the stock sold and the cost to the concessionaire. Whereas this is conceptually easy to imagine, in practice it is difficult to administer. Hidden from the airport can be a variety of markdowns, discounts, rebates, deductions, and commissions that make the gross margin figure an unreliable guide to profit.

Percentage of net margin is calculated on the margin between the sale price of the stock and the cost to the concessionaire of buying and selling that stock. Net margin is even more difficult to compute than gross margin. The airport is drawn into discussions and probably arguments concerning the concessionaire's overhead, salaries, commission, management expenses, and so on. Neither gross nor net margin, therefore, can be recommended as a basis for tariff setting.

Percentage of turnover is the most frequently used form of tariff, largely because it is more simple to monitor than other methods, turnover being a relatively straightforward figure that can be obtained from the concessionaire's books. The percentage can be in the form of a single rate applicable on all levels of turnover or a progressive rate, increasing as turnover increases. In most cases, increased turnover is due as much to increased passenger or traffic flow as to the business initiatives of the concessionaire. When the turnover is used as a basis for tariff calculation, care must be taken to ensure that satisfactory minimum profit levels are left for the concessionaire in the face of the types of business downturns that can occur when traffic levels fluctuate.

Fixed plus variable tariff arrangements are less common. Under this system the most common structure is a fixed tariff plus a percentage of turnover above some agreed threshold level. A tariff of this nature can ensure that over a fixed period of time, a certain minimum level of return is guaranteed to the airport, with progressive increases as turnover increases. An arrangement of this type may be useful where high start-up costs in the nature of fixtures or furnishings must be provided by the airport for a speculative business where turnover is hard to estimate.

An unsuccessful concession is of little value to the airport; management should, therefore, recognize that the best form of tariff structure is one that gives good service levels to the customer, adequate financial incentives to the concessionaire, and high returns to the airport. Securing the optimum tariff structure requires much thought and sensitive negotiation skills.

6.10 QUALITY OF SERVICE

Although the concessions at airports operate as independent and usually iden-tifiably named businesses, the implications of a poorly run concession are quite different from those that would accrue to a poorly run business in the general community. At the airport, trading rights are granted exclusively so the cus-tomer is, to a degree, captive. It is largely the airport that will receive com-plaints concerning poorly run concessions, and it is the airport's image that is tarnished by poor service levels. Consequently, most airports write their con-cessionary contracts in such a way that strictly enforceable service levels are defined and methods by which quality of service is to be measured are stated.

Some airports ensure an internal environmental quality by providing and controlling all fixtures and fittings, requiring the concessionaire to move into finished premises. Any alterations are at the discretion of the airport and are carried out to the airport's satisfaction. Other ways in which service levels are controlled are by

- Accounting checks
- Commercial operation checks

Accounting checks give the airport access to accounts and balance sheets. The continuing financial viability of the concessionaire can be monitored in this way.

Commercial operation checks are carried out to determine the operational levels of service. Typically, monitoring is carried out on staffing levels, prices, hours of operating, cleanliness, staff appearance and behavior, customer wait-ing lines, exchange rates given, range of articles available, and customer com-plaints.

6.11 TERMINATION OF CONCESSION

Termination of a concession can be brought about in a number of ways.

1. *Normal termination.* In most cases the termination of the concession takes place in a normal and predictable manner at the end of the contract period. Normal termination is generally to the advantage of both parties in that the term of the contract is fixed and the contract conditions clearly state the financial implications at expiry.
2. *Termination by airport.* Contracts must indicate on what grounds termination of the contract can be brought about by the airport. The two most common grounds are for operational purposes and dismissal.

   Operational grounds for contract termination include requiring the building for other purposes, building demolition, or transfer of operations to another site. *Dismissal* of the concessionaire can take place when there are serious violations of the contract with respect to service, nonpayment of invoices and charges, or intentional misrepresentation of balance sheets and accounts to avoid payment of concessionary charges.
3. *Termination by concessionaire.* Termination by the concession contractor can take place due to death of the contractor in the case of a personal contract and by bankruptcy or voluntary liquidation of a contracting firm.

Contracts should define the implications of premature termination on both the contractor and the airport.

6.12 EXAMPLE OF THE TERMS AND CONDITIONS FOR A DUTY-FREE CONCESSION

The following is an example of the terms and conditions of contract for a duty-free concession at an airport.

ORIONVILLE INTERNATIONAL AIRPORT AUTHORITY
ORIONVILLE AIRPORT

Operation of Duty-Free and Tax-Free Shop—Terms and Conditions of Contract

1. *Definition of Terms Used in These Conditions*

   In these Conditions, the following expressions have the meanings indicated:

   a. "The Airport Authority" or "The Authority" means the Orionville International Airport Authority.

b. "The Contractor" means the firm or company whose offer shall have been accepted.

c. "The Chief Executive" means the Chief Officer or any person or persons acting for him for the time being of the Orionville International Airport Authority.

d. "The County Treasurer" means the Treasurer of the Orionville City County Council.

e. "The Agreement" means the formal Agreement referred to in Paragraph 39 of these Terms and Conditions of Contract together with the documents forming the offer and acceptance thereof and all other documents incorporated therewith.

f. "The premises" or "the shop" means the premises or the shops that will be allocated to the contractor as indicated in the covering letter that accompanies and forms part of these documents or such other premises as the Authority may subsequently require the contractor to occupy.

g. The headings to these Conditions shall not affect the interpretation thereof.

2. *Interpretation of Conditions*

Nothing in these Terms and Conditions shall be deemed to create a tenancy of the premises concerned, nor does acceptance of the Conditions confer upon the contractor any right to the exclusive use of occupation of the premises or any part thereof or any exclusive rights in relation to the articles to be sold or to the provision of the services covered by the contract on the Airport as a whole.

3. *Rights of Contractor under Agreement*

Under the Terms of the Agreement, the contractor will be given the right to display and sell in the duty-free and tax-free shops at Orionville Airport (hereinafter referred to a "the shops") to entitled departing passengers (as defined by Government Customs and Excise) boarding aircraft from Orionville Airport at prices exclusive of Tax and/or Duty, as applicable, liquor (as defined in Clause 4 hereof), cigarettes, cigars, and tobacco, and such goods as perfumes, glass and chinaware, cigarette lighters, watches, pens, jewelry, leather goods, sunglasses, china, onyx and silver-plate giftware, and such other goods as may from time to time be allowed by Government Customs and Excise and agreed by the Authority that would be dutiable or taxable if sold otherwise than to such persons as before mentioned. The Department of Industry may require the contractor to offer for sale domestically made goods of the same categories as any imported goods offered for sale.

4. *Definition of Liquor*

For the purposes of the Agreement, the expression "liquor" shall mean duty-free wines, spirits, and liqueurs and shall exclude all beers, ales, lagers, and other malted liquors that may properly be considered under the general title of "beers."

5. *Hours of Opening*

The contractor will be required to keep the shops open daily (including Sundays) at all times when departing or transit passengers are in the International Departure Lounge prior to embarking on their flights. By virtue of the Shops (Airports) Act 1962 and the Orionville Airport Shops Order 1962 (S.I. 1962/2161), Part 1 of the Shops Act 1950 (which relates to hours of closing) does not apply to the duty-free and tax-free shop.

6. *Licenses*

The contractor will be required to provide at his own expense any licenses that may be necessary to enable his business to be performed legally.

7. *Provision of Equipment by the Contractor*

The contractor may be required to provide at his own expense all movable furniture, furnishings, equipment, appliances, and utensils necessary for the operation of the premises to the standard required the Authority, subject, in the case of furniture and furnishings, to the Authority's approval thereof. The contractor will also be required to provide, repair, maintain, and replace as required and at his own expense any item of fixed equipment considered necessary over and above the fixed equipment provided by the Authority that is in situ at the time when the contractor enters upon the premises for the purpose of commencing business.

The supply and fitting of replacement electric light bulbs or fluorescent tubes in the premises occupied by the contractor will be carried out by the Authority and the cost thereof recharged to the contractor. Such supply and fitting may be carried out by the contractor provided that the replacement bulbs or tubes are of a pattern approved by the Authority, that the fitting thereof is undertaken at the contractor's risk, and that on alterations or modifications are carried out to the electric light fittings installed in the premises.

The contractor will be responsible for complying with the provisions of the Offices, Shops, and Railway Premises Act 1963 (or the relevant Factories Acts) relating to fire precautions in the premises. This will include the provision and maintenance at his own expense of such fire-fighting equipment as may be considered necessary for the adequate protection of the premises by the local Fire Authority and any additional fire-fighting equipment the Authority considers should be installed to meet any special fire hazard it adjudges to exist therein.

8. *Payment for Services*

The contractor will be required to pay the Authority for all electrical energy consumed or used on the premises at a tariff equivalent to the tariff pertaining locally.

Such telephone facilities as the Authority considers necessary are installed in the premises for the use of the contractor, who will be responsible for the payment of all charges in respect of instrument and line rentals and for all calls originating from the instruments concerned.

9. *Insurance of Premises and Payment of Rates*

The Authority will insure the premises and the equipment belonging to the Authority against fire and will pay all real estate taxes and charges levied by the Water Authority. All other impositions and outgoings will be payable by the contractor.

10. *Repairs and Maintenance*

The contractor will be expected to use the premises and the installations and any fixed equipment provided therein with all due care and for the purposes only of the Agreement referred to in Paragraph 39 of these Terms and Conditions of Contract.

Repairs and maintenance of the premises and of the installations and any fixed equipment provided therein by the Authority, together with the replacement of any item the Authority has undertaken or may subsequently undertake to supply, will be carried out by the Authority at its own expense *provided* that such repairs, maintenance, or replacement are necessitated by fair wear and tear. Repairs, maintenance, or replacement, the necessity for which is in the opinion of the Authority attributable to misuse, negligence, or omission on the part of the contractor or his servants or agencies, will be carried out by the Authority and the cost thereof recharged to the contractor.

11. *Use of Premises*

The contractor will be required to use the premises for the sole purpose of selling and exhibiting for sale the commodities specified by the Authority or providing the services so specified and will not sell, exhibit, or expose for sale any goods or articles or provide services or any other description without the written consent of the Authority.

12. *Indemnities*

The contractor will be required to indemnify the Authority against

a. Any loss or damage to the property of the Authority (other than fair wear and tear; see Paragraph 10).

b. All actions, proceedings, claims, costs, and demands for personal injury (including injury resulting in death) or for damage or loss to property that may be made against the Authority or any of its servants or agents by any person (including any servant or agent of the Authority or of the contractor) arising out of or in connection with anything done, permitted, or omitted in or upon the premises or elsewhere on the Airport in the exercise of the rights granted to them.

Provided that this clause shall not apply in respect to any personal injury (including injury resulting in death) or loss of or damage to property that the contractor is able to show was not caused by the neglect or default of the contractor or of any servant or agent of his or by any circumstances within his or their control. *And further provided* that if any such injury, loss, or damage giving rise to a claim against the Authority or their servants or agents as aforesaid is shown by the contractor to have been caused in part by the neglect or default of any other person (including any servant or agent of the Authority), the liability of the contractor under this clause in respect of such injury, damage, or loss shall not include any proportion of the total sum payable in respect thereof that is properly attributable to that person's neglect or default.

13. *Policies of Insurance*

The contractor will be required to take out with Insurers or Underwriters approved by the city Treasurer a policy or policies of insurance covering in terms satisfactory to the City Treasurer all claims covered by the indemnity contained in Paragraph 12 and will produce for the City Treasurer's inspection at any time the policy or policies and the receipt for the last premium paid in respect thereof. The contractor will be required to assign to the Authority all sums that may become due from their Insurers in respect of the indemnity referred to or any claim to which the same may apply.

14. *Cleaning of Premises*

The contractor will be required to keep the premises and any area adjoining thereto that he may be permitted by the Authority to utilize for the display of merchandise and any showcases, racking, and shelving in a wholesome, clean, and tidy condition at all times to the satisfaction of the Authority. In the event of the contractor not wishing any of the cleaning referred to above to be carried out by his own staff, the Authority will arrange for the work to be carried out by its cleaning contractors on a rechargeable basis.

15. *Access by the Airport Authority*

The contractor will be required to permit the Authority, its officers, or its servants to enter the premises at all reasonable times to satisfy itself that the terms of the Agreement are being complied with, or for the purpose of carrying out repairs to or replacement of fixtures and fittings belonging to the Authority, or to inspect such fire-fighting appliances as shall have been installed in accordance with the provisions of Clause 7 of these Terms and Conditions of Contract, without—insofar as fire-fighting appliances are concerned—relieving the contractor of responsibility for ensuring that such appliances are in good working order at all times.

16. *Decoration*

The Authority will have the right at its absolute discretion to decorate the interior and exterior of the premises in such color schemes as it may select. The contractor will not be permitted to carry out any alterations to the decor of the premises or erect any signs, notices, or informative media, either temporary or permanent, without the prior approval in writing of the Authority.

17. *Provisions of Heating and Lighting Installations*
The contractor will not be permitted to add to or interfere with the systems for heating, electric lighting, and power supply without the prior approval in writing of the Authority.

18. *Space Heating*
The Authority will be responsible for providing reasonable heating of the premises during each seven-month period from 1 October to 30 April, but the Authority will not be liable for damages or otherwise for any temporary or unavoidable breakdown in such service.

19. *Corrupt Practices and Fair Wages Resolutions*
The contractor will be required to observe and fulfill the obligations upon contractors referred to in Standing Orders 45 and 46 of the Airport Authority included in the tender documents of which these Terms and Conditions form a part.

20. *Restrictions upon Assignment and Subletting*
The contractor will not be permitted to sublet, assign, or part with possession of the premises or of any part thereof.

21. *Advertisements*
The contractor will not be permitted to advertise or permit any advertising or display or cause to allow to be displayed or affixed in or about the premises any poster, placard, notice, or sign for the purpose of advertisement except for such purposes and on such occasions as shall be authorized in writing by the Authority.

22. *Responsibilities for Stock*
The Authority will not be in any way responsible for any stock or other property of the contractor that may be placed or left by him on the premises or elsewhere at the Airport.

23. *Restriction of Access of the Public*
Without prejudice to Paragraphs 12 and 13 hereof, the Authority does not give any warranty or assurance as to the condition, safety, or suitability for any purpose of the premises or any part thereof or in any way guarantee the continued use and operation of the Airport and may at any time and from time to time at its sole discretion close or restrict the access of the public to the Airport or to any part thereof, including the shop premises, or forbid the entry of any person or persons to the same for such periods as they may deem necessary without incurring liability to the contractor in respect of any disturbance or reduction in or loss of business consequent

thereon, *provided* that in the event of closure of the Airport, the Authority may at the request of the contractor review any payment that may be due from him, and consent to make such reduction in it as in its sole discretion shall consider fair and reasonable having regard to the circumstances.

24. *Payment to the Authority of Percentage(s) of Gross Takings*

The contractor, in consideration of the financial benefit to be derived from the performance of his obligations under the terms of the Agreement and from the use of the premises, facilities, and equipment provided by the Authority, will be required to state the percentage of the gross takings that he is prepared to pay to the Authority in respect of each category of merchandise. Applicants may, if they desire, submit a range of offers based upon contract periods ranging between a minimum period of three years and a maximum period of ten years. The percentage(s) offered may, if the contractor so desires, be subject to the payment of guaranteed annual minimum sums irrespective of the amount of gross annual takings.

The expression "gross annual takings" as used in this clause shall include

a. The amount of any takings in cash
b. The retail value of any goods sold on credit during the period concerned
c. The cash value of any consideration received that is related directly or indirectly to the sale of duty-free and tax-free goods, including all advertising and promotional allowances

25. *Keeping of Books of Account*

The contractor will be required to keep such books and accounts and maintain such cash-control systems as the City Treasurer or the Airport Authority consider necessary and will produce these books when called upon to do so for the inspection of the City Treasurer, any of his duly authorized officers, or any duly authorized officer of the Airport Authority.

26. *Analysis of Sales*

The contractor will be required to supply to the Authority, within twenty-one days from the end of each calendar month, a sales analysis in sufficient detail as to allow the Authority to effectively control and monitor the operation of the duty-free and tax-free sales. Details of unit sales for individual brands will be required.

27. *Payment of Guaranteed Minimum Sum*

Payment of the guaranteed annual minimum amount(s) referred to in Paragraph 24 of these Terms and Conditions of Contract will be made to the City Treasurer in twelve separate monthly installments in advance commencing on 1 December 1992 and thereafter on the first day of each month during the period of the concession contract. The payment of the balance, if any, based on the percentages of turnover, will be made together with a return of gross takings for each category of goods to the City Treasurer by the 21st of the month following that in which the business concerned was transacted. If such payments are not received by the City Treasurer within seven days of the due date (whether formally demanded or not), the contractor will be required to pay, additionally, interest based on the period from the due date on the sums outstanding at the First National Bank Base Lending rate plus 4 percent per annum.

In order to avoid total payments by the contractor exceeding the amount due to the Authority at any point in time, the amounts due on a percentage basis will be calculated cumulatively at each month end throughout the accounting year.

28. *Payment of Customs Charges*

The contractor will be responsible for the payment of *all* charges made by Customs and Excise for official attendance at the shops or Bonded Store or such charges as may be incurred in connection with the examination of documents relating to the computerized cash-control system.

29. *Standard of Service to be Provided*

The contractor will be required to the best of his ability and at such times as may be lawfully required by the Authority to display and sell the categories of goods defined by the Authority to all entitled passengers wishing to avail themselves of the facilities provided and shall so conduct the said business that the general standards of the same, including those of the goods sold, the prices charged therefore, and the service given shall be to the satisfaction of the Authority. The contractor will be required to sell and supply only such brands of liquor, cigarettes, cigars, and tobacco as may have been approved by the Authority and shall sell and supply such brands only in such units and at such prices as shall have been so approved. The brands displayed and sold should at all times include recognized market-brand leaders, and the contractor should ensure that such brand leaders are given adequate and prominent display in the area available for this purpose. The contractor should indicate the brand leaders that he proposes to stock in the various categories of goods and must ensure that these are available at all times.

The contractor will be required to state the numbers and types of staff he intends to employ and whether these staff would be full-time or part-time.

The contractor will also be required to ensure that all staff employed by him at the Airport are persons of integrity who have the requisite skill and experience for the efficient and safe performance of their duties.

The contractor will also be requested to ensure that at all times the number of staff on duty is adequate for the efficient operation of the concession in all aspects of its operation, including bonded store.

30. *Prices to be Charged*
   a. All duty-free prices will be regularly reviewed, taking into account factors such as
      i. The effects of price changes on sales volumes
      ii. Prices charged at other Airports and by airlines
      iii. Normal prices prevailing in the community
   b. When selling prices are increased, the concessionaire will be allocated his original percentage margin of the new selling price.
   c. Cost price increases occurring between the regular selling price reviews will be added to current selling prices, thus maintaining the cash take of the Airport Authority and Concessionaire.
   d. The contractor will be required from time to time to supply, in confidence, to the Authority details of the net cost price of any goods sold, inclusive of discounts or other allowances.

31. *Payment for Purchase of Duty-Free Goods*
   This clause authorizes the contractor to accept payment in foreign currency for goods purchased but excludes the right for him to deal in currency that is reserved for the Authority.
   a. *Foreign currencies.* The contractor will be required, subject to the withdrawal of such facilities at times of currency instability as determined by the Authority, to accept all foreign currencies bought and sold by the National Clearing Banks by way of payment for goods sold in the duty-free shop. A charge may be made for this service by offering a rate of exchange that shall be not more than 2 percent below the rate quoted by the bank at the Airport, or such other banks as may be specified by the Authority, to purchase a particular currency on a particular day. The contractor will be required to display a notice to this effect in the duty-free shop, and up-to-date exchange rate sheets must be available for inspection at the cash tills at all times.
   b. *Credit cards.* The contractor will be required to accept the recognized range of credit cards in lieu of cash for goods sold in the duty-free shop but will have the right to withdraw this facility if he is able to show to the Authority that it is reasonable to do so.

32. *Provision of Brochures*
   The contractor will be required to produce and make available to passengers, at his own expense, an adequate supply of up-to-date brochures, giving details of merchandise sold and information regarding the duty-free allowances permitted on entry into the countries to which passengers are traveling. Subject to the Agreement of the Airport Authority, these brochures may be separate or combined. Additionally, the contractor will be required to provide, at his own expense, sufficiently attractive display media for such brochures and/or information sheets, the design of this

facility to be approved by the Authority. The contractor will also be required, at his own expense, to provide carrier bags, the design and standard of which will be subject to approval by the Airport Authority.

33. *Alternative Premises*

The Authority may, by giving not less than fourteen days notice in writing, require the contractor to vacate the whole or any part of the premises, in which event the Authority shall permit the contractor to occupy alternative premises that, in the opinion of the Authority, are suitable for the needs of the contractor and that he will be required to occupy on the same terms as set out herein.

34. *Storage of Dangerous Materials*

The contractor will be required to ensure that at no time does he store or keep on the premises any explosive material or petroleum spirit or any highly inflammable substances whatsover or any goods of a hazardous nature *provided always* that nothing in this connection shall prohibit the contractor from keeping and having in the premises with the prior written consent of the Authority reasonable quantities of such things as are normally required in premises used for the purposes hereby authorized.

35. *Safety*

The contractor will be required to comply with any reasonable requirements of the Authority directed to the safety of the premises or the premises of which they form a part or the safety of customers or passengers.

36. *Security Systems*

The contractor will be required to install and maintain, at his own expense and subject to the prior approval of the Authority, any burglar alarm system or other security system that he feels is necessary for the safe conduct of his business.

37. *Movement of Vehicles*

The routing and positioning on the Airport of the vehicles operated by the contractor and his suppliers will at all times be subject to the control of the Authority and the contractor and his suppliers will be required to comply with all traffic regulations on the Airport, whether statutory or by virtue of a directive of the Chief Executive.

38. *Duration of Agreement*

The Agreement will commence on 1 December 1992 and will be in force for a period of not less than three years and not exceeding ten years. The term will be as negotiated with the successful applicant and will be stated in the Airport Authority's formal letter of acceptance of offer.

39. *Formal Agreement*

The contractor will be required to enter into an Agreement to be prepared by the Secretary of the Orionville International Airport Authority embodying the preceding conditions and such other conditions as the Secretary may consider to be necessary for the purpose of safeguarding the interests of the Authority in the premises and so as to ensure that the business carried on in the premises is conducted in a proper manner to the satisfaction of the Authority.

40. *Termination of Agreement*

The Agreement between the Authority and the contractor may be terminated

a. By either party thereto, giving to the other not less than six calendar months notice in writing at any time, or

b. By the Authority at any time forthwith in the event of the contractor failing to carry out any of his obligations under the Agreement, such termination to be without prejudice to any rights of the Authority under the Agreement accrued prior to such termination.

The contractor will be required, on the expiration or sooner determination of the Agreement, to yield up the premises with the fittings, fixtures, and installations therein (except such trade and other fixtures and fittings as shall have been provided by the contractor) in good and tenantable repair and condition and to make good to the satisfaction of the Authority any damage occasioned to the premises by reason of the removal of such contractor's fixtures and fittings. The Authority may at its absolute discretion accept this agreed sum in lieu of making good any or all of the items referred to in this paragraph.

John Doe
Secretary
Orionville International Airport Authority
June 1992

REFERENCES

1. *Manual on Commercial Activities.* Paris: International Civil Airports Association, 1979.

7

Financial Management Information Systems

7.1 PURPOSES OF FINANCIAL MANAGEMENT SYSTEMS

Just as the art of generalship relies on sound military intelligence, good management can be based only on good information. Wise decision making by a management team necessitates a continuous flow of accurate and timely information to the decision makers in a manner that ensures that necessary choices and actions can be based on as complete an information set as is necessary at the time. Considered management and well-designed information systems go hand-in-hand in the modern airport business environment.

Information systems for decision making are not new. There are biblical references to the use of informants by the ancient Israelites to provide intelligence to their generals prior to battle. Caesar documents the information-gathering activities of reconnaissance patrols and spies in his accounts of the Gallic Wars and the conquest of Britain. With the rise of trading houses in medieval Europe, commercial information was passed by letter and word of mouth to advise merchants on market opportunities, and even rudimentary double-entry bookkeeping evolved to record the status of business and to inform merchants of the availability of profit, capital, and cash. Business records date back to the earliest times. There are many extant examples of the business records of the builders of the tombs in the Egyptian Valley of the Kings that would, in their day, have served as rudimentary information systems.

Modern financial management information systems serve much the same purpose as these early examples. They differ greatly in substance, in that they support much more sophisticated and complex business organizations, they provide information to a more complex set of decision makers, and they must work in a substantially shortened time frame. Nevertheless, it should never be forgotten that the logistics that supported the construction of such huge enterprises as the Pyramids, Hadrian's Wall, and the Great Wall of China were all backed by written information systems that were used to assemble large quantities of matériel and moved large numbers of skilled and unskilled labor to complete complex constructions according to some preplanned design.

Modern business practice has for a long time recognized that throughout the life of a business, decisions must be made that will affect the profitability of the enterprise. These decisions are based on information concerning the historic and current performance of the enterprise and the skills and expertise of the management. Some of these decisions determine the long-term direction in which the enterprise will be headed. These are *strategic* in nature and are usually infrequently made. With respect to a particular choice of direction, such strategic decisions might be made once a year or even less frequently. *Tactical* decisions, which decide not the direction of the enterprise but rather the general manner in which existing strands of effort are to be carried out, are made more frequently, often on a monthly or quarterly basis. *Day-to-day* decisions are necessary to ensure the smooth execution of the business in the light of unplanned and random variations during operation.

Airports are enterprises that generate both revenues and expenditures. To do so they must use labor and capital in the form of investments in facilities and other assets. Whether or not the airport is expected to run at a profit, this usage of labor and capital to generate revenues and expenditures makes the airport a business and therefore amenable to better decision making and higher financial efficiency with the aid of a comprehensive financial information system. In common with other modern businesses, airports can benefit from using computer-based information technology that gives rapid access to the current status of the finance system. Modern financial information systems differ from ancient systems in the scale and scope of information available and the speed and ease with which that information can be accessed.

The scope of a modern financial information system is extensive. An individual airport or an airport-operating group (such as the New York–New Jersey airports, BAA, or Aéroports de Paris) could be expected to have a system covering at least the following areas:

1. Expenditure control
   - *Budgeting.* Past, current, and projected future expenditure levels
   - *Budgeting control.* Expenditures to date versus budgeted figures and updated forecasts of annual expenditure versus annual budget
   - *Expenditure procedures.* Authorizations for spending, authorization limits, and flagging for overspending or exceeding authorization

- *Labor analysis.* Budgeted labor and costs and actual labor and costs to date and projected over the financial year
- *Policy review.* Flagging of areas in which there is a consistent pattern of either overspending or underspending from budget
- *Unit measurement.* Calculation of performance indicators with respect to expenditures: for example, unit costs per passenger, per traffic unit, or per movement

2. Income control
   - *Budgeting.* Past, current, and projected future income levels
   - *Budgetary control.* Income to date versus budgeted figures and updated forecast of annual revenues versus annual budget
   - *Activity relationship.* Relationship between income, net income, and level of activity in terms of passengers processed, traffic units carried, and the like

3. Asset control
   - Asset register
   - Depreciation policy: for example, straight line or declining balance
   - Individual asset records and returns
   - Project appraisal: techniques to be used and inputs and outputs

4. Credit control
   - Debtor accounts: procedure for raising accounts and method of handling
   - Level of age of debt (disaggregate by individual transaction, aggregate by company or individual, total over all accounts)

5. Financial control
   - Cash-flow status
   - Daily balances
   - Long-term borrowing
   - Sources and application of funds

6. Accounts
   - Profit and loss: past and current
   - Balance sheet: past and current

7.2 DECISION MAKERS WHO NEED INFORMATION

The exact design of a financial information system is dependent on the structure of the organization to be served and the levels at which various data outputs are required. As indicated in earlier chapters, airports and airport groups vary significantly in structure, depending on the country in which they operate, their size, and the local jurisdiction and political structure. Some airports are, effectively, simply operating departments within a local, state, or central government and, as such, are components of a civil service administration. Other facilities are operated by semiautonomous public authorities; still others are private companies that, in some cases, are publicly owned. Most airport administrations are responsible for one airport only; however, many airports around the world are operated as part of an airport group. Notable in the last category are the facilities operated by the Port Authority of New York and New Jersey (John F. Kennedy, La Guardia, Newark, and Teterboro), BAA, Aéroports de Paris, and Los Angeles. In this section it will be assumed that the system under discussion is geared to a multiairport authority in the public sector. The differences between this and other modes of operation are not so great that the reader cannot infer how the comments must be reinterpreted for the private company or single-airport situation.

Within an operating authority for a multiairport system, administrators and managers have different responsibilities and, consequently, require different data from any information system.

1. *Chairperson or president of the authority.* The chairperson is responsible for the long-term strategic view of the authority, current and long-term viability and profitability, economic social and environmental impact, political viability, expansion of individual facilities, and the development or purchase of new facilities. As such, the chairperson requires information on the current status of cash flow, profit and loss, budgets, assets, and overall performance, both systemwide and for individual airports.

2. *Managing director.* Being responsible for the overall operation of all airports, the managing director requires systemwide and facility-specific information to the same degree as the chairperson. The managing director is, however, less concerned with the political, economic, and social considerations. With overall operational responsibility, the managing director requires knowledge of the financial and operational performance of the major functional areas of each airport, which are usually grouped into individual budget centers. On a nonfinancial basis, the managing director also requires aggregate operational information to assist in the major decisions with respect to the operation and development of all facilities.

3. *Director of finance.* As the financial expert advising the Airport Authority Board, the director of finance requires financial information aggregated across the system and disaggregated by individual airport. Typically, the director of finance needs historical, current, and projected data on cash flow, profit and loss, budgets, assets, and performance. Data within each facility should also be available by individual budget centers. Additionally, this director requires information on corporate financial performance indicators such as self-financing ratio, debt/asset ratio, assets/liabilities ratio, and so on.

4. *Other directors.* Depending on the structure of the governing board of the authority, the responsibilities of the individual directors may vary. For example, the director of planning, if there is one, requires data related to assets, current and projected profit and loss, borrowings, and so on, also on a systemwide and facility basis. The director of commercial development requires information on concessionary contracts, current and projected profit and loss, assets, borrowings, and the like, also on a systemwide and facility basis.

5. *Airport general managers.* General managers require systemwide data only on a general and highly aggregated level. For their own facilities the requirement is much more specific: cash flows, profit and loss, budget, assets, and detailed performance data. The general manager also needs access to data related to individual cost and budget centers.

6. *Airport finance manager.* As the responsible manager of finance at an individual airport, the airport finance manager requires data on cash flows, profit and loss, budgets, assets, and the detailed performance of individual cost and budget centers. Summaries of miscellaneous recoverable charges, outstanding debts, and so on are also required.

7. *Airport line managers.* Managers such as the chief engineer, operations manager, and terminal manager require overall airport budgets, budgets of the budget and cost centers for which they are responsible, and performance criteria in the form of revenues and expenses for the same. They also require operational data in terms of passengers, movements, and work-load units for comparison of actual and forecast conditions. Line managers require information on unusual expenditures such as those incurred for overtime, snow clearance, or hired machinery or labor.

8. *Nonairport requirements.* The output needs for any statutory or regulatory requirement that information be reported can and should be built into the financial information system. Typically such reports are to the following bodies:
   • The Civil Aviation Authority
   • The government for corporate taxation or for reports to any controlling monopolies commission

9. *Airlines.* Where airline charges are computed on a residual or compensatory cost basis, the financial information system should be designed to show the figures used in the calculation of charges. Within the European Community, commission requirements for a more transparent indication of airport costs to airlines, for the purpose of justifying airport charges, will increasingly require the use of information systems to provide this data. Thus, it is clear that whatever the basis for computing charges, transparency of costs is becoming a universal requirement.

7.3 INFORMATION REQUIRED

To enable the various levels of management to monitor and influence the financial performance of the airport group, information is provided in a variety of levels of aggregation or disaggregation. To do this, activities are grouped so that they can be monitored by a cost center, budget center, profit center, individual airport, or airport group.

A *cost center* is usually the most disaggregate level of activity used for the control of elements of budgets. For example, replacement of failed electrical bulbs in a concession area would be charged to the minor electrical maintenance cost center for the terminal area. The term is not, however, well defined. In the United States, for example, it is not unusual to have the terminal and the airfield defined as cost centers. A *budget center* is a more aggregate grouping of transactions related to the operating budget of an individual manager. In the case stated previously, the budget center could be associated with the general electrical maintenance of the terminal and landside, an area budgeted and monitored by the chief electrical engineer. *Profit centers* are associated with the revenue-generating areas of the airport, where budgets reflect targets for various identifiable activities. For example, two different profit centers in the terminal area could be the following:

Concessions (shopping): duty-free and tax-free shops, speciality shops and bookshop
Concessions (services): restaurants, bars, snack bars, hotel reservations, car rental, valet, shoeshine

Managers of a single airport within a group have an interest in the separate identification and assignment of revenues and expenditures to an individual facility. For example, within large airport groups such as those operating in the Paris, London, New York, and Los Angeles areas, the revenues and expenditures of each airport are presented on an individual facility basis.

General managers and policy boards of airport groups additionally require information consolidated across the entire airport group.

The output from an airport financial management information system is likely to include at least the following if it is to enable managers to make necessary decisions:

1. Current income, revenues, costs and profitability statements, both monthly and cumulative from the beginning of the financial year, with
   a. Income and expenditure by cost center
   b. Income and expenditure by budget center

   c. Income and expenditure by profit center
   d. Income and expenditure by individual airport
   e. Consolidated income and expenditure by airport group
2. Current rate of spending and progress on capital development, monthly and cumulative to date, with reprojections of the anticipated month-end and year-end totals, in comparison with budget
3. Availability of funds, current and future, with cash-flow projections
4. Degree of capacity utilization
5. Service standards
6. Competition for scarce resources
7. Progress and slippage on projects and developments

7.4 FINANCIAL INDICATORS USED

A financial information system will provide managers with a variety of indicators, depending on the nature of decisions to be taken. *Strategic* indicators are required for policies with medium- to long-term effects; *tactical* indicators assist in decision making for the short and medium term. Immediate- and very-short-term courses of action are based on *day-to-day* data that advise the manager of the current status of the enterprise.

1. *Strategic indicators.* A number of indicators are useful for long-term policy making. They are likely to include the following.
   a. *Return on capital investment*
      i. For the airport group as a whole
      ii. For individual airports
      iii. for individual projects (discount cash flow or other life-cycle-costing methods)
   b. *Payback period.* Some analysts use this rather imprecise method for investment appraisal. It can be useful to compare small investments of very limited economic life, where the form of cash flows is somewhat similar. In general, however, payback analysis should be avoided in favor of more exact methods based on discount cash-flow methods.
   c. *Self-financing ratio*
   d. *Current assets/liabilities*
   e. *Debtors ratio.* The ratio of debt owed to the airport or group to current assets
   f. *Creditors ratio.* The ratio of debt owed by the airport or group to current assets
2. *Tactical indicators.* These indicators are used for short- to medium-term control of the business.
   a. Income per passenger or work-load unit (WLU)

    b. Costs per passenger or work-load unit

    c. Income per unit or facility or throughput (for example, income per square meter or square foot, income per available parking space)

    d. Cost per unit of facility or throughput

    e. Gross profit on sales

    f. Rate of return on sales

    g. Percentage of concessionary sales

    h. Overtime hours/normal hours ratio

3. *Day-to-day indicators.* These indicators are used for continuous control of costs and expenditures:

    a. Cash flows

    b. Revenue flows

    c. Expenditure flows

    d. Actual and budgeted revenues and expenditures

    e. Outstanding debtors and location of debt

    f. Outstanding creditors and location of credit

4. *Target indicators* (agreed at national, state, or local government level, as appropriate, in the case of a public airport)

    a. Return on capital

    b. Cost improvements

    c. Productivity improvements

    d. Level of service criteria (for example, equipment availability, complaints, and compliments)

As financial control systems become more sophisticated and computer software and memory continue to become available at less cost, the use of financial indicators will almost certainly increase at all levels of management. A more complete discussion of performance indicators is given in Chapter 9.

7.5 PRESENTING FINANCIAL INDICATORS

Whereas some day-to-day financial management decisions must be made on current data, many more strategic judgments require the provision of information at much longer time intervals. For example, cash-flow decisions with an airport group may be made by the treasury function on daily balances see Section 3.4. Major decisions related to the commissioning of large development projects must take a longer-term view of revenues and expenditures. The outputs of a financial information system are related to the monthly, annual, quarterly, and even daily positions of the business. The following are required of an airport group:

1. *Monthly* airport results
   a. Profit and loss accounts for the month and cumulative to date
   b. Budget out-turn statement
   c. Concessionary and other income by profit or revenue centers
2. *Monthly* consolidated group results
   a. Profit and loss account for the month and cumulative
   b. Cash flow for the month and cumulative
   c. Adjusted and budgeted income and expenditures for the balance of the financial year, projecting yearly out-turn
3. *Monthly* profit and loss (revenues and expenditures) accounts of management contracts by others)
4. *Annual* budget submissions for each of next five years, with indicators of costs and revenues per passenger, per movement, per employee, and per unit of capital employed
5. *Quarterly* activity cost statements: for example, traffic, commercial, parking lots, and ground access where maintenance is the responsibility and under the budgetary control of the chief engineer (Such statements serve to provide guidance on the profitability of these services and help to establish prices to be charged.)
6. *Daily* current balances and cash flows at all individual airport facilities and consolidated group figures
7. *Ad hoc situations:* on-off decisions on the profitability of optional courses of action based on historic cost and revenue figures held by central accounts

7.6 DATA TO BE PROCESSED

A successful and efficient airport enterprise is likely to operate with a financial management system based on budgetary control. Such a system permits managers continually to evaluate actual performance with respect to that which has been anticipated in budgetary planning. The concept of detailed budgetary control introduced the notions of cost centers, profit centers, and budget centers. In actual practice these three phases are often used with a great deal of imprecision to mean very much the same thing. An attempt will be made here to define them differently according to the way in which they are used at some airports, without the pretense that such definitions would have universal acceptance.

A *cost center* refers to a particular area of activity where the boundaries of the activity are well defined and to which costs which are incurred and the revenues obtained can be identified with some precision and certainty. The activity involved may or may not be loss-making in nature (for instance, public relations, which often nominally loses money, versus commercial rentals, which are clearly profitable).

A *budget center* can be defined as an area of activity under the control of an administrator who prepares and manages a budget encompassing the entire scope of that activity. According to this definition, a budget center comprises a number of cost centers.

A *profit center* is a less well defined term that is often used to denote a range of activities within the airport that earn revenue and therefore are potentially profitable, such as commercial activities, airside traffic, and ground transportation. Such broadly defined areas frequently cover several budget centers. The usage of the term *profit center* in this wider sense defines broad areas where a more commercial attitude to revenues and expenditures will either increase profits or reduce net losses.

Accurate accounting of revenues and expenditures is obtained by the use of cost-center codes. Proper budgetary control is obtained by ensuring that direct expenditure can be allocated to a particular cost center only on the authorization of the manager responsible for the budget appropriate to that cost center. Similarly, indirect costs and revenues accrued must be agreed to be correct prior to allocation. Table 7–1 shows the form of allocation of cost-center codes to budget centers for one European airport group comprising a number of independently operating airports. The parameters of this particular system were as follows:

Income:	120 financial types
Expenditure:	100 financial types
Cost centers:	200 financial types
Budget centers:	35 financial types

All income and expenditure are accrued to individual cost centers, each of which is linked to a budget center. A fully centralized cost and financial accounting system operates on an income earned–work done basis rather than on cash received–cash paid. A centralized computer installation handles input both from remote terminals in the individual airports and terminals in the central accounts office.

The system provides procedures for landing fees, wages and salaries, credit control, bill paying, project control, fixed assets, and costing. Additionally, all systems provide whatever is necessary for monthly profit and loss and budget out-turn statements and daily cash flows.

TABLE 7–1. Example of Cost Center and Budget Center Allocation Coding

| Cost Center Code Number | Airside Safety and Operations Engineering | Cost Center Codes | | | | | | |
| | | Associated Budget Center No. | | | | | | |
		Airport No. 1	Airport No. 2	Airport No. 3	Airport No. 4	Airport No. 5	Airport No. 6	Airport No. 7
E001	Chief engineer, DCE and staff	27	17	14	12	13	10	15
E002	Engineering stores, staff and stock	27	6	14	4	13	10	15
E101	Repayment works services	28	18	15	13	14	11	16
E201	Civil engineer and staff	27	17	14	12	13	10	15
E202	Domestic water service	29	19	18	14	15	12	17
E203	Fire mains	29	19	18	14	15	12	17
E204	Roads	29	17	14	14	8	10	17
E301	E & M engineer and staff	27	17	14	12	13	10	15
E401	Electrical distribution	30	21	17	15	17	13	18

8

Life-Cycle Costing

8.1 INTRODUCTION

Life-cycle costing is an assessment of a procurement or project option in which all the significant benefits or costs of ownership are considered in monetary terms over the economic life of the option. As such it is narrower in its terms of reference than benefit-cost analysis, in which attempts are usually made to attribute costs and benefits to intangible factors such as, for example, saved travel time, increased noise impact, or increased employment opportunity. Life-cycle costing is, therefore, an efficient and valuable tool for selecting among very similar options but cannot properly be used to select among a number of options that have numerous and differing externalities. The principal objectives of the methodology are as follows:

1. To select on an economic basis an optimum solution to a problem involving a number of available solution options
2. To provide a single, clearly defined framework of analysis that will lead to repeatable results and is regarded as both fair and logical
3. To force a manager to derive explicit rather than intuitive assumptions, rendering the final option choice objective and avoiding subjectivity

Conceptually, life-cycle costing seeks to minimize the total costs of a procurement or project over the whole of its life cycle. It is assumed that all other aspects and implications of choice (such as social, political and moral) are generally similar, and differences are, therefore, insignificant and ignorable. The method can be used at any phase of a project: planning, design, procurement or construction, operations or maintenance, and retirement. Benefits

147

from its use decrease exponentially with time as one moves through the life cycle of the project under consideration. Maximum benefits are assured by applying the method early in the planning phase; there is little benefit to be gained from utilizing the method in the closing stages of the economic life of a project or of procured material.

8.2 APPLICATION TO AIRPORT MANAGEMENT

Figure 8–1 indicates how life-cycle costing forms an integral part of *cost effectiveness* analysis, which additionally requires consideration of *system performance* and *system effectiveness*. In the context of the airport manager, life-cycle costing typically involves the consideration of the following costs:

1. Acquisition or construction cost
2. Operational cost
3. Supporting technology costs, including training
4. Maintenance costs
5. Disposal costs

The form of analysis used at airports is usually different from that used in production industries in that there are no costs associated with product research, development, and production. This more conventional form of analysis may, however, be required in some project areas. For example, if an analysis were to be made on whether an information system should be purchased from a contractor or developed internally within the airport by its own staff, research and development costs would need to be taken into account for the latter option.

8.3 INTERACTION BETWEEN TIME AND MONEY

The computation of life-cycle costs is complicated by the fact that time and money are interrelated, because the value of money is time-dependent. This can be demonstrated by two simple examples:

Example

In 1624, the Indians sold Manhattan to the Dutch for $24 and a barrel of rum. If those Indians had been able to deposit that money in a bank at a deposit rate of 8 percent per annum untaxed, there would have been $48,000 billion in their account in 1992.

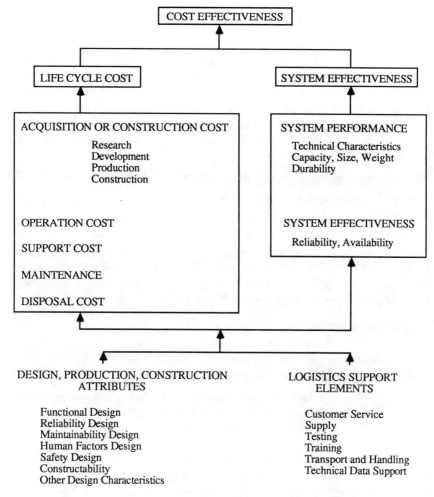

FIGURE 8–1. Cost effectiveness in the context of airport management

Example

If an individual is told that he or she will receive a lottery prize of $10,000 today, the individual is naturally delighted. If the payment is to be made tomorrow, there is no significant different in his or her delight. Should the payment be deferred to 31 December next year, the individual's pleasure is somewhat less. However, if payment is to be 25 years from now, his or her joy is considerably diminished. As the payment time stretches to 50 years or 100 years ahead, delight changes to indifference.

In the first case, if the average prevailing interest rate over the 368 years was 8 percent, then $24 in 1624 is entirely equivalent to $48,000 billion in 1992. In the second case, the amount of money is identical throughout the time period considered, i.e., $10,000. However, the perceived value changes over time; the rate at which the value of money is perceived to change over time is termed the *discount rate*. This rate is essential to the computation of life-cycle costs.

8.4 METHODS FOR EVALUATION[1]

Because the perceived value of various sums of money depends on the time at which they are expended or received, the life-cycle costs of a project cannot be obtained directly by totaling the actual cash flows (1). Rather, discounted cash flows must be used. If all cash flows are collapsed into one single monetary value or ratio, it is possible to make a simple, single-parameter evaluation. Four different methods of analysis are available (2):

1. Net present worth
2. Equivalent uniform net annual return
3. Benefit-cost ratio
4. Internal rate of return

At first sight, the four methods may appear to be quite different, but in reality the underlying rationale is similar, and the methods, with similar assumptions, lead to identical conclusions. *Benefit-cost ratio* has been used extensively by U.S. government authorities since its adoption by the U.S. Corps of Engineers, under congressional mandate, at the time of the Depression. It is used as a way of showing that the benefits accruing from public works projects exceed actual and environmental costs of construction, maintenance, and operation.

Other managers prefer to consider the relationship of average annual benefits to average annual costs in the form of net annual benefits or costs, because these can be related to annual budgeting costs. The *equivalent uniform net annual return* method is useful in this case.

The total costs and benefits over the life of a project are more clearly presented by calculations of *net present value*. This method is, therefore, preferred by managers wishing to have some feeling for total costs.

---

[1] Section 8.4 is reprinted from Reference 1. Copyright © 1989 John Wiley & Sons. Reprinted by permission of John Wiley & Sons, Inc.

Internal rate of return analysis is found useful by others because it provides clear and direct comparisons for the earning power of invested capital. In that all methods lead to the selection of the same project under identical assumptions, all are appropriate in an evaluation procedure, and in some situations the manager may wish to use more than one method to provide additional output information.

Net Present Worth (NPW)

Net present worth analysis permits a comparison of the total equivalent benefits and costs across the total economic life of the project. The actual costs at periodic points of time are treated as cash flows, which are discounted to equivalent worths at the zero-time point. The interest rate used in this discounting process is likely to be the minimum attractive rate of return over the period of analysis. In some cases, the discount rate is set either by governmental or by corporate policy. The net present worth is, by definition, the difference between net present benefits and net present costs. At a selected discount rate, a project is considered economically viable if the net present worth is positive, because it earns more than the minimum attractive rate of return. Where mutually exclusive options are under consideration, the project with the largest net present worth is chosen, all other things being equal.

In the simplest case, a project could be a single cash flow, *C*, at time zero, bringing a benefit, *B*, *n* years later, as shown here.

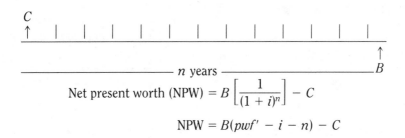

$$\text{Net present worth (NPW)} = B \left[\frac{1}{(1 + i)^n} \right] - C$$

$$\text{NPW} = B(pwf' - i - n) - C$$

where C = cost
         B = benefit
         i = minimum attractive rate of return
         n = period of project analysis
$(pwf' - i - n)$ = present worth factor for a single benefit at discount rate i
                   for a period of n years

Where a single project cost produces a uniform flow of annual benefits, the cash-flow diagram is of the following form:

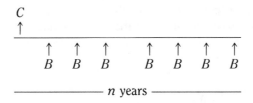

In this case the calculation of net present worth is made from the following equation:

$$\text{NPW} = B\left[\frac{(1 + i)^n - 1}{i(1 + i)^n}\right] - C$$

$$= B(pwf - i - n) - C$$

where
B = annual benefit
C = initial cost
i = minimum attractive rate of return
n = period of project analysis
$(pwf - i - n)$ = present worth factor for a series of uniform benefits at discount rate i for a period of n years

In the general case, both costs and benefits will be irregular cash flows over the whole time period of analysis. The general equation can be written for an irregular cash-flow diagram.[2]

$$\text{NPW} = \sum_{k=0}^{n} B_k\left[\frac{1}{(1 + i)^k}\right] - \sum_{k=0}^{n} C_k\left[\frac{1}{(1 + i)^k}\right]$$

$$\text{NPW} = \sum_{k=0}^{n} B_k(pwf' - i - k) - \sum_{k=0}^{n} C_k(pwf' - i - k)$$

[2] For a complete treatment of how interest formulas are computed, see (2).

Equivalent Uniform Net Annual Return (EUNAR)

The equivalent uniform net annual return can be calculated directly from the net present worth by multiplying the NPW by the capital recovery factor. This factor is the compound interest relationship that converts a cash flow at time zero into a series of uniform flows over a defined time period—in this case, the analysis period. The relationship is shown by the following equations and cash-flow diagram.

$$A = \text{NPW} \left[\frac{i(1 + i)^n}{(1 + i)^n - 1} \right]$$

or

$$A = \text{NPW}(crf - i - n)$$

where
A = equivalent uniform net annual return
NPW = net present worth
i = minimum attractive rate of return
n = period of project analysis
$(crf - i - n)$ = capacity recovery factor for discount rate i for a period of n years

It can be seen that the equivalent uniform net annual return is the amount by which the uniform annual benefits exceed the uniform annual costs when discounted according to a minimum rate of return. Provided that this difference is positive, the project is economically advisable, since economic benefits outweigh costs at an attractive rate of return. Mutually exclusive alternative projects can be evaluated by comparison of the uniform annual net returns. The project with the higher net return is more desirable.

Benefit-Cost Ratio (B/C)

One of the most widely used forms of economic analysis is the benefit-cost ratio. As the name implies, the method determines the ratio of benefits to costs after each has been discounted comparably with respect to time at the minimum attractive rate of return. Those projects with B/C ratios greater than 1.0

are economically viable, whereas those with ratios below 1.0 are not. The ratio is computed from comparably discounted cash flows and can be applied either to equivalent uniform annual costs and benefits or to present worth of costs and benefits. This equivalency is illustrated by the following cash-flow diagrams and equations, where the redundancy of the capital-recovery factor in the second form of the ratio is obvious.

$$\begin{array}{ccccccc}
C_0 & C_1 & C_2 & C_k & C_{n-1} & C_n & \text{Present worth of costs} \\
\downarrow & \downarrow & \downarrow & \downarrow & \downarrow & \downarrow & \downarrow \\
\equiv & & & & & & \\
\uparrow & \uparrow & \uparrow & \uparrow & \uparrow & \uparrow & \uparrow \\
B_0 & B_1 & B_2 & B_k & B_{n-1} & B_n & \text{Present worth of benefits}
\end{array}$$

Using present worth values, we have

$$B/C = \text{benefit-cost ratio} = \frac{\displaystyle\sum_{k=0}^{n} B_k \left[\frac{1}{(1+i)^k}\right]}{\displaystyle\sum_{k=0}^{n} C_k \left[\frac{1}{(1+i)^k}\right]} = \frac{\displaystyle\sum_{k=0}^{n} B_k(pwf' - i - k)}{\displaystyle\sum_{k=0}^{n} C_k(pwf' - i - k)}$$

Using equivalent uniform annual benefits and costs yields

$$B/C = \frac{(crf - i - n)\displaystyle\sum_{k=0}^{n} B_k(pwf' - i - k)}{(crf - i - n)\displaystyle\sum_{k=0}^{n} C_k(pwf' - i - k)}$$

Internal Rate of Return

One method of economic evaluation that makes no internal assumption concerning the minimum attractive rate of return on investment is called the *internal rate of return* method. In evaluating the economic feasibility of a scheme, the analyst computes, by trial-and-error methods, the discounting rate that exactly equalizes the discounted benefits and the discounted costs. Although it is more usual to equalize the present worths of costs and benefits, the method can also be applied to equivalent uniform annual cash flows, since these can be calculated directly from present worths. It can be seen that the internal rate of return is the interest rate r that satisfies the following equation of cash flows:

$$B_0 \quad B_1 \quad B_2 \qquad B_k \qquad B_{n-1} \quad B_n$$
$$\downarrow \quad \downarrow \quad \downarrow \qquad \downarrow \qquad \downarrow \qquad \downarrow$$

$$\uparrow \quad \uparrow \quad \uparrow \qquad \uparrow \qquad \uparrow \qquad \uparrow$$
$$C_0 \quad C_1 \quad C_2 \qquad C_k \qquad C_{n-1} \quad C_n$$

$$0 = \sum_{k=0}^{n} B_k \frac{1}{(1+r)^k} - \sum_{k=0}^{n} C_k \frac{1}{(1+r)^k}$$

Provided that the internal rate of return exceeds some externally set minimum attractive rate of return, the scheme is judged to be economically feasible. The relative attractiveness of alternative schemes can be related directly to the size of their internal rates of return.

8.5 ANALYSIS PERIOD AND DISCOUNT RATE

Before life-cycle costing can be carried out, a number of assumptions must be made for analytical purposes. Two of the most important are the determination of the period over which the analysis is to be made and the discount rate to be used.

It is common practice to link the economic life of a project to the physical life of the facility in question. The following physical lives are frequently used:

Buildings	25–30 years
Rigid pavements	25 years
Flexible pavements	20 years
Drainage	40–50 years
Land	Infinite
Computers	5–10 years
Fittings and fitments	10 years

When life-cycle costing is carried out for the major elements of airports, periods of thirty-five to forty years are not inappropriate, because the physical lives of major construction elements can reach thirty years and the time to complete planning design and construction requirements can easily stretch to ten years. The analyst must, however, bear in mind that this analysis period is entirely incompatible with accurate forecasting. Whereas the initial capital costs of such long-term projects are reasonably well estimated, the predicted annual expenses and revenues become unreliable as the forecast period extends. This is true for all applications of life-cycle costing, but it is especially true when the method is applied to the aviation industry, where technological, social, and political changes have made long-term forecasts extremely unreliable (3). As explained in Section 8.1, the method is inappropriate in cases where different options have different external effects that are, for the purposes of the analysis, unquantified and therefore ignored. The effect of externalities is exacerbated over long periods; consequently the analyst should be wary of using life-cycle costing over an extended analysis period.

Another argument against the use of life-cycle costing over long periods of time comes from the nature of discounting and the discount rate. Since the mid-1960s, high interest rates have been commonly used in the Western market economies as a measure to counter inflation. Discount rates used in life-cycle costing analysis must necessarily reflect secularly high interest. However, as indicated in Section 8.3, over long periods high discount rates can virtually eliminate large effects, provided that they are sufficiently distant in the future. This can be exemplified by an investment of $10 million dollars that engenders what may be considered as a catastrophic loss of $200 million forty years ahead. If the discount rate is 5 percent, the present value is $28.4 million. If the discount rate is 20 percent, however, its effect is a mere $140,000. Clearly the use of discounting is anomalous to long-term planning, which requires a comprehensive evaluation methodology (4).

8.6 EFFECTS OF TAXATION, DEPRECIATION, MORTGAGES, AND INFLATION

Taxation

In the analyses shown in this chapter, taxation is ignored, because in most countries airports are public bodies that pay no taxes. Where taxation is encountered, it must be treated as a cash flow on the expenditure side. Any tax reliefs that are claimed as a result of the project can be treated as revenues.

Depreciation

Depreciation is an accounting device that does not involve a cash flow. It can, therefore, be ignored in life-cycle costing analysis. The exception to this is where the obtained salvage value is different from the depreciated or book value of the asset. If the airport pays taxes, the salvage value must be modified by a capital loss or gain based on the difference between actual and depreciated value. This capital loss or gain will attract a tax rebate or charge, which must be treated as a cash flow.

Mortgages

Where capital expenditure is financed by a loan, the repayments over the life of the mortgage should be used as cash flows, rather than the capital sum which must be regarded only as a transfer payment.

Inflation

Inflation must be ignored in life-cycle costing analysis. It is taken into account automatically in the discount rate. Future costs and revenues are estimated in terms of current prices. In fact, of course, they may be inflated, but the correctly chosen discount rate, when applied in the course of the analysis, brings them to an appropriate present worth. There is no way of overcoming the effect of an incorrect estimate of the discount rate. If it is chosen too low, then the true benefit of an early capital investment to take advantage of real depreciation of payments for capital recovery is underestimated. Conversely, if the discount rate is set too high, real benefits are overestimated.

In theory, the discount rate should account for the average rate of inflation over the life of the project plus the "true annual rate of interest." This true value is the rate that would pertain in a society where inflation was zero. Perhaps the closest approximation to this value of interest was obtained in Europe between 1815 and 1914, when inflation was practically zero for almost a century. Interest rates in those times were only 2 to 2½ percent. It is appropriate to summarize this discussion by stating that during inflationary times, life-cycle costing analysis is best conducted only over short analysis periods. In times of very high inflation, life-cycle costing analysis is likely to be very misleading.

8.7 EXAMPLE OF PROCEDURE

Example 8-1   Selection of Floor Covering in Leased Concession Areas

A decision has to be made on the selection of floor covering for a terminal concessionary area that will be leased out on a series of leases for an estimated 20 years. After that time, it is considered that the terminal will be obsolete and operations will have to move to a new terminal on another site. Two types of floor covering are considered suitable. Industrial carpeting has an installation cost of $100 per square meter, an economic life of five years, and an annual cleaning and maintenance cost of $10 per square meter. Alternatively, a cheaper, more durable rubberized floor covering could be used at an installation cost of $80 per square meter, with an economic life of 10 years. There is, however, a high maintenance and cleaning cost associated with this product. Annually this is expected to be $20 per square meter. The area involved is 10,000 m², and the discount rate in current use for a twenty-year economic life is 10 percent. Assume that the floor coverings have no salvage value and that removal and re-preparation costs at the time of renewal are 10 percent of installation costs.

Solution: Calculate the net present value of the costs of each alternative over the total economic life of the concession, twenty years.

Installation costs:	Carpet	$100/m²
	Rubber	$ 80/m²
Maintenance and cleaning costs:	Carpet	$ 10/m²/annum
	Rubber	$ 20/m²/annum
Renewal periods:	Carpet	5 years
	Rubber	10 years
Renewal costs:	Removal and re-preparation, 10 percent of installation costs for both types of floor covering.	

Alternative 1: Carpeting

Cost	Present Value
Installation:	
10,000 m² × $100/m² × (*pwf'* − 10 − 0)	$1,000,000
Maintenance and cleaning:	
10,000 m² × $10/m² × (*pwf* − 10 − 20)	
= 10,000 × 10 × 8.514	$851,000
Replacement at end of years 5, 10, and 15, including removal of old carpet and preparation:	
Year 5: 10,000 m² × 1.1 × $100/m² × (*pwf'* − 10 − 5)	
= 10,000 × 1.1 × 100 × 0.6209	$682,990
Year 10: 10,000 m² × 1.1 × $100/m² × (*pwf'* − 10 − 10)	
= 10,000 × 1.1 × 100 × 0.3855	$424,050
Year 15: 10,000 m² × 1.1 × $100/m² × (*pwf'* − 10 − 15)	
= 10,000 × 1.1 × 100 × 0.2394	$263,340
Total present value of costs for carpeting	$3,221,780

Alternative 2: Rubber floor covering

Cost	Present Value
Installation:	
10,000 m² × $80/m² × (*pwf'* − 10 − 0)	$800,000
Maintenance and cleaning:	
10,000 m² × $20/m² × (*pwf* − 10 − 20)	
= 10,000 × 20 × 8.514	$1,702,800
Replacement at end of year 10, including removal of old flooring and preparation:	
10,000 m² × 1.1 × $80/m² × (*pwf'* − 10 − 10)	
= 10,000 × 1.1 × 80 × 0.3855	$339,240
	$2,842,040

Decision: Even though cleaning and maintenance costs are higher, the total life-cycle cost of the rubber floor covering is $379,740, or 11.7 percent less expensive in terms of net present worth than the carpeting alternative.

8.8 CASH-FLOW METHOD AND SPREADSHEET ANALYSIS

The form of method of analysis described in Section 8.7 is sometimes referred to as the *formula method.* In this form of analysis each individual cash flow or series of cash flows is considered separately and discounted back to time zero. An alternative form of analysis that has become widely used following the introduction of computers is the *cash-flow* method.

In this form of computation, the individual cash flows are considered on a year by year basis. A net cash flow is computed for an individual year by summing individual cash flow elements. The net cash flow for the year is then discounted back to time zero, and the net present value of the project or investment is computed by summing the discounted annual present values over the project life. The method is best understood by a simple example.

Example 8–2

An investment of $50,000 is made in a computer, which is expected to produce annual savings in operational costs of $20,000 per annum. Maintenance costs are $1,000 for the first three years and $3,000 after that. Salvage value after five years is $5,000, this period being considered the economic life of the machine in technological terms. The discount rate is 15 percent. Compute the net present value of the investment.

Solution: The analysis is carried out as indicated in Table 8–1, on a line-by-line or year-by-year basis. Using the indicated discount rate of 15 percent, the net present value of the investment is $14,040.

The system has the advantage that it easily permits the introduction of several discount rates to permit sensitivity testing and internal rate of return analysis.

The cash-flow method is a particularly suitable application of spreadsheet analysis; spreadsheets are widely available in software for microcomputers. Existing software programs using the cash-flow format have a number of options, which can be very rapidly accessed:

1. Projects or procurement programs can be evaluated rapidly at various discount rates.
2. The internal rate of return can be computed very rapidly.

TABLE 8–1. Analysis of Computer Investment Using Cash-flow Method

Year	Capital Costs	Maintenance Costs	Operational Savings	Salvage Receipts	Net Cash Flow	Discount Factor ($pwf' - i - n$) $i = 15$	Present Value of Cash Flow
0	(50,000)				(50,000)	1.0000	(50,000)
1		(1,000)	20,000		19,000	0.8696	16,522
2		(1,000)	20,000		19,000	0.7561	14,366
3		(1,000)	20,000		19,000	0.6575	12,493
4		(3,000)	20,000		17,000	0.5718	9,721
5		(3,000)	20,000	5,000	22,000	0.4972	10,938
						Total net present value	14,040

160

3. Graphical representations of the investment project can be generated with ease. Typically, these are in the form of annual cash flows or annual expenditure/revenue graphs.

Example 8–3   Use of Lotus 1-2-3 Software

The Metropolis Development Corporation wants to evaluate two different projects related to building a hotel on the grounds of Oriana Airport.

Project I: Initial investment of $13.5 million, with $8 million invested in construction and so on in year 1 and $5.5 million invested in year 2. Annual net operating profits, excluding refurbishment and renovation, of $2 million/annum for twenty years, with refurbishment costs of $200,000/annum and a major refit of $1.5 million in the eleventh year of operation. Salvage costs at the end of the project estimated at $6.5 million.

Project II: Initial investment of $25 million, with $15 million invested in the first year and $10 million in the second year. Annual net operating profit, excluding refurbishment and renovation, estimated at $3.9 million/annum for the twenty-year operational period. Refurbishment costs of $600,000/annum, with a major renovation cost of $2.5 million in the eleventh year of operation. Salvage value is estimated at $5 million.

Solution: For the purposes of this example, the net present value of the two projects are compared at discount rates of 5 percent, 10 percent, and 15 percent. Furthermore, the internal rates of return of the two projects are also calculated.

The inputs of costs and income are put in using Lotus 1-2-3 software in the form shown in Table 8–2. Net present values of three discount rates are output in Table 8–3 and 8–4, and the internal rate of return is computed as 11.26 percent for Project I in Table 8–5 and 10.72 percent for Project II in Table 8–6. Graphical representations of cost-income for both projects are shown in Figures 8–2(a) and (b). Figure 8–3 indicates the projected cash flows for both projects in graphic form.

8.9 CASE STUDY OF AIRPORT REDEVELOPMENT

Example 8–4   Upgrading and Redevelopment of the Airport Terminal Building, Elizabethville Airport

Statement: The existing air terminal building at Elizabethville Airport, a sketch of which is shown in Figure 8–4, dates back to the late 1940s. Since the

TABLE 8–2. Inputs to Lotus 1-2-3 Spreadsheet

METROPOLIS DEVELOPMENT CORPORATION: INVESTMENT APPRAISAL

YEAR	PROJECT I COST	PROJECT I INCOME	PROJECT II COST	PROJECT II INCOME
1	£8,000,000.00	£0.00	£15,000,000.00	£0.00
2	£5,500,000.00	£0.00	£10,000,000.00	£0.00
3	£200,000.00	£2,000,000.00	£600,000.00	£3,900,000.00
4	£200,000.00	£2,000,000.00	£600,000.00	£3,900,000.00
5	£200,000.00	£2,000,000.00	£600,000.00	£3,900,000.00
6	£200,000.00	£2,000,000.00	£600,000.00	£3,900,000.00
7	£200,000.00	£2,000,000.00	£600,000.00	£3,900,000.00
8	£200,000.00	£2,000,000.00	£600,000.00	£3,900,000.00
9	£200,000.00	£2,000,000.00	£600,000.00	£3,900,000.00
10	£200,000.00	£2,000,000.00	£600,000.00	£3,900,000.00
11	£200,000.00	£2,000,000.00	£600,000.00	£3,900,000.00
12	£200,000.00	£2,000,000.00	£600,000.00	£3,900,000.00
13	£1,700,000.00	£2,000,000.00	£3,100,000.00	£3,900,000.00
14	£200,000.00	£2,000,000.00	£600,000.00	£3,900,000.00
15	£200,000.00	£2,000,000.00	£600,000.00	£3,900,000.00
16	£200,000.00	£2,000,000.00	£600,000.00	£3,900,000.00
17	£200,000.00	£2,000,000.00	£600,000.00	£3,900,000.00
18	£200,000.00	£2,000,000.00	£600,000.00	£3,900,000.00
19	£200,000.00	£2,000,000.00	£600,000.00	£3,900,000.00
20	£200,000.00	£2,000,000.00	£600,000.00	£3,900,000.00
21	£200,000.00	£2,000,000.00	£600,000.00	£3,900,000.00
22	£200,000.00	£8,500,000.00	£6,000,000.00	£8,900,000.00

TABLE 8–3. Project I Output (Lotus 1-2-3 Spreadsheet)

PROJECT I NET PRESENT VALUE
===

YEAR	COST	INCOME	CASH FLOW
1	£8,000,000.00	£0.00	(£8,000,000.00)
2	£5,500,000.00	£0.00	(£5,500,000.00)
3	£200,000.00	£2,000,000.00	£1,800,000.00
4	£200,000.00	£2,000,000.00	£1,800,000.00
5	£200,000.00	£2,000,000.00	£1,800,000.00
6	£200,000.00	£2,000,000.00	£1,800,000.00
7	£200,000.00	£2,000,000.00	£1,800,000.00
8	£200,000.00	£2,000,000.00	£1,800,000.00
9	£200,000.00	£2,000,000.00	£1,800,000.00
10	£200,000.00	£2,000,000.00	£1,800,000.00
11	£200,000.00	£2,000,000.00	£1,800,000.00
12	£200,000.00	£2,000,000.00	£1,800,000.00
13	£1,700,000.00	£2,000.000.00	£300,000.00
14	£200,000.00	£2,000,000.00	£1,800,000.00
15	£200,000.00	£2,000,000.00	£1,800,000.00
16	£200,000.00	£2,000,000.00	£1,800,000.00
17	£200,000.00	£2,000,000.00	£1,800,000.00
18	£200,000.00	£2,000,000.00	£1,800,000.00
19	£200,000.00	£2,000,000.00	£1,800,000.00
20	£200,000.00	£2,000,000.00	£1,800,000.00
21	£200,000.00	£3,000,000.00	£1,800,000.00
22	£300,000.00	£3,500,000.00	£8,300,000.00

NPV at 05%			£8,165,298.25
NPV at 10%			£1,210,625.97
NPV at 15%			(£2,539,483.08)

original building was constructed, there have been numerous additions and modifications. The structure in its current condition is very shabby. It is currently carrying more than twice the peak-hour passenger loading that it can comfortably handle and continuing traffic growth is expected, but only if additional facilities can be provided. The existing building is difficult to modify to acceptable modern standards because of numerous structural elements, such as bearing walls and building columns. In developing a number of options for bringing the air terminal up to standards acceptable for the 1990s three principle options have been developed.

Option 1. Expand existing building with extensive structural renovation. Existing public car parking and aircraft apron areas will also be utilized and expanded.

TABLE 8–4. Project II Output (Lotus 1-2-3 Spreadsheet)

PROJECT II NET PRESENT VALUE

YEAR	COST	INCOME	CASH FLOW
1	£15,000,000.00	£0.00	(£15,000,000.00)
2	£10,000,000.00	£0.00	(£10,000,000.00)
3	£600,000.00	£3,900,000.00	£3,300,000.00
4	£600,000.00	£3,900,000.00	£3,300,000.00
5	£600,000.00	£3,900,000.00	£3,300,000.00
6	£600,000.00	£3,900,000.00	£3,300,000.00
7	£600,000.00	£3,900,000.00	£3,300,000.00
8	£600,000.00	£2,900,000.00	£2,300,000.00
9	£600,000.00	£3,900,000.00	£3,300,000.00
10	£600,000.00	£3,900,000.00	£3,300,000.00
11	£600,000.00	£3,900,000.00	£3,300,000.00
12	£600,000.00	£3,900,000.00	£3,300,000.00
13	£3,100,000.00	£3,900,000.00	£800,000.00
14	£600,000.00	£3,900,000.00	£3,300,000.00
15	£600,000.00	£3,900,000.00	£3,300,000.00
16	£600,000.00	£3,900,000.00	£3,300,000.00
17	£600,000.00	£3,900,000.00	£3,300,000.00
18	£600,000.00	£3,900,000.00	£3,300,000.00
19	£600,000.00	£3,900,000.00	£3,300,000.00
20	£600,000.00	£3,900,000.00	£3,300,000.00
21	£600,000.00	£3,900,000.00	£3,300,000.00
22	£600,000.00	£8,900,000.00	£8,300,000.00

NPV at 05%   £14,329,291.00
NPV at 10%   £11,208,052.62
NPV at 15%   (£5,161,424.16)

164

TABLE 8–5. Project I Internal Rate of Return (Lotus 1-2-3 Spreadsheet)

PROJECT I INTERNAL RATE OF RETURN

COST	INCOME	CASH FLOW	GUESS	IRR –I
£8,000,000.00	£0.00	(£8,000,000.00)	8.00%	11.26%
£5,500,000.00	£0.00	(£5,500,000.00)		
£200,000.00	£2,000,000.00	£1,800,000.00		
£200,000.00	£2,000,000.00	£1,800,000.00		
£200,000.00	£2,000,000.00	£1,800,000.00		
£200,000.00	£2,000,000.00	£1,800,000.00		
£200,000.00	£2,000,000.00	£1,800,000.00		
£200,000.00	£2,000,000.00	£1,800,000.00		
£200,000.00	£2,000,000.00	£1,800,000.00		
£200,000.00	£2,000,000.00	£1,800,000.00		
£200,000.00	£2,000,000.00	£1,800,000.00		
£1,700,000.00	£2,000,000.00	£300,000.00		
£200,000.00	£2,000,000.00	£1,800,000.00		
£200,000.00	£2,000,000.00	£1,800,000.00		
£200,000.00	£2,000,000.00	£1,800,000.00		
£200,000.00	£2,000,000.00	£1,800,000.00		
£200,000.00	£2,000,000.00	£1,800,000.00		
£200,000.00	£2,000,000.00	£1,800,000.00		
£200,000.00	£2,000,000.00	£1,800,000.00		
£200,000.00	£2,000,000.00	£1,800,000.00		
£3,500,000.00	£3,500,000.00	£8,300,000.00		

NPV at 11.26%   £0.00

165

TABLE 8–6. Project II Internal Rate of Return (Lotus 1-2-3 Spreadsheet)

PROJECT II INTERNAL RATE OF RETURN

COST	INCOME	CASH FLOW	GUESS	IRR – I
£15,000,000.00	£0.00	(£15,000,000.00)	8.00%	10.72%
£10,000,000.00	£0.00	(£10,000,000.00)		
£600,000.00	£3,900,000.00	£3,300,000.00		
£600,000.00	£3,900,000.00	£3,300,000.00		
£600,000.00	£3,900,000.00	£3,300,000.00		
£600,000.00	£3,900,000.00	£3,300,000.00		
£600,000.00	£3,900,000.00	£3,300,000.00		
£600,000.00	£3,900,000.00	£3,300,000.00		
£600,000.00	£3,900,000.00	£3,300,000.00		
£600,000.00	£3,900,000.00	£3,300,000.00		
£600,000.00	£3,900,000.00	£3,300,000.00		
£3,100,000.00	£3,900,000.00	£800,000.00		
£600,000.00	£3,900,000.00	£3,300,000.00		
£600,000.00	£3,900,000.00	£3,300,000.00		
£600,000.00	£3,900,000.00	£3,300,000.00		
£600,000.00	£3,900,000.00	£3,300,000.00		
£600,000.00	£3,900,000.00	£3,300,000.00		
£600,000.00	£3,900,000.00	£3,300,000.00		
£600,000.00	£3,900,000.00	£3,300,000.00		
£600,000.00	£3,900,000.00	£3,300,000.00		
£600,000.00	£8,900,000.00	£8,300,000.00		

NPV at 10.72%   (£0.00)

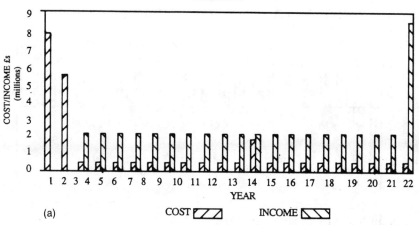

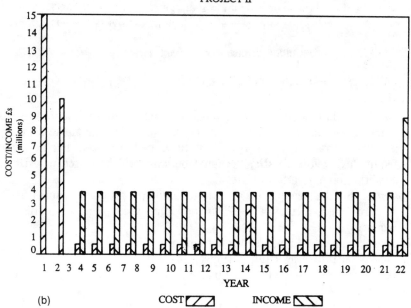

FIGURE 8–2. (a) Cost versus income graph—Project I; (b) Cost versus income graph—Project II

PROJECTED CASH FLOW GRAPH
PROJECTS I & I I

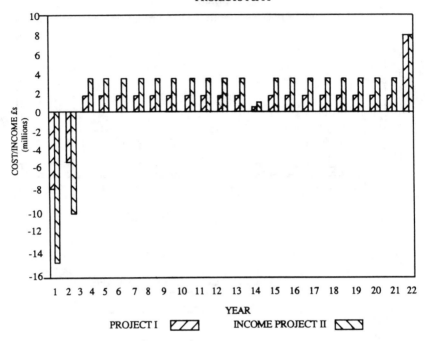

FIGURE 8–3. Cash flows—projects I and II

Option 2. Build new passenger terminal building just to the east of existing building, relocating the general aviation facilities. Existing public car parking and aircraft apron areas will continue to be utilized, but they will require expansion. Existing terminal building will be leased in existing condition on a long-term lease.

Option 3. Build a new passenger terminal building close to the main 04-22 runway, south of runway 14-32, in the largely vacant land area. This will require

1. New terminal building and aircraft apron
2. New parallel taxiway south of runway 14-32
3. New access road to the new terminal site via the vacant area of the site west of treshold 14

With this option it is anticipated that there will be savings in operational costs to the airlines due to lower taxiing costs. Because these do not accrue directly to the airport and because landing fees will not be raised to retrieve these benefits, they are not included in this analysis. With this option, it is

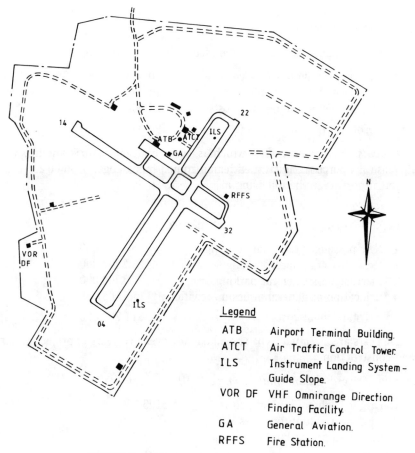

FIGURE 8–4. Elizabethville Airport—existing layout

also assumed that the existing terminal building would be leased on a long-term lease in its existing condition without capital improvement.

The analysis is done over a useful project life of fifteen years, using compound interest tables A8–1 to A8–4 in the appendix to this chapter.

Option 1
Capital costs, including all project-management costs:

1. Renovate existing terminal building	$5,200,000
2. Extend aircraft apron	$700,000
3. Increase car parking	$100,000
Total capital costs	$6,000,000

These costs are assumed to be spread equally over two years of project design and construction phase.

Increased operating and maintenance (OM) costs (annual)

1. Larger-terminal building costs $20,000
2. Increased aircraft apron costs $3,000
3. Increased car-parking-area costs $2,000

    Total annual increased OM costs $25,000

Benefits. Passenger traffic, which is currently 200,000 pax/annum, will increase at 4 percent annually, with an income per passenger of $6.00 accruing to the airport. (See the following.)

Option 2
Capital costs, including all project-management costs:

1. New passenger terminal building $7,500,000
2. Extend aircraft apron $900,000
3. Increase passenger car parking $300,000
4. Relocation of general aviation activities $3,000,000

    Total capital costs $11,700,000

These costs are assumed to be spread equally over two years of project design and construction.

Increased operating and maintenance (OM) costs (annual)

1. Larger terminal building costs $105,000
2. Larger aircraft apron costs $11,000
3. Increased car parking area costs $5,000

    Total annual increased OM costs $121,000

Benefits

1. Rental from lease of existing terminal building (annual) $200,000
2. With better terminal facilities, passenger traffic will increase at 5% annually with an income per passenger of $7.00 accruing to the airport. (See the following.)

Option 3
Capital costs, including all project-management costs:

1. New passenger terminal building $7,500,000
2. New aircraft apron $1,600,000
3. Car parking $600,000
4. New access facilities $1,600,000

5. Drainage	$700,000
6. New taxiway	$1,800,000
Total capital costs	$13,800,000

Increased operating and maintenance (OM) costs (annual):

1. Larger terminal building costs	$105,000
2. Larger aircraft apron costs	$11,000
3. Increased car parking area	$5,000
4. Access, additional costs	$5,000
5. Drainage, additional costs	$3,000
6. Taxiway, additional costs	$4,000
Total annual increase OM costs	$133,000

Benefits

1. Rental from lease of existing
   terminal building (annual) $200,000
2. With improved airside facilities
   and better terminal facilities,
   passenger traffic will increase
   at 7% annually, with an income per passenger of $8.00
   accruing to the airport. (See
   the following.)

Because of uncertainty with respect to technological change, the economic project life is assumed for all three options to be fifteen years, with zero salvage value of facilities at the end of that period. It is recognized that after fifteen years of use, some of these facilities may still have useful life.

Table 8–7 shows projected passenger growth and the associated new income to the airport under the assumptions adopted for the three options under analysis.

Tables 8–8 through 8–10 show a year-by-year stream of benefits in cash-flow terms, also indicating the discounted net cash-flow stream.

Conclusions: None of the three options is economically attractive at a discount rate of 10 percent over the fifteen-year economic life of the project. If other considerations indicate that continued and expanded air transport service is desirable, Option 1 is marginally more economic than Option 3. Given the uncertainty of forecasts and the much higher levels of service that could be provided by Option 3, it is likely that this option would be selected for long-term development, recognizing that—considered in financial terms only—it is a marginally less economic option.

TABLE 8–7. Projected Passenger Growth and Associated Income at Elizabethville Airport for Various Options

Year	Option 1 Growth	Option 1 Income ($)	Option 2 Growth	Option 2 Income ($)	Option 3 Growth	Option 3 Income ($)
1	8,000	48,000	10,000	70,000	14,000	112,000
2	16,320	97,920	20,500	143,500	28,898	231,184
3	84,973	149,838	31,525	220,675	45,501	364,008
4	33,972	203,932	43,101	301,707	62,159	497,272
5	43,331	259,986	55,256	386,792	80,510	644,080
6	53,064	318,384	68,019	476,133	100,146	801,168
7	63,186	379,116	81,420	569,940	121,156	969,248
8	73,714	442,284	95,491	668,437	143,637	1,149,096
9	84,466	506,796	110,266	771,862	167,692	1,341,536
10	96,049	576,294	125,779	880,453	193,430	1,547,440
11	107,890	647,340	142,068	994,476	220,970	1,763,504
12	120,206	721,236	159,171	1,114,197	250,438	2,003,504
13	133,015	798,090	177,130	1,239,910	281,969	2,255,752
14	146,335	878,010	195,986	1,371,902	315,707	2,525,656
15	160,189	961,134	215,786	1,510,502	351,806	2,814,448
16	174,596	1,047,576	236,575	1,656,025	390,433	3,123,464
17	189,580	1,137,480	258,404	1,808,828	431,763	3,454,104
18	205,163		281,324		475,986	
19	221,370		305,390		523,306	
20	238,225		330,660		573,937	
21	255,754		357,193		628,112	
22	273,984		285,052		686,080	

8.10 SENSITIVITY ANALYSIS

The precision of the figures generated by life-cycle costing studies should not be imputed to convey an accuracy of computation or subsequent analysis. It must be recognized that many assumptions go into any analysis and the accuracy and reliability of the answer may be sensitive to these assumptions. Therefore, adequate decision making is likely to be possible only when *sensitivity analysis* is carried out, because for some situations, the result of the analysis depends on the particular combination of assumptions.

Sensitivity analysis should be carried out by repeating the analysis under conditions of varied assumptions, using low and high estimates of the various factors. In life-cycle costing, assumptions must be made relative to

The discount rate
The level and timings of cash flows (benefits, revenues, and costs)

TABLE 8–8. Analysis Table for Option 1

Option 1

Year	Capital Cost	Additional O and M Costs	Rents	Incremental Passenger Revenues	Net Cash Flow (NCF)	$pwf' - i - n$ ($i = 10\%$)	Present Value of Cash Flow
0	(3,000,000)				(2,952,000)	1.0000	(2,683,663)
1	(3,000,000)			48,000	(2,902,080)	0.9091	(2,398,279)
2				97,920		0.8264	
3		(25,000)		149,838	124,838	.7513	93,791
4		(25,000)		203,832	178,832	.6830	122,142
5		(25,000)		259,986	234,986	.6209	145,902
6		(25,000)		318,384	293,384	.5645	165,615
7		(25,000)		379,116	354,116	.5132	181,732
8		(25,000)		442,284	417,284	.4665	194,663
9		(25,000)		506,796	481,796	.4241	204,330
10		(25,000)		576,294	551,294	.3855	212,523
11		(25,000)		647,340	622,340	.3505	218,130
12		(25,000)		721,236	696,236	.3186	221,821
13		(25,000)		798,090	773,090	.2897	223,964
14		(25,000)		878,010	853,010	.2633	224,598
15		(25,000)		961,134	936,134	.2394	224,110
16		(25,000)		1,047,576	1,022,576	.2176	222,512
17		(25,000)		1,137,480	1,112,480	.1978	220,048
						Total net present value	(2,206,061)

173

TABLE 8-9. Analysis Table for Option 2

Option 2

Year	Capital Cost	Additional O and M Costs	Rents	Incremental Passenger Revenues	Net Cash Flow (NCF)	pwf' – i – n (i = 10%)	Present Value of Cash Flow
0						1.0000	
1	(5,850,000)			70,000	(5,780,000)	.9091	(5,254,598)
2	(5,850,000)			143,500	(5,706,500)	.8264	(4,715,852)
3		(121,000)	200,000	220,675	299,675	.7513	225,146
4		(121,000)	200,000	301,707	380,707	.6830	260,023
5		(121,000)	200,000	386,792	465,792	.6209	289,210
6		(121,000)	200,000	476,133	555,133	.5645	313,373
7		(121,000)	200,000	569,940	648,940	.5132	333,036
8		(121,000)	200,000	668,437	747,437	.4665	348,679
9		(121,000)	200,000	771,862	850,862	.4241	360,851
10		(121,000)	200,000	880,453	959,453	.3855	369,869
11		(121,000)	200,000	994,476	1,073,476	.3505	376,253
12		(121,000)	200,000	1,114,197	1,193,197	.3186	380,153
13		(121,000)	200,000	1,239,910	1,318,910	.2897	382,088
14		(121,000)	200,000	1,371,902	1,450,902	.2633	382,022
15		(121,000)	200,000	1,510,502	1,589,502	.2394	380,527
16		(121,000)	200,000	1,656,025	1,735,025	.2176	377,541
17		(121,000)	200,000	1,808,828	1,887,828	.1978	373,412
						Total net present value	(4,818,267)

TABLE 8–10. Analysis Table for Option 3

Option 3

Year	Capital Cost	Additional O and M Costs	Rents	Incremental Passenger Revenues	Net Cash Flow (NCF)	$pwf' - i - n$ ($i = 10\%$)	Present Value of Cash Flow
0	(6,900,000)					1.0000	
1	(6,900,000)			112,000	(6,788,000)	.9091	(6,170,971)
2				231,184	(6,668,816)	.8264	(5,511,109)
3		(133,000)	200,000	364,008	431,008	.7513	323,816
4		(133,000)	200,000	497,272	564,272	.6830	385,398
5		(133,000)	200,000	644,080	711,080	.6209	441,510
6		(133,000)	200,000	801,168	868,168	.5645	490,081
7		(133,000)	200,000	969,248	1,036,248	.5132	531,802
8		(133,000)	200,000	1,149,096	1,216,096	.4665	567,309
9		(133,000)	200,000	1,341,536	1,408,536	.4241	597,360
10		(133,000)	200,000	1,547,440	1,614,440	.3855	622,367
11		(133,000)	200,000	1,763,504	1,830,504	.3505	641,592
12		(133,000)	200,000	2,003,504	2,070,504	.3186	659,663
13		(133,000)	200,000	2,255,752	2,322,752	.2897	672,901
14		(133,000)	200,000	2,525,656	2,592,656	.2633	682,646
15		(133,000)	200,000	2,814,448	2,881,448	.2394	689,819
16		(133,000)	200,000	3,123,464	3,190,464	.2176	694,245
17		(133,000)	200,000	3,454,104	3,521,104	.1978	696,474
					Total net present value		(2,985,097)

175

The period of analysis
The timings of renewals, replacements, and refurbishment
Estimates of economic life
Salvage values or removal costs

The basic analysis is made using most likely values of the parameters for the calculation, and the sensitivity of the decision is then tested against variations in those parameters.

APPENDIX

Following are tables that list compound interest factors for 5-, 10-, 15-, and 20-percent compound interest. These tables apply to the case study of airport redevelopment described in Section 8.9.

TABLE A8-1. 5% Compound Interest Factors

	Single Payment			Uniform Series			
n	Compound Amount Factor, $caf' - i - n$	Present Worth Factor, $pwf' - i - n$	Sinking Fund Factor, $sff - i - n$	Capital Recovery Factor, $crf - i - n$	Compound Amount Factor, $caf - i - n$	Present Worth Factor, $pwf - i - n$	n
1	1.0500	0.9524	1.000 00	1.050 00	1.000	0.952	1
2	1.1025	0.9070	0.487 80	0.537 80	2.050	1.859	2
3	1.1576	0.8638	0.317 21	0.367 21	3.153	2.723	3
4	1.2155	0.8227	0.232 01	0.282 01	4.310	3.546	4
5	1.2763	0.7835	0.180 97	0.230 97	5.526	4.329	5
6	1.3401	0.7462	0.147 02	0.197 02	6.802	5.076	6
7	1.4071	0.7107	0.122 82	0.172 82	8.142	5.786	7
8	1.4775	0.6768	0.104 72	0.154 72	9.549	6.463	8
9	1.5513	0.6446	0.090 69	0.140 69	11.027	7.108	9
10	1.6289	0.6139	0.079 50	0.129 50	12.578	7.722	10
11	1.7103	0.5847	0.070 39	0.120 39	14.207	8.306	11
12	1.7959	0.5568	0.062 83	0.112 83	15.917	8.863	12
13	1.8856	0.5303	0.056 46	0.106 46	17.713	9.394	13
14	1.9800	0.5051	0.051 02	0.101 02	19.599	9.899	14
15	2.0789	0.4810	0.046 34	0.096 34	21.579	10.380	15
16	2.1829	0.4581	0.042 27	0.092 27	23.657	10.838	16
17	2.2920	0.4363	0.038 70	0.088 70	25.840	11.274	17
18	2.4066	0.4155	0.035 55	0.085 55	28.132	11.690	18
19	2.5270	0.3957	0.032 75	0.082 75	30.539	12.085	19
20	2.6533	0.3769	0.030 24	0.080 24	33.066	12.462	20
21	2.7860	0.3589	0.028 00	0.078 00	35.719	12.821	21
22	2.9253	0.3418	0.025 97	0.075 97	38.505	13.163	22
23	3.0715	0.3256	0.024 14	0.074 14	41.430	13.489	23

24	13.799	44.502	0.072 47	0.022 47	0.3101	3.2251	24
25	14.094	47.727	0.070 95	0.020 95	0.2953	3.3864	25
26	14.375	51.113	0.069 56	0.019 56	0.2812	3.5557	26
27	14.643	54.669	0.068 29	0.018 29	0.2678	3.7335	27
28	14.898	58.403	0.067 12	0.017 12	0.2551	3.9201	28
29	15.141	62.323	0.066 05	0.016 05	0.2429	4.1161	29
30	15.372	66.439	0.065 05	0.015 05	0.2314	4.3219	30
31	15.593	70.761	0.064 13	0.014 13	0.2204	4.5380	31
32	15.803	75.299	0.063 28	0.013 28	0.2099	4.7649	32
33	16.003	80.064	0.062 49	0.012 49	0.1999	5.0032	33
34	16.193	85.067	0.061 76	0.011 76	0.1904	5.2533	34
35	16.374	90.320	0.061 07	0.011 07	0.1813	5.5160	35
40	17.159	120.800	0.058 28	0.008 28	0.1420	7.0400	40
45	17.774	159.700	0.056 26	0.006 26	0.1113	8.9850	45
50	18.256	209.348	0.054 78	0.004 78	0.0872	11.4674	50
55	18.633	272.713	0.053 67	0.003 67	0.0683	14.6356	55
60	18.929	353.584	0.052 83	0.002 83	0.0535	18.6792	60
65	19.161	456.798	0.052 19	0.002 19	0.0419	23.8399	65
70	19.343	588.529	0.051 70	0.001 70	0.0329	30.4264	70
75	19.485	756.654	0.051 32	0.001 32	0.0258	38.8327	75
80	19.596	971.229	0.051 03	0.001 03	0.0202	49.5614	80
85	19.684	1 254.087	0.050 80	0.000 80	0.0158	63.2544	85
90	19.752	1 594.607	0.050 63	0.000 63	0.0124	80.7304	90
95	19.806	2 040.694	0.050 49	0.000 49	0.0097	103.0357	95
100	19.848	2 610.025	0.050 38	0.000 38	0.0076	131.5013	100

TABLE A8–2. 10% Compound Interest Factors

	Single Payment		Uniform Series			
n	Compound Amount Factor, caf' – i – n	Present Worth Factor, pwf' – i – n	Sinking Fund Factor, sff – i – n	Capital Recovery Factor, crf – i – n	Compound Amount Factor, caf – i – n	Present Worth Factor, pwf – i – n	n
1	1.1000	0.9091	1.000 00	1.100 00	1.000	0.909	1
2	1.2100	0.8264	0.476 19	0.576 19	2.100	1.736	2
3	1.3310	0.7513	0.302 11	0.402 11	3.310	2.487	3
4	1.4641	0.6830	0.215 47	0.315 47	4.641	3.170	4
5	1.6105	0.6209	0.163 80	0.263 80	6.105	3.791	5
6	1.7716	0.5645	0.129 61	0.229 61	7.716	4.355	6
7	1.9487	0.5132	0.105 41	0.205 41	9.487	4.868	7
8	2.1436	0.4665	0.087 44	0.187 44	11.436	5.335	8
9	2.3579	0.4241	0.073 64	0.173 64	13.579	5.759	9
10	2.5937	0.3855	0.062 75	0.162 75	15.937	6.144	10
11	2.8531	0.3505	0.053 96	0.153 96	18.531	6.495	11
12	3.1384	0.3186	0.046 76	0.146 76	21.384	6.814	12
13	3.4523	0.2897	0.040 78	0.140 78	24.523	7.103	13
14	3.7975	0.2633	0.035 75	0.135 75	27.975	7.367	14
15	4.1772	0.2394	0.031 47	0.131 47	31.772	7.606	15
16	4.5950	0.2176	0.027 82	0.127 82	35.950	7.824	16
17	5.0545	0.1978	0.024 66	0.124 66	40.545	8.022	17
18	5.5599	0.1799	0.021 93	0.121 93	45.599	8.201	18
19	6.1159	0.1635	0.019 55	0.119 55	51.159	8.365	19
20	6.7275	0.1486	0.017 46	0.117 46	57.275	8.514	20
21	7.4002	0.1351	0.015 62	0.115 62	64.002	8.649	21
22	8.1403	0.1228	0.014 01	0.114 01	71.403	8.772	22
23	8.9543	0.1117	0.012 57	0.112 57	79.543	8.883	23

24	9.8497	0.1015	0.011 30	0.111 30	88.497	8.985	24
25	10.8347	0.0923	0.010 17	0.110 17	98.347	9.077	25
26	11.9182	0.0839	0.009 16	0.109 16	109.182	9.161	26
27	13.1100	0.0763	0.008 26	0.108 26	121.100	9.237	27
28	14.4210	0.0693	0.007 45	0.107 45	134.210	9.307	28
29	15.8631	0.0630	0.006 73	0.106 73	148.631	9.370	29
30	17.4494	0.0573	0.006 08	0.106 08	164.494	9.427	30
31	19.1943	0.0521	0.005 50	0.105 50	181.943	9.479	31
32	21.1138	0.0474	0.004 97	0.104 97	201.138	9.526	32
33	23.2252	0.0431	0.004 50	0.104 50	222.252	9.569	33
34	25.5477	0.0391	0.004 07	0.104 07	245.477	9.609	34
35	28.1024	0.0356	0.003 69	0.103 69	271.024	9.644	35
40	45.2593	0.0221	0.002 26	0.102 26	442.593	9.779	40
45	72.8905	0.0137	0.001 39	0.101 39	718.905	9.863	45
50	117.3909	0.0085	0.000 86	0.100 86	1 163.909	9.915	50
55	189.0591	0.0053	0.000 53	0.100 53	1 880.591	9.947	55
60	304.4816	0.0033	0.000 33	0.100 33	3 034.816	9.967	60
65	490.3707	0.0020	0.000 20	0.100 20	4 893.707	9.980	65
70	789.7470	0.0013	0.000 13	0.100 13	7 887.470	9.987	70
75	1 271.8952	0.0008	0.000 08	0.100 08	12 708.954	9.992	75
80	2 048.4002	0.0005	0.000 05	0.100 05	20 474.002	9.995	80
85	3 298.9690	0.0003	0.000 03	0.100 03	32 979.690	9.997	85
90	5 313.0226	0.0002	0.000 02	0.100 02	53 120.226	9.998	90
95	8 556.6760	0.0001	0.000 01	0.100 01	85 556.760	9.999	95
100	13 780.6123	0.0001	0.000 01	0.100 01	137 796.123	9.999	100

TABLE A8–3. 15% Compound Interest Factors

	Single Payment		Uniform Series				
n	Compound Amount Factor, $caf' - i - n$	Present Worth Factor, $pwf' - i - n$	Sinking Fund Factor, $sff - i - n$	Capital Recovery Factor, $crf - i - n$	Compound Amount Factor, $caf - i - n$	Present Worth Factor, $pwf - i - n$	n
1	1.1500	0.8696	1.000 00	1.150 00	1.000	0.870	1
2	1.3225	0.7561	0.465 12	0.615 12	2.150	1.626	2
3	1.5209	0.6575	0.287 98	0.437 98	3.472	2.283	3
4	1.7490	0.5718	0.200 26	0.350 27	4.993	2.855	4
5	2.0114	0.4972	0.148 32	0.298 32	6.742	3.352	5
6	2.3131	0.4323	0.114 24	0.264 24	8.754	3.784	6
7	2.6600	0.3759	0.090 36	0.240 36	11.067	4.160	7
8	3.0590	0.3269	0.072 85	0.222 85	13.727	4.487	8
9	3.5179	0.2843	0.059 57	0.209 57	16.786	4.772	9
10	4.0456	0.2472	0.049 25	0.199 25	20.304	5.019	10
11	4.6524	0.2149	0.041 07	0.191 07	24.349	5.234	11
12	5.3503	0.1869	0.034 48	0.184 48	29.002	5.421	12
13	6.1528	0.1625	0.029 11	0.179 11	34.352	5.583	13
14	7.0757	0.1413	0.024 69	0.174 69	40.505	5.724	14
15	8.1371	0.1229	0.021 02	0.171 02	47.580	5.847	15
16	9.3576	0.1069	0.017 95	0.167 95	55.717	5.954	16

n						n
17	6.047	65.075	0.165 37	0.015 37	0.0929	10.7613	17
18	6.128	75.836	0.163 19	0.013 19	0.0808	12.3755	18
19	6.198	88.212	0.161 34	0.011 34	0.0703	14.2318	19
20	6.259	102.444	0.159 76	0.009 76	0.0611	16.3665	20
21	6.312	118.810	0.158 42	0.008 42	0.0531	18.8215	21
22	6.359	137.632	0.157 27	0.007 27	0.0462	21.6447	22
23	6.399	159.276	0.156 28	0.006 28	0.0402	24.8915	23
24	6.434	184.168	0.155 43	0.005 43	0.0349	28.6252	24
25	6.464	212.793	0.154 70	0.004 70	0.0304	32.9190	25
26	6.491	245.712	0.154 07	0.004 07	0.0264	37.8568	26
27	6.514	283.569	0.153 53	0.003 53	0.0230	43.5353	27
28	6.534	327.104	0.153 06	0.003 06	0.0200	50.0656	28
29	6.551	377.170	0.152 65	0.002 65	0.0174	57.5755	29
30	6.566	434.745	0.152 30	0.002 30	0.0151	66.2118	30
31	6.579	500.957	0.152 00	0.002 00	0.0131	76.1435	31
32	6.591	577.100	0.151 73	0.001 73	0.0114	87.5651	32
33	6.600	664.666	0.151 50	0.001 50	0.0099	100.6998	33
34	6.609	765.365	0.151 31	0.001 31	0.0086	115.8048	34
35	6.617	881.170	0.151 13	0.001 13	0.0075	133.1755	35
40	6.642	1 779.090	0.150 56	0.000 56	0.0037	267.8635	40
45	6.654	3 585.128	0.150 28	0.000 28	0.0019	538.7693	45
50	6.661	7 217.716	0.150 14	0.000 14	0.0009	1 083.6574	50
∞	6.667		0.150 00				∞

TABLE A8–4. 20% Compound Interest Factors

| | Single Payment | | | | | Uniform Series | | |
	Compound Amount Factor, $caf - i - n$	Present Worth Factor, $pwf - i - n$		Sinking Fund Factor, $sff - i - n$	Capital Recovery Factor, $crf - i - n$	Compound Amount Factor, $caf - i - n$	Present Worth Factor, $pwf - i - n$	n
1	1.2000	0.8333		1.000 00	1.200 00	1.000	0.833	1
2	1.4400	0.6944		0.454 55	0.654 55	2.200	1.528	2
3	1.7280	0.5787		0.274 73	0.474 73	3.640	2.106	3
4	2.0736	0.4823		0.186 29	0.386 29	5.368	2.589	4
5	2.4883	0.4019		0.134 38	0.334 38	7.442	2.991	5
6	2.9860	0.3349		0.100 71	0.300 71	9.930	3.326	6
7	3.5832	0.2791		0.077 42	0.277 42	12.916	3.605	7
8	4.2998	0.2326		0.060 61	0.260 61	16.499	3.837	8
9	5.1598	0.1938		0.048 08	0.248 08	20.799	4.031	9
10	6.1917	0.1615		0.038 52	0.238 52	25.959	4.192	10
11	7.4301	0.1346		0.031 10	0.231 10	32.150	4.327	11
12	8.9161	0.1122		0.025 26	0.225 26	39.581	4.439	12
13	10.6993	0.0935		0.020 62	0.220 62	48.497	4.533	13
14	12.8392	0.0779		0.016 89	0.216 89	59.196	4.611	14
15	15.4070	0.0649		0.013 88	0.213 88	72.035	4.675	15
16	18.4884	0.0541		0.011 44	0.211 44	87.442	4.730	16

n						n
17	22.1861	0.0451	0.009 44	0.209 44	105.931	4.775	17
18	26.6233	0.0376	0.007 81	0.207 81	128.117	4.812	18
19	31.9480	0.0313	0.006 46	0.206 46	154.740	4.844	19
20	38.3376	0.0261	0.005 36	0.205 36	186.688	4.870	20
21	46.0051	0.0217	0.004 44	0.204 44	225.026	4.891	21
22	55.2061	0.0181	0.003 69	0.203 69	271.031	4.909	22
23	66.2474	0.0151	0.003 07	0.203 07	326.237	4.925	23
24	79.4968	0.0126	0.002 55	0.202 55	392.484	4.937	24
25	95.3962	0.0105	0.002 12	0.202 12	471.981	4.948	25
26	114.4755	0.0087	0.001 76	0.201 76	567.377	4.956	26
27	137.3706	0.0073	0.001 47	0.201 47	681.853	4.964	27
28	164.8447	0.0061	0.001 22	0.201 22	819.223	4.970	28
29	197.8136	0.0051	0.001 02	0.201 02	984.068	4.975	29
30	237.3763	0.0042	0.000 85	0.200 85	1 181.882	4.979	30
31	284.8516	0.0035	0.000 70	0.200 70	1 419.258	4.982	31
32	341.8219	0.0029	0.000 59	0.200 59	1 704.109	4.985	32
33	410.1863	0.0024	0.000 49	0.200 49	2 045.931	4.988	33
34	492.2235	0.0020	0.000 41	0.200 41	2 456.118	4.990	34
35	590.6682	0.0017	0.000 34	0.200 34	2 984.341	4.992	35
40	1 469.7716	0.0007	0.000 14	0.200 14	7 343.858	4.997	40
45	3 657.2620	0.0003	0.000 05	0.200 05	18 281.310	4.999	45
50	9 100.4382	0.0001	0.000 02	0.200 02	45 497.191	4.999	50
∞			0.200 00	0.200 00		5.000	∞

REFERENCES

1. Wright, P., and N. Ashford. *Transportation Engineering.* 3d ed. New York: John Wiley, 1989.
2. Grant, E.L., W. Grant Ireson, and R.S. Leavenworth. *Principles of Engineering Economy.* 7th ed. New York: John Wiley, 1985.
3. Kanafani, A. *Transportation Demand Analysis.* New York: McGraw-Hill, 1983.
4. Ashford, N., and J.M. Clark. "An Overview of Transport Technology Assessments." *Transportation Planning and Technology* 3, no. 1, 1974.

9

Performance Indicators

9.1 NEED FOR PERFORMANCE INDICATORS

Many, if not most, airports are in a position of either monopoly or semimonopoly. Furthermore, especially with larger operations, the conditions within which the airport functions are peculiar to that facility. The fact that, in general, full or near monopoly exists should not be construed to imply that most airports abuse this situation by using resources wastefully or by price gouging, phenomena that are often associated with a monopoly. The majority of airports are within the publicly owned sector and have a tradition of public service. Profits, charges, and wages are consequently generally lower than in much of the privately owned sector of aviation, and service levels are at least as high. In the current political climate, which frequently and incorrectly assumes that public services are wasteful per se, it is important to develop and use measures that can demonstrate the performance of an airport over time and can be used to compare the operation of one facility against another.

Even if all airports were to become private companies, the position of monopoly or semimonopoly would not, under conditions of normal profitable competition, necessarily lead to optimal performance. High profit levels may mask wasteful consumption of resources, which have been provided in the past with public monies and have been written down to have little asset value. Equally, high profit levels may indicate poor service levels to the airport's clientele: the airlines and the passengers. In fact, few airports exist in an environment in which pure competition can be considered to exist. Inevitably, a number of constraints will exist to inhibit or hinder direct competition between airports. These may be political, economic, social, regulatory, technical, or geographical (1). Such special conditions, which may exist at any airport that otherwise belongs to an apparently typical cross section of similar airports, mean that comparison among airports is usually difficult and frequently is not really possible even with sophisticated performance measures. These measures can, however, be of considerable assistance in making comparisons of relative performance across time at any one airport, since they will indicate possible changes in efficiency or levels of service.

9.2 HISTORIC USE OF PERFORMANCE MEASURES

Rudimentary forms of performance measures have been used in the airport industry for many years. Annual reports of airports have regularly recorded, on a historic basis, annual passenger and freight throughputs, annual air transport movements (ATMs), and total movements, financial turnover, and profits or losses. Improvements on these figures on a year-to-year basis have routinely been accepted as indicators of improved performance.

A more structured approach was adopted by the former British Airports Authority, which in the early 1980s, prior to privatization, published the British Airports Authority Performance Review (2). This review, which was issued in conjunction with the annual report, contained key financial statistics for the reported year. Additionally the BAA reported on the status and changes in

Trading profit and rate of return on capital
Total terminal passengers
Total income; traffic income; trading income
Total air transport movements
Total expenditure
Total cargo and mail tonnage

Additionally, performance was measured against agreed-upon government targets. For example, for the financial year 1984–1985 the report commented on the following targets, which had been agreed upon between the BAA and government in 1984 to run for the period 1983–1986.

1. *To achieve, on the average, a minimum annual rate of return on average net assets of 3 percent plus one-fifth of the annual percentage growth in terminal passengers on a cumulative basis in each successive year:* In 1984–1985 BAA's target of return was 6.3 percent, made up of 4.1 percent of the year before plus one-fifth of the 11 percent traffic growth (2.2 percent); 6.9 percent was achieved.
2. *To reduce costs (at constant prices and excluding depreciation) per terminal passenger by ½ percent per year plus an additional reduction equiva-*

lent to two-fifths of the percentage growth in terminal passengers over the three-year period:

Costs per Passenger

1982–1983	Base year	£4.87
1983–1984	Target	£4.73
1983–1984	achieved	£4.63
1984–1985	Target	£4.49
1984–1985	achieved	£4.31

3. *To increase the number of terminal passengers per payroll hour by ½ percent a year plus two-fifths of the percentage growth in terminal passengers over the three-year period:*

Passengers per Payroll Hour

1982–1983	Base year	2.60
1983–1984	Target	2.68
1983–1984	achieved	2.80
1984–1985	Target	2.81
1984–1985	achieved	3.12

Other nonfinancial indicators were considered:

1. Analysis of passenger comments with respect to catering, baggage, and other BAA facilities as well as nonspecific areas:
   Complaints
   Compliments
2. Runway closure
3. Availability of mechanical equipment in sensitive passenger areas or service:
   Passenger conveyors
   Escalators
   Elevators in terminals and parking lots
   Loading bridges

Although the published indicators were set groupwide, senior management set individual targets for each of the seven constituent airports of the BAA group. This was clearly necessary in a situation where there were extremely profitable elements (Heathrow) and other facilities that could not conceivably be expected to break even (Prestwick). It should be noted that up to the early 1980s, all airports in the BAA group were either only marginally profitable operations or were substantial losers with respect to traffic income. The trading profit of the entire group was derived from the profit on commercial (nonaeronautical) income at Heathrow. Given substantial cross subsidization within the group, targets for performance indices varied widely among individual airports.

To encourage senior management at the individual airports to achieve performance targets, salaries were strongly linked to performance. Up to 40 percent of the senior manager's salary depended on achieving all targets. Failure to achieve two major targets would result in a zero performance-linked bonus. This policy provided an extremely strong incentive to senior management at the individual airports. To ensure that the concept of achieving performance targets was pervasive in the system, incentive bonuses of up to a maximum of 20 percent of their total salaries were paid to middle managers. Targets for middle managers at individual airports were set locally by the senior airport staff. These targets ensured that if met, the individual airport would achieve its own targets within the group.

For the remainder of the discussion in this chapter, only financial performance indicators will be considered. A more complete treatment of the structuring of general performance monitoring at airports is given in (3).

9.3 STUDIES OF FINANCIAL PERFORMANCE INDICATORS

Arguing for the more widespread use of financial performance indicators, a number of studies have been carried out by several researchers, showing the relative performance of various airports in cross-sectional studies. These studies are often flawed by the inability of those carrying out the work to ensure complete compatibility of data bases, the need in some cases for sweeping assumptions to provide a basis for comparison, and the temporal limitation of the data base with respect to time. With respect to the last point, the cross-sectional comparison is necessarily made at one point in time, and conclusions could well vary if the time frame used were different.

During the 1980s, two major studies on the comparative financial performance of airports were carried out in Europe. In 1987, Doganis and Graham published an analysis of the performance of 24 major European airports from 11 different countries, using 17 different economic performance criteria (1). In 1989, Assailly produced an analytical study of 33 French airports (4) using 18 performance indicators. These two studies, although covering much of the same ground, were in practice quite different in nature. The Doganis and Graham work related to a number of large airports throughout the extent of western Europe. Because these airports were selected from a large number of countries, the techniques of financing and even the method of financial reporting showed marked differences among the various facilities. A number of assumptions therefore had to be made to provide a measure of compatibility to the analysis. The work by Assailly, on the other hand, was carried out on a set of data that was of a much more homogeneous nature in that all data were derived from airports funded under the French system of financing and financial reporting. The airports varied greatly in scale of operation, ranging from Aéroports de Paris, with 33.6 million passengers in the analysis year 1986, to Valence, with 42,000 passengers in the same year.

Financial performance indicators have been developed in five main areas:

1. Costs
2. Revenue
3. Labor productivity
4. Capital productivity
5. Financial profitability

Table 9–1 compares the Doganis indicators with those of the ITA according to this five-tier classification. In some cases, the criteria are identical, but there are also significant differences. The British study, concentrating as it did on the larger European airports, necessarily took freight operations into consideration. This was done by the use of work-load units (WLUs), which were considered equal to one passenger or 100 kg of freight. The French study, dealing generally with very much smaller airports, developed its measures in terms of passenger throughput, ignoring freight. This assumption in a study largely dominated by small airports with insignificant freight operations presented only slight problems with respect to internal compatibility of data for the few large airports under consideration. Direct comparisons between the findings of two studies is, however, difficult.

Doganis presents *performance profiles* for each of the various airports, whereby each individual performance indicator is measured against the industry average, which is normalized to the value 100. In this case, the industry average was accepted to be the average of the sampled airports. It was then possible to obtain a visual comparison of overall performance by directly comparing the graphic profiles, such as those for Vienna and Amsterdam in Figures 9–1 and 9–2. An alternative way of using the data is to rank a number of airports according to performance in one indicator and to examine an airport within the range of observed values and with respect to the industry average, as shown in Figure 9–3.

Cross comparisons can be made between airports using performance indicators, but such comparisons can be misleading. It is entirely understandable that senior management and directors on the boards of individual airports want to improve performance to match that of the best in the industry. However, great care must be taken that the comparisons made are founded on truly

TABLE 9–1. Classification of Cross-sectional Performance Measuring

	Institut du Transport Aérien	Doganis and Graham
Costs:		
	Total cost per passenger	Total costs per WLU
	Personnel costs per passenger	Personnel costs per WLU
	Capital costs per passenger	Capital costs per WLU
	Personnel costs/value added ratio	.
	Capital costs/value added ratio	.
	Personnel costs per employee	.
	Debt/gross revenue ratio	Operating costs per WLU
	.	
	.	
	.	
Revenue:		
	Gross revenue per passenger	Gross revenue per WLU
	Aeronautical revenue per passenger	.
	Nonaeronautical revenue per passenger	.
		.
	Ground support service revenue per passenger	Gross revenue/expenditure ratio
	.	
	.	
	.	
Labor productivity:		
	Gross revenue/employee	Gross revenue per employee
	Value added/employee	.
	Passengers/employee	.
		.
	.	WLU per employee
	.	Value added per unit personnel costs
Capital productivity:		
	Assets per passenger	Assets per WLU
	Assets/gross revenue ratio	.
	.	.
	.	Profit/net assets ratio
	.	Value added per unit capital cost
Financial profitability:		
	Operating income/gross revenue ratio	.
	Operating income/passenger	.
	.	Profit/revenue ratio
	.	Value added per unit staff and capital costs

Indicator

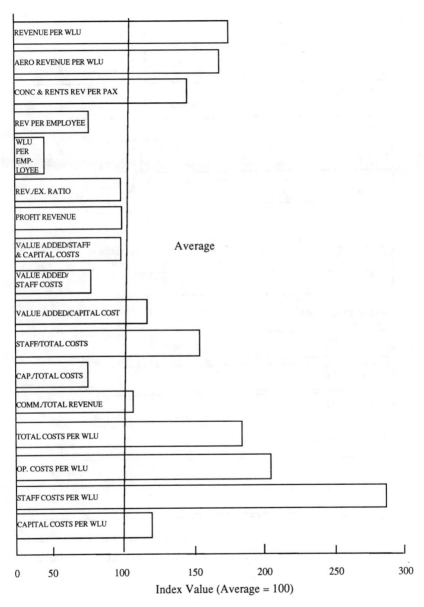

FIGURE 9–1. Performance profiles—Vienna (Source: Rigas Doganis and Anne Graham. *Airport Management: The Role of Performance Indicators*. Research Report No. 13. Transport Studies Group, Polytechnic of Central London, 1987.)

Indicator

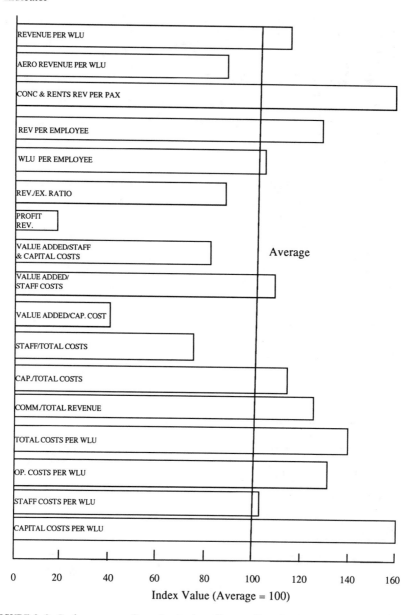

FIGURE 9–2. Performance profiles—Amsterdam (Source: Rigas Doganis and Anne Graham. *Airport Management: The Role of Performance Indicators.* Research Report No. 13. Transport Studies Group, Polytechnic of Central London, 1987.)

Airport

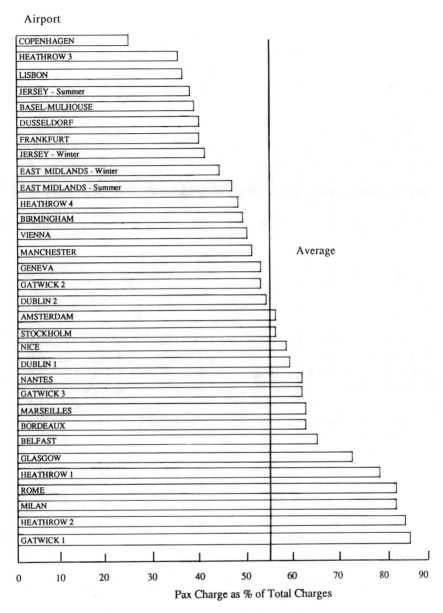

FIGURE 9–3. Passenger charges as a percentage of total airport charges (Source: Rigas Doganis and Anne Graham. *Airport Management: The Role of Performance Indicators.* Research Report No. 13. Transport Studies Group, Polytechnic of Central London, 1987.)

comparable data. In many airports, the range of encompassed activities and duties varies greatly. The way in which assets, loans, and grants, for example, have been treated can differ so greatly in substance that true comparisons are almost impossible. Even in the matter of salaries and wages, the differing procedures between civil service practice and private or quasi-governmental authorities can make comparisons of personnel costs virtually meaningless.

Those cross comparisons felt to be possible can be most powerfully presented in terms of graphical or statistical data used in conjunction with other performance indices or variables.

Examples of two variable relationships are drawn from (1) and (4) and are shown in Figures 9–4 and 9–5. Figure 9–4 shows a European-wide comparison of the revenue/expenditure ratio with the index of international charges. The simple regression line shown has the following form (1):

$$\frac{\text{Revenue}}{\text{Expenditure}} = -0.796 + 0.2079 \ln\left(\frac{\text{international}}{\text{charges index}}\right) \tag{9-1}$$

$$R^2 = 0.522$$

Since approximately only one-half of the variation of the data is explained by this equation, the relationship is not considered to be strong. Visually this is demonstrated by the scatter of points around the graph.

An even less strong relationship is demonstrated in Figure 9–5, where the graph shows the association between unit nonaeronautical revenues and international traffic share. The form of the equation in this case is (4)

$$\frac{\text{Nonaeronautical revenues}}{\text{per passenger}} = 7.37 + 0.208\left(\frac{\text{international}}{\text{traffic share}}\right) \tag{9-2}$$

In other cases relationships are found between more directly associated variables, and these are noted to be much more strongly correlated.

For example, there are very strong relationships between total airport costs, total revenues, and passenger throughput (4):

$$\text{Total cost} = 0.29 + 0.0426(\text{passenger traffic}) \tag{9-3}$$

$$R^2 = 0.966$$

$$\frac{\text{Aeronautical}}{\text{revenues}} = -0.346 + 0.019(\text{passenger traffic}) \tag{9-4}$$

$$R^2 = 0.976$$

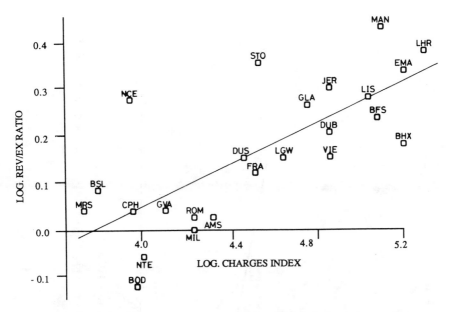

FIGURE 9–4. Relationship between revenue/expenditure ratio and airport charges (Source: Rigas Doganis and Anne Graham. *Airport Management: The Role of Performance Indicators.* Research Report No. 13. Transport Studies Group, Polytechnic of Central London, 1987.)

$$\text{Nonaeronautical revenues} = -1.98 + 0.0235(\text{passenger traffic}) \qquad (9–5)$$

$$R^2 = 0.94$$

$$\text{Total revenues} = -2.34 + 0.0426(\text{passenger traffic}) \qquad (9–6)$$

$$R^2 = 0.962$$

These strong relationships were able to be defined in the ITA study because the data base was from one year and concerned only one currency; additionally, the airports were entirely within one country and used essentially one system of financing. Cross comparisons between countries are much more difficult.

9.4 AGGREGATE AND DISAGGREGATE DATA

A general rule of analysis that has wide application outside the range of financial matter is that the use of disaggregate data is preferable to the use of

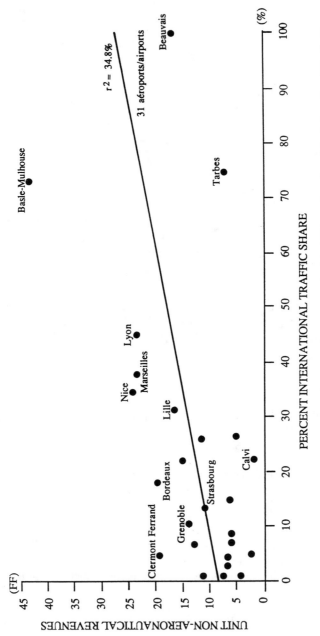

FIGURE 9–5. Unit Nonaeronautical revenues (excluding ground support services) in 1986 as a function of the International Traffic Share (Source: Adapted from Reference 4.)

aggregated information. In the course of aggregation, there is a general tendency to obscure the true variations in underlying data. Consequently, the aggregate relationships observed are less reliable than they at first appear, and the conclusions that may be drawn from them are not as robust as they seem. These considerations are equally true when applied to the matter of performance indicators. The more disaggregated the data, the more reliable the indicator becomes and the easier it is to make comparison among airports. There are, however, a number of difficulties:

1. Disaggregated data, if published, can result in the widespread dissemination of commercially sensitive data. As has been stated elsewhere, in the increasingly commercial atmosphere in which airports operate, the tendency of airports has been to make published financial data less transparent rather than more so and to restrict researchers' access to nonpublished data.
2. Revenues are often, by their nature, relatively easily assigned to cost centers. The accrual of revenue to a particular activity is, for the most part, either obvious or can be apportioned in a reasonably uncontroversial manner. With costs, the situation is not so easy. For example, apportioning building operational and maintenance costs in terminal concession areas is not carried out on a basis that is universally agreeable. It has been argued for many years that BAA and BAA plc have consistently overstated commercial profits, due to the manner in which costs attributable to commercial operations have been apportioned. In that traffic profits have been understated to the same degree, if the same argument is applied, the matter is not very important if the figures are to be used only to monitor performance. However, where there is no generally accepted manner of cost attribution, comparisons between airports are difficult.
3. Because financial matters are rich in data, the degree of possible disaggregation is high. Some level of aggregation is necessary to ensure that the amount of performance-monitoring data does not become unmanageable. Indices being examined by a manager should be aggregated to a level that balances the scale of the activity being managed.

Where possible the top management team at an airport should have access to current information costs and revenues, disaggregated into aeronautical, nonaeronautical, and commercial cost centers. Top and middle management will have an interest in overall performance indicators on an airportwide basis. Middle management will, however, be much more interested in the performance of individual cost centers.

9.5 AGGREGATE FINANCIAL PERFORMANCE INDICES

Performance criteria, as previously described, are helpful not only for evaluating a facility's operating efficiency on a year-to-year basis, but also—with judicious use—for cross comparison among facilities. There is, however, a wider application by financial analysts who use fiscal criteria to evaluate the financial viability of airports. Here, also, great care must be taken in making cross comparisons among airports, because the different financial bases in terms of grants, low-interest loans, credits, and permitted amortization can make real cross comparison difficult.

The Congressional Budget Office has suggested four indicators for evaluating the finances of U.S. airports operating with both the compensatory and residual approach to pricing (5, 6). These four indicators are widely used by investment advisers—for example, bond-rating agencies—to assess the efficiency of public enterprises:

Operating ratio
Net take-down ratio
Debt-to-asset ratio
Debt service safety margin

The first two indicators are a measure of the availability of revenues surplus to the requirements of regular operating expenses. The second two indicators are used to measure an operation's ability to support borrowing, both existing and new, for capital investment.

Operating ratio is derived by dividing operating expenses by operating revenue. Measuring the share of operating revenue consumed by operating expenses, a high ratio indicates very little surplus revenue available for capital spending. Conversely, a low ratio is taken as a measure of financial strength and possibly efficiency. (The reader must take care to realize that operating revenues and expenses in the CBO's terminology include the commercial non-aeronautical operations.)

$$\text{Operating ratio} = \frac{\text{operating expenses}}{\text{operating revenue}}$$

Net take-down ratio is computed by subtracting operating expenses from total revenue and dividing the result by total revenues. Although similar in concept to the operating ratio, the net take-down ratio is a slightly broader measure of residual airport revenues after subtraction of operating expenses, in that nonoperating revenues are included.

$$\text{Net take-down ratio} = \frac{\text{total revenue} - \text{operating expenses}}{\text{total revenue}}$$

Debt-to-asset ratio is a measure of the total assets provided by creditors. It is computed in the following manner:

$$\text{Debt-to-asset ratio} = \frac{\dfrac{\text{gross}}{\text{debt}} - \dfrac{\text{bond principal}}{\text{reserves}}}{\dfrac{\text{net fixed}}{\text{assets}} + \dfrac{\text{working}}{\text{capital}}}$$

Low debt-to-asset ratios are considered desirable, because creditors have the assurance that asset coverage of debt is high. This is particularly important in the U.S. market, where assets provide the bond holders' security for outstanding bonds.

Debt service safety margin is a measure of the proportion of revenues available to service new debt and the availability of a safety net should the airport experience unusually low revenues. It is defined in the following way:

$$\frac{\text{Debt service}}{\text{safety margin}} = \frac{\dfrac{\text{total}}{\text{revenues}} - \dfrac{\text{operating}}{\text{expenses}} - \dfrac{\text{debt}}{\text{service}}}{\text{total revenues}}$$

In applying these criteria to U.S. airports, Lewis found strong statistical evidence that the compensatory approach to the financial management of airports led to more efficient and financially strong results than the residual approach (5, 6). It was felt that the added earning power made possible by the compensatory approach permitted the pursuit of revenue opportunities and created strong incentives for revenue maximization. Statistical analysis indicated that those airports operating under compensatory rules had operating revenues that were better by approximately 10 percent, net take-down ratios that were better by 24 percent, and debt service safety margins at twice the level of residual operations (6). There are two possible reasons for this better showing:

1. Airports in relatively stronger positions with respect to the travel market are more likely to use the compensatory approach.
2. Operating efficiency and financial performance are improved by using the compensatory approach.

There is strong evidence that the latter rationale is correct, but there still remains some room for doubt in the matter, and the argument over the two systems is certain to continue.

In the United Kingdom, financial criteria were developed at the time of the privatization of the regional airports for evaluating the business plans that were required to be presented to government. The following indicators were used:

1. *Ratio of debt to equity* (not to exceed 30 : 70)
2. *Ratio of interest payments to operating profits* (the limit set on this in the long term not to exceed 33 percent)
3. *Ratio of current assets to liabilities* (set to be greater than 2 : 1)

9.6 INCOME AND FINANCIAL PERFORMANCE INDICES OF THE 1990s

In the last ten years many airports, urged to take a more "commercial attitude," have begun to pay considerably more attention to fiscally related performance indices. For example, in the early 1990s Schipol set itself four major, companywide financial targets:

1. Cost of capital: 10 percent per annum or less
2. Equity/debt ratio: 1.5 minimum
3. Return on assets: 6 percent
4. Cash flow/interest requirement ratio: 3.0 minimum

In the wake of the commercial climate promoted by privatization, BAA plc devised a range of fiscal performance measures for its airports within the airport group. These were grouped into three classifications; those related to *income,* to *staffing and costs,* and to *finance.*

I. Income ratios
   A. *Traffic charges per passenger.* This measure of the overall level of traffic charges is recognized as having little to do with efficiency, since the level is largely set by exogenous factors.
   B. *Traffic charges/total turnover.* This index measures the degree to which the airport relies on traffic income for its business.
   C. *Commercial income per passenger.* Comprising both income from concessions and car parking, this measure monitors the airport's total commercial income per passenger.
   D. *Concession income per passenger.* This index measures the airport's ability to generate concessionary income. Included within this ratio are incomes from duty- and tax-free sales, tax-paid sales, catering, car rental, advertising, banking and exchange facilities, plus other concessionary services.

E. *Duty and tax-free income per international departing passenger.* Due to the changing nature of traffic within the Economic Community in relation to the internal market regulations, this measure is important. It monitors the income from sales of duty- and tax-free goods per international departing passenger.

F. *Other concessions income per passenger.* Income from concessions other than those associated with duty- or tax-free sales—e.g., catering, car rental, banking, exchange, tax-paid retailing and advertising—is included in this category. Car-parking concessionary income is excluded.

G. *Car-parking income per passenger.* This category involves income from public car parking per passenger. This income is very highly dependent on the location of the airport, the type of passenger, and the access facilities provided in terms of public transport.

H. *Other income per passenger.* This category is a measure of income performance from noncommercial or concessionary areas. Typically, property and agricultural income would be grouped in this index.

II. Staffing and cost ratios (Care must be used to ensure that comparisons from year to year or between years are made on a basis of true comparability.)

A. *Staff costs per staff member.* This is a measure of the average wage level at the airport.

B. *Passengers per staff member.* This ratio is a measure of staff productivity.

C. *Staff costs per passenger.* This index is a measure of overall employee cost per unit of output, not including WLUs of freight.

D. *Other direct costs per passenger.* This index is a measure of other cash costs per unit of output.

E. *Property costs per passenger.* This measure includes real estate taxes, utilities, cleaning, car-parking management, and busing costs.

F. *Maintenance and equipment costs per passenger.* This index is a measure of equipment operational and maintenance costs.

G. *General costs per passenger.* This measure is largely related to policing costs.

H. *Intercompany costs per passenger.* In terms of the BAA operation, all charges from other airports and the corporate office are included here. For airports owned by municipalities or local authorities, their charges would accrue to this ratio.

III. Financial ratios to shareholders and financial risk

A. *Earnings/share (EPS).* This index is a measure of profits after tax and appropriate pre-earnings adjustments are made.

B. *Dividends/share.* The amount of earnings paid out in the form of dividends to shareholders is measured by this index.
C. *Dividend cover.* This is the proportion of earnings paid out in dividend. It is equivalent to the EPS divided by the dividend/share.
D. *Interest cover.* This index is a measure of the degree to which a company can finance its current debt from its current trading determined by dividing trading profit by interest payments.
E. *Debt/equity.* This index is a measure of the financial risk of an airport company.

At a more disaggregate level, some performance indices are monitored by individual airports on a month-by-month moving annual basis within the overall group. These include the following:

Yield per passenger (£)
Cost per passenger (£)
Duty-free/tax-free per international departure passenger (£)
Commercial income per passenger (£)
Total income per passenger (£)
Maintenance cost per passenger (£)
Trading profit per passenger (£)
Staff cost per employee (£)
Trading profit per employee (£)
Return on fixed assets (percent)
Return on capital employed (percent)
Debtors/creditors
Cash flow predividend and debtor/creditor movement (£M)

Under the 1986 Airports Act in the United Kingdom, regulation of the monopoly position of BAA with respect to aviation-related charges is attained by control of the operating charges of the South East England airports by the Civil Aviation Authority (CAA). This is achieved in consultation with another more financially oriented body, the Monopolies and Mergers Commission (MMC), which examines the financial position of the BAA and other airport companies every five years. The first of these reports relating to the major London airports was published in June 1991; in the course of this report, the performance indicators discussed in this section were examined in depth (7). In that this report can provide source material, the reader should examine the Commission's report in detail. Although narrowly related to the performance of three major British airports, the document provides a universally applicable framework for appraising financial performance.

9.7 CONCLUSIONS

Most airports in the world have made little use of general performance indicators that relate to the facility's performance in a variety of fields: operations, environment, economic, financial, sociopolitical, and so on (3). Where internally monitored indicators have been set, these in the past have been largely operational, with only crude measures being constructed in the financial area. The worldwide commercialization of airports is a movement that has gathered great momentum since the mid-1980s. Regardless of whether the majority of airports within an individual system are likely to end in the private sector (unlikely in the United States) or are to remain forever entirely in the public domain (unlikely in Europe), commercialization is a trend that intrinsically must cause a relative de-emphasis of the operational aspects of the facilities in favor of the commercial aspects. This factor, combined with the need to provide transparencies of revenues and expenditures to ensure reasonable charges in the monopoly situation, will most certainly mean that financial performance indicators will, in the future, be in much wider use than is current practice.

REFERENCES

1. Doganis, R., and Anne Graham. *Airport Management: The Role of Performance Indicators.* Transport Studies Group Report No. 13. London: Transport Studies Group, Polytechnic of Central London, January 1987.
2. *British Airports Authority Performance Review 1982/3.* London: British Airports Authority, 1983.
3. Ashford, N., H.P.M. Stanton, and C.A. Moore. *Airport Operations.* London: Pitman Publishing, 1991.
4. Assailly, C. *Airport Productivity.* Paris: Institut du Transport Aérien, 1989.
5. Lewis, D. *Airport Ownership and Financial Management.* Ottawa: James Hickling Management Consultants, April 1988.
6. *Financing U.S. Airports in the 1980s.* Washington, D.C.: Congressional Budget Office, April 1984.
7. *MMC2 The Monopolies and Mergers Commission, BAA plc, A Report on the Economic Regulation of the South East Airports Companies, (Heathrow Airport Ltd., Gatwick Airport Ltd., and Stansted Airport Ltd.).* London: Civil Aviation Authority, 1991.

10

Business Plans

10.1 NEED FOR A BUSINESS PLAN

Increased commercialization of airports has required a more continual monitoring of corporate activity to provide better conformity of company practices
to stated company objectives. Where airports have been run by public employees as part of the central or local civil service structure, the objectives of the
airport as a corporate entity frequently were unstated; if stated, these objectives
were submerged within the general ethos of public service. Even where the
management structure of the airport was an autonomous body reporting to a
political body or to a minister, for example, the general ethos of public service
pertained. Commercial profit in many cases was not considered to be a particularly important corporate objective.

Typically, for an airport operating within the public-service sector, the
objectives of the administration, often unstated, would comprise the following:

1. To promote aviation activity
2. To supply facilities in reasonable balance with demand
3. To attain a balance between actual and estimated budgets
4. To maintain growth in close approximation to forecasts
5. To sustain a level of capital expenditure within the resources of the controlling government

To this were added, in some cases, economic and performance criteria such as
the following:

6. To obtain a minimum rate of return on the value of assets

7. To achieve minimum levels of performance with respect to performance criteria (see Chapter 9)

The business plan is an integral part of the overall corporate plan. Unlike the airport master plan, which is a document defining the long-term strategy for airport development, the business plan is a short- to medium-term document. In it is contained a statement of the corporate objectives and ethos. In private companies, these objectives are determined by shareholders; the strategies by which they are to be attained are determined by managers. In the case that objectives are not being met, it is the strategies or even the managers that must be changed, not the objectives.

In the private company, as opposed to the public-service organization, the principal corporate objective is usually to generate the greatest return on shareholders' capital subject to the constraint that the company discharges its social and ethical obligations to society. The authors have decided that the propriety or advisability of privatizing all or part of an airport's business will not be discussed here. The answers to such questions of privatization lie in the political and social plane rather than the financial. However, it is now generally recognized that there is a current perception in the Western democracies and in the emerging democracies, especially in central and eastern Europe, that

1. Airport service levels to passengers and airlines can be increased by the introduction of the commercial ethic.
2. Airports should, in most cases, by financially self-sufficient in the long term, and their capital expenditure requirements can be generated from income.
3. The aviation industry is sufficiently mature in its structure that governmental regulation of the commercial aspects is largely unnecessary and that the mechanism of the private market can best supply the air travel needs of the public.

Whether the private market can live up to the aspirations of the free-market theorists will be proved by experience. This will have to be observed over many years; it will be a long time before the effects of the dead hand of governmental economic regulation will cease to be discernible.

10.2 PREPARATION OF A BUSINESS PLAN

Business planning should be considered as a continuing process. Once prepared, the business plan requires frequent reexamination to ensure that the plan continues to reflect the business environment in which the airport must operate.

The initial plan involves the following key steps:

1. A statement of the airport's business aims and objectives
2. A market analysis of the demand for air transport at the airport, identifying underlying trends
3. An assessment of the degree of competition within the market for airport business and an evaluation of the airport's strengths and weaknesses with respect to competing airports
4. Determination of the services to be offered or the sector of the market to be attacked
5. A statement of the measures to be taken by the airport to market and sell its services
6. Determination of the impact of proposed measures on the management and operations of the airport
7. Preparation of financial forecasts, estimation of required resources, and an indication of how resources are to be used

10.3 CASE STUDY OF A BUSINESS PLAN FOR PRIVATIZATION OF A REGIONAL AIRPORT

The underlying material for this case study was made available to the authors by a British regional airport at the time of privatization of that facility as required by the British Airports Act of 1987. To preserve confidentiality of the figures, the case study is set in a scenario of a fictitious northern European island republic, Erehwon, which has a number of regional airports plus several airports in the general vicinity of Queenstown, the capital. It is assumed that the Erehwon Civil Aviation Authority (ECAA) is responsible for gathering aviation statistics and guiding governmental aviation policy decisions. In the newly privatized climate, individual airports are responsible to their owners (shareholders) for decisions on the running of the airports. The currency of the country will, for purposes of clarity, be assumed to be the U.S. dollar.

Centralia International Airport (CIA) is a private company. All shares of the company are owned by a public body, the Centralia Regional Authority, which is made up of four local governments: Wessex, Midshire, East Lampton, and Norbury. The case study indicates the form of business plan that is likely to have been produced by management at the time of privatization of the airport in 1988. All accounts up to the end of the financial year 1988–1989 show the airport operating as a public body. Subsequent accounts are for a privatized facility.

Figure 10–1 shows the island of Centralia, with the three capital city airports in the vicinity of the capital, Queenstown. CIA's principal competition

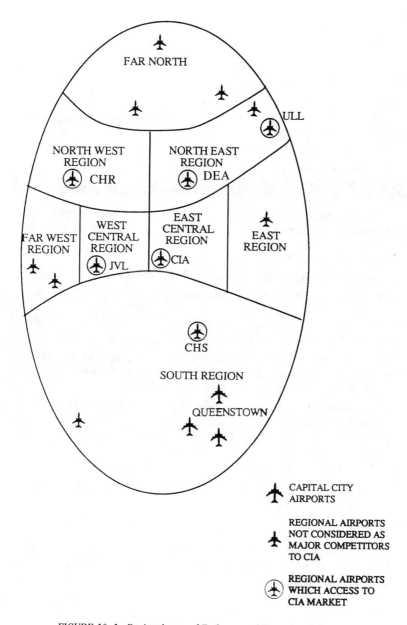

FIGURE 10-1. Regional map of Erehwon and its regional airports

comes from services supplied through airports at Chase (CHS), Jonesville (JVL), Deal (DEA), Chester (CHR), and Ulltown (ULL).

Business Climate

Background

A number of factors influence the market of air transport demand at Centralia International Airport (CIA).

- State of the national economy
- National and local unemployment levels
- Population growth
- Inflation and wage levels
- International exchange rates
- International political environment
- Industrial relations climate
- Surface transport network
- Local summer climate during vacation periods

For example, the international charter market saw a national drop of between 6 percent and 10 percent in the central region of the country in 1988 compared with 1987. CIA was particularly affected, with a 21 percent fall in annual passenger throughput. This drop was attributed to the following:

- A good Erehwonian summer in 1987 and poor publicity for Mediterranean resorts encouraged holidays at home in 1988
- Flights to other airports in the Centralia region were consolidated
- An extended strike occurred in the Centralia gold mines, a basic industry in the region. This affected regional disposable income
- SUNDOWNERS, CIA's leading tour operator, exhibited poor performance both locally and nationally

CIA's Markets

CIA's markets are domestic, scheduled international, chartered international, and cargo destined mainly to the central Erehwon area. Table 10–1 shows the market share of nearby airports.

The growth in the number of CIA's terminal passengers is shown in Table 10–2. This growth rate exceeds the national and regional growth rates in Erehwon.

The terminal share of scheduled domestic and international services has remained relatively stable. International services in the region are supplied primarily by Jonesville and Chester airports.

TABLE 10–1. Passenger/Cargo at Central Erehwon Airports, 1988

	Domestic (000s)	International		Cargo (tonnes)	Workload[a] Units (000s)	Percentage Share (%)
		Schedule (000s)	Charter (000s)			
CIA	846	213	1,719	43,788	3,261	9
Jonesville (JVL)	1,281	1,158	2,463	16,578	5,085	15
Chester (CHR)	4,341	2,952	10,869	95,625	19,215	56
Deal (DEA)	741	171	477	1,023	1,401	4
Chase (CHS)	81	102	4,569	38,334	5,175	15
Ulltown (ULL)	150	90	99	27	339	1
	7,440	4,686	20,196	195,294	34,476	100

[a] 1 work load unit = 1 passenger or 90 kg of cargo.

Source: ECAA Airport statistics

In 1984 a 50 percent rebate in cargo traffic charges induced significant cargo traffic growth, putting CIA into third position in all Erehwon noncapital airports in cargo, behind only Chester and Fast, an airport on the nearby island of Nire. Table 10–3 (which, unlike Table 10–1, includes mail) shows the dramatic growth in cargo traffic.

The use of CIA as a base for a major regional freight carrier and the choice of the airport as one of the republic's two main distributional hubs for the Erehwon Post Office has allowed the airport to establish itself as a major air freight center, to a degree independent of the economy of the central region itself.

Competition
Table 10–4 shows the competitive position of CIA in the central region of Erehwon. In the absence of geographical bias, the strongest competition to CIA's development would come from airports with a record of profitability and a strongly established operating base. In this case, Chester, with 18 million passengers, nearly 100,000 tonnes of cargo, and a total surplus in the 1986–1987 financial year of $27.6 million, is the leading competitor. Jonesville is a strong competitor, with more than 4.8 million terminal passengers in 1987.

Table 10–5, however, indicates that proximity to market base does give some protection, showing that passengers strongly tend to use nearby airports.

Financial History
Tables 10–6 and 10–7 indicate recent financial performance and capital investment, respectively, at CIA.

TABLE 10-2. CIA's Terminal Passengers 1982–1987

	1982		1983		1984		1985		1986		1987	
	000s	%	000s	%	000s	%	000s	%	000s	%	000s	%
Domestic	639	32	663	30	813	31	843	29	870	27	846	30
International												
scheduled	252	13	222	10	234	9	204	7	201	6	213	8
chartered	1,110	55	1,332	60	1,578	60	1,836	64	2,172	67	1,719	62

Source: ECAA Airport statistics

TABLE 10–3. Cargo Traffic in the Central Erehwon Airports, 1982–1987

| | Cargo (tonnes) | | | | | | Average Annual Growth Rate, |
Airport	1982	1983	1984	1985	1986	1987	1982–1987
Chester	72,708	85,923	70,950	73,395	86,442	95,625	5.6%
CIA	20,034	10,665	19,539	23,505	38,913	43,707	16.9%
Chase	39,014	33,984	35,385	31,422	41,082	38,334	−0.4%
Jonesville	9,012	7,851	6,561	9,786	13,374	16,578	+13.0%
Deal	1,146	867	1,029	1,089	912	1,023	−2.2%
Ulltown	180	186	162	141	219	27	−31.6%

Source: ECAA Airport statistics

Planning Assumptions

Economic Conditions

The plan envisages the same economic conditions as those assumed in the Erehwon Civil Aviation Authority's "Air Traffic Forecasts for the Republic of Erehwon," 1988.

Marketing Assumptions

- CIA will have no capacity constraints in any market sector.
- There will be no radical change in the nature of airlines or operators at CIA.
- There is adequate capacity on routes to the capital city, Queenstown, to preclude changes to aircraft or frequencies in the next five years.
- CIA's market share of domestic traffic will remain constant.
- CIA's pricing policy will remain as competitive as it is currently.
- Scheduled international flight increases will tend to occur in other Central Erehwon airports.
- Any moves toward deregulation will cause airlines to concentrate their operations at larger airports, following the experiences gained from U.S. deregulation.
- The Erehwon Post Office (EPO) will continue to operate its overnight air services from at least two distribution centers.
- Cargo will continue to increase at a strong growth rate.

Traffic Forecasts

- Three percent per annum increases in passengers to Queenstown Airports (compare with 1.4 percent to 3.7 percent estimated by ECAA)

TABLE 10–4. Summary of Competitive Situation

Airport	Terminal Passengers 1987 (000s)	Annual Percent Change 1982–1987	Cargo (tonnes) 1987	Annual Percent Change 1982–1987	Total Surplus (Deficit) 1986–1987 ($ mill.)	Operating Surplus (Deficit) 1986–1987 ($ mill.)	Operating Surplus (Deficit)/Income 1986–1987 ($ mill.)	24-hour Operation	No. of Destinations				
									IT	Sched. Dom.	Sched. Europe	Cargo Dom.	Cargo Europe
CIA	2,775	7	43,701	17	8.1	10.8	38	Yes	39	8	2	10	4
Jonesville	4,902	1	16,578	13	7.5	9.9	23	Yes	47	15	16	4	5
Chester	18,162	7	95,625	6	27.6	46.5	29	Yes	86	18	29	—	4
Deal	1,389	5	1,023	–2	(0.3)	2.7	31	0700–2200	14	13	5	—	—
Chase	4,758	–5	38,334	0	5.7	10.5	23	Yes	40	4	1	3	6
Ulltown	339	25	27	–32	(0.6)	(0.3)	–2	0700–2200	1	10	4	—	—

TABLE 10–5. Percentage Share of Passengers by Origin/Destination 1985

Passenger Origin/Destination by Region	Domestic			International Schedule			International Charter		
	CIA (%)	JVL (%)	CHR (%)	CIA (%)	JVL (%)	CHR (%)	CIA (%)	JVL (%)	CHR (%)
East central	81	12	7	42	45	13	59	22	19
West central	6	83	11	2	82	16	10	72	18
Northeast	32	2	66	6	3	91	16	—	84
Northwest	—	—	100	—	—	100	1	—	99
Far north	—	7	93	—	4	96	—	4	96
Far west	1	20	79	—	30	70	—	31	69
East	54	33	13	—	14	86	—	51	49
South	18	36	46	17	61	22	12	28	60

- Three percent per annum increases in passengers to other domestic airports (compare with 3.1 percent to 5.3 percent estimated by ECAA)
- Three percent per annum increases in passengers on international scheduled flights (compare with ECAA forecasts of 3 percent to 9 percent)
- Eight percent per annum increases in international charger passengers (compare with ECAA forecasts of 3 percent to 9 percent; forecast based on much improved performance of SUNDOWNERS and a general diversification regionally of the charter market to the benefit of regional airports)
- Five percent per annum increases in mail in 1988–1989 and 1989–1990 and 3 percent thereafter, based on EPO's assessment of mail growth
- Twenty percent per annum increases in freight in 1988–1989 and per annum thereafter 10 percent (This reflects growth of express parcels' market and is more conservative than CIA's leading carrier's forecast.)

Personnel

Upon privatization the company will have 700 jobs. Due to the need to transfer internally into the airport's own organization some support service jobs currently supplied by local government, this will grow to 750 jobs.

In the first five years the number of jobs will continue to grow to 803, an increase of 7 percent.

Some activities will still be contracted out:

Civil engineering
Architecture
Legal
Real estate

TABLE 10–6. Operating Income, Expenditure, and Surplus 1982–1983 to 1987–1988 at Centralia International Airport

	1982–1983 $ (mill.)	1983–1984 $ (mill.)	1984–1985 $ (mill.)	1985–1986 $ (mill.)	1986–1987 $ (mill.)	1987–1988 $ (mill.)
Operating income	14.4	18.0	21.9	25.8	29.7	28.8
Operating expenditures	11.4	12.9	16.2	17.1	19.2	20.7
Operating surplus	3.0	5.1	5.7	8.7	10.5	8.1
Surplus as percent of income	20.8	28.3	26.0	34.9	35.4	28.1

Source: CIA Annual Reports

216

TABLE 10–7. Capital Investment 1982–1983 to 1987–1988 at Centralia International Airport

	1982–1983	1983–1984	1984–1985	1985–1986	1986–1987	1987–1988
Capital Investment in $ (mill.)	5.7	4.8	4.2	3.9	3.9	9.0

Source: CIA Annual Reports

These will be for initial periods of two years, after which the position will be reviewed. Financial projections assume continued contracting out.

Facilities
The following planned capital program is envisaged.

Passenger Facilities
1989–1990   Expansion of international departure lounge—$0.75 million
1993–1994 to 1994–1995   Further expansion of passenger terminal to meet passenger growth—$6.0 million

Cargo-related Facilities
1989–1990   Apron phase 1—$2.15 million
1990–1991   Apron phase 2—$1.5 million
1992–1993   Apron phase 3—$1.8 million
1990–1991   Access road dedicated to cargo—$0.75 million

Operational and Security Requirements
1989–1990 to 1991–1992   Replacement and expansion of airport operational systems—$1.2 million
1990–1991   Cat II approach lighting to runway 30, installation of RESA and arrestor bed—$0.75 million
1992–1993   ILS Cat II and runway extension to runway 12—$1.15 million

Environmental Requirements
1989–1990 to 1990–1991   Land acquisitions—$1.2 million

Finance
The following assumptions are made:

• Increases in price levels at 4 percent per annum
• Increases in pay levels at 6 percent in 1989–1990 and 4 percent per annum thereafter

Business Strategy

The business strategy is evolved following a clear definition of the company's goals and objectives, and actions are indicated under

Corporate status
Management structure and systems
Market strategy

The principal goal of the company is to operate an international airport and to engage in such activities as are necessary to encourage individuals and businesses to make the fullest use of the airport and its facilities in order to maximize profitability within the constraints of safety, security, and service standards.

This statement leads to the following corporate policies:

- To maintain high standards of safety and security
- To encourage customer loyalty
- To be a good employer
- To be a good neighbor
- To operate efficiently
- To contribute to the local economy

These policies are interpreted in the following ways.

Safety and Security
The company will maintain the highest possible standards of safety for aircraft, passengers, and airport staff having due regard to the requirements of the ECAA's airport licensing regulations, criteria prescribed by ICAO, and the requirements of the Health and Safety at Work Act and any other relevant legislation.

The company will, in cooperation with appropriate government departments and agencies, ensure the highest practicable standards of security against terrorism and crime, bearing in mind the responsibilities of tenants and operators for the security of their own leased premises, property, aircraft, and equipment.

Customer Service
The company will seek to encourage customer loyalty by improving and extending the range and quality of services offered to customers by the company directly and also by its concessionaires and contractors.

Facilities will, as far as possible, be designed and provided according to anticipated demand and by reference to space and service standards defined by the board of directors to ensure that no more than 5 percent of annual passengers experience substandard conditions.

Labor

The company will strive to ensure, as a good employer, fair pay and conditions of service for employees and to encourage a working partnership leading to higher productivity and higher standards of service to customers through proper arrangement for participation, consultation, and negotiation and to promote security of employment.

The company will make appropriate pension provisions for its employees.

Environmental Considerations

The company will operate, as far as possible, in harmony with the communities adjoining the airport and will seek to maintain a balance of interest between those communities and the needs of air transport.

The company will take all practicable steps to monitor aircraft noise levels and to alleviate nuisance arising therefrom.

Steps will also be taken to minimize the visual intrusion of airport development in the local environment.

Financial and Commercial Policy

The company aims to operate efficiently and to ensure as far as possible that it meets the financial and performance targets set down by the board of directors from time to time.

A competitive and commercial approach will be adopted to ensure the effective utilization of the company's assets and opportunities and to provide the required financial returns.

These policies will be supported by a pricing strategy that will seek to ensure that charges are consistent with the need to generate sufficient revenue to enable the company to operate and develop its facilities in a competitive industry.

The company is committed to the concept of development of income from sources other than aircraft landing and parking fees and will aim to maximize profit in its commercial affairs.

Of the facilities and services provided at airports, some are unique to the airport environment, such as air traffic and ground movement control, and these should be provided by the company. Others, such as shops, banks, and parking lots, are common throughout the land. It is company policy that these latter services should be provided by the company or under contract or concession by specialist organizations with appropriate experience.

The company seeks to encourage the development of comprehensive air cargo facilities at Centralia International Airport. In doing so, it seeks to provide significant new employment in the area, and it is anticipated that the cost of such development will be supported by outside capital. The company will further provide adequate operational facilities to encourage the development of a broad range of air cargo activities that support industry in the region. These improved distribution facilities are viewed as a contribution to the effectiveness of industry within the region, enabling it to compare more adequately.

Local Economy

The company acknowledges the importance of its role in the stimulation of the local economy by generation of employment and by the spending power it creates and recognized its contribution to the prosperity of the locality.

Corporate Status

The airport company will be registered as a public limited company trading under the name of Centralia International Airport plc. The company's registered office will be at the airport administration headquarters at Centralia International Airport.

The company will have an authorized and issued share capital of $87 million, which will be publicly traded.

As part of the capital structure of the company, loans up to $30 million will be established between the company and one of its former owners, Wessex County Council.

Management Structure

The board of directors will have nine members; of these, six will act in a nonexecutive capacity. Four will be appointed by the local authorities of Wessex, Midshire, East Lampton, and Norbury. The three executive directors will be the managing director, the finance and commercial director, and the technical director.

Below board level, a division structure will be established with five divisional managers:

Director of finance and chief accountant
Director of commercial activities
Director of personnel and administration and company secretary
Director of operations
Director of engineering

The total initial staff will be 750. Figures 10–2 and 10–3 show organograms of the staffing structure prior to privatization and immediately afterwards.

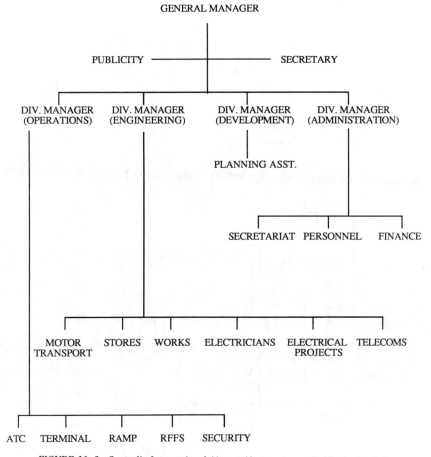

FIGURE 10–2. Centralia International Airport (Organogram—Public Authority)

Management Systems

With the establishment of a management structure that ensures that all activities essential to the business are provided in the company, a new management system will be required to accommodate functions transferred from Wessex County Council, which as the major owner provided most support functions.

An information technology strategy is being developed, it incorporates the following:

- Coordination of all operational, financial, and commercial systems requirements

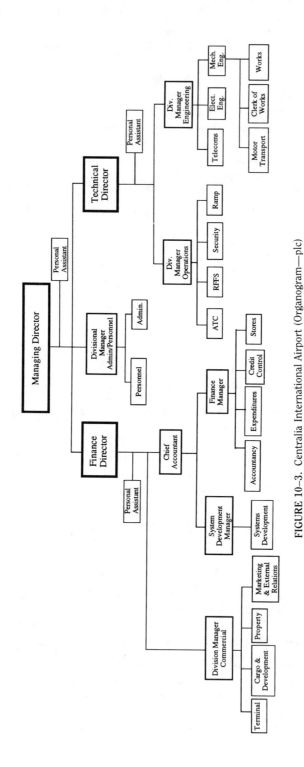

FIGURE 10–3. Centralia International Airport (Organogram—plc)

- Integration of systems and standardization of hardware and software
- Emphasis on commercial rather than tailor-made software packages
- High usage of report generation and interrogation by airport staff
- Centralization of responsibility for information technology within the organizational structure
- Full system implementation for April 1990

Market Strategy
Marketing will focus on

- International inclusive tour (IT) sector
- Overnight air cargo market

IT sector marketing activity will be addressed to

- Traveling public via information on airports services and facilities
- Travel agents via information on CIA's resources and requirements
- Tour operators via developing close working relationships to foster an environment conducive to the growth of IT

Cargo activity will be encouraged by publicizing facilities to express parcel operators and the Erehwon Post Office and by providing high standards of service with respect to delays and facilities to counter attempts by competing airports to weaken CIA's cargo base. Charges will be kept competitive to encourage both the IT and cargo sectors.

Physical and Financial Projections

Passengers
Table 10–8 shows forecasts of the passenger throughput through 1994. The share taken by International Charter is forecast to increase by 1 percent each year from 70 percent in 1989–1990 to 75 percent in 1993–1994.

Air Transport Movements
Table 10–9 shows air transport movement (ATM) forecasts for the same period. Within the totals, international charter and cargo ATMs are forecast to increase by 28.2 percent and 24.3 percent, respectively, whereas domestic ATMs will remain constant.

TABLE 10–8. Passenger Forecasts 1989–1990 to 1993–1994

	1989–1990	1990–1991	1991–1992	1992–1993	1993–1994
Passengers (000s)	3,876	4,122	4,383	4,665	4,968

TABLE 10–9. Total Air Transport Movements 1989–1990 to 1993–1994

	1989–1990	1990–1991	1991–1992	1992–1993	1993–1994
ATMs	99,600	102,450	106,500	110,550	114,900

Staffing

The staffing forecasts are as follows:

	1989–1990	1990–1991	1991–1992	1992–1993	1993–1994
Staffing	750	765	780	791	803

A breakdown of the staffing levels is shown in Table A10–4 in the appendix to this chapter.

Profit and Loss

Table 10–10 shows a summary of the forecast profit and loss accounts for the years 1989–1990 to 1991–1992. These are prepared in accordance with the Companies Act of 1985 and differ from the local-authority format previously used for the airport's accounts. The major differences lie in the areas of depreciation and the treatment of interest charges and taxation, as shown in Table A10–1.

TABLE 10–10. Summary Profit and Loss Accounts

	1989–1990	1990–1991	Increase/ (Decrease)	1991–1992	Increase/ (Decrease)
	($000s)	($000s)	%	($000s)	%
Operating income	38,916	42,810	10.0	46,956	9.7
Operating expenditure	(33,327)	(35,271)	5.8	37,596	6.6
Operating profit before interest and tax	5,589	7,539	34.9	9,360	24.2
Interest on investment	366	210	(42.6)	648	208.6
Interest payable	3,657	3,726	1.9	3,675	(1.4)
Profit before tax	2,298	4,023	75.1	6,333	57.4
Tax	(804)	(1,407)	75.0	(738)	57.4
Profit after tax	1,494	2,616	75.1	4,119	57.5
Extraordinary items	(300)	—	—	—	—
Net profit	1,194	2,616	119.1	4,119	57.5

TABLE 10–11. Cash Flow in Years 1989–1990 and 1990–1991 in $000s

| | Start-up | 1989–1990 | | | | 1990–1991 | | | |
		Q1	Q2	Q3	Q4	Q1	Q2	Q3	Q4
Net cash movements	8,100	408	−6,669	1,495	−2,829	−237	2,748	2,637	−2,856
Balance at end of period	8,100	8,508	1,839	3,324	495	258	3,006	5,643	2,787

TABLE 10–12. Balance Sheet Forecasts as of 31 March

	Opening $000s	1990 $000s	1991 $000s	1992 $000s
Fixed assets	119,355	121,770	122,325	118,893
Net current assets	36	168	3,438	1,638
Total capital employed	119,391	121,938	125,763	120,531
Financed by:				
Deferred taxation	180	984	2,394	1,389
Long-term debt	31,359	31,908	31,707	31,266
Capital grant	—	—	—	—
Shareholders' funds	87,852	89,046	91,662	87,876
Total	119,391	121,938	125,763	120,531

Forecast operating profit increases from $5.6 million in 1989–1990 to $7.5 million in 1990–1991 and $9.4 million in 1991–1992. These profits represent 14. 3 percent, 17.6 percent, and 19.9 percent, respectively, of operating income—performance that may appear poor in terms of the operating surpluses prior to privatization. These surpluses do, however, reflect a charge for depreciation, which was absent from the local-government accounts. In local-government accounting, loan repayments are broadly equivalent to depreciation. They are not charged against operating surpluses but are met by the constituent local authority from the distributed operating surpluses.

Interest on long-term borrowing is constant throughout the planning period; no repayment of initial debt is contemplated.

The airport as a plc (an incorporated private company) is also liable for corporation tax.

Cash Flow

Table 10–11 on the previous page summarizes the cash-flow position until the end of the fourth quarter of the financial year 1990–1991. The significant outflow of funds in the second quarter of 1989–1990 is due to a distribution of surpluses generated in 1988–1989. This is a unique situation that will not be repeated. The minimum cash position anticipated is $258,000 at the end of the first quarter of 1990–1991. Thereafter, the situation improves.

Balance Sheet

Table 10–12 summarizes the opening and forecast balance sheets as of 31 March 1989, 1990, 1991, and 1992.

Financial Criteria

The ECAA Letter of Guidance for airports about to privatize recommends that the ratio of debt to equity should not exceed 30 : 70. In the forecast period, this ratio is 26 : 74 for CIA.

The Letter of Guidance also recommends that interest payments should not exceed 33 percent of sustainable operating profits. For CIA this figure is 59 percent in 1989–1990, 47 percent in 1990–1991 and 32 percent in 1991–1992, a downward trend indicating conformity in the short to medium term.

The rate of current assets to liabilities is also within the 2 : 1 ratio that the government requires should not be exceeded in business plans submitted at the time of privatization.

APPENDIX

Following are tables detailing Centralia International Airport's projected profit and loss accounts, balance sheets, capital investment, and staffing forecasts.

TABLE A10–1. Centralia International Airport: Forecast Profit and Loss Accounts

	Actual 1985–1986 $000s	Actual 1986–1987 $000s	Actual 1987–1988 $000s	Forecast 1988–1989 $000s	1989–1990 $000s	1990–1991 $000s	1991–1992 $000s
Operating Income							
1. Traffic Charges							
Landing and Parking							
(a) Int. pass. ATMs	} 8,679	5,784	4,956	6,654	7,311	8,151	8,931
(b) Dom. pass. ATMs		1,944	2,067	2,031	2,109	2,193	2,280
(c) Cargo ATMs		990	1,110	1,263	1,362	1,512	1,719
(d) Mail ATMs		258	288	324	339	354	372
(e) Other a/c movements		1,221	1,167	1,113	1,236	1,254	1,269
Passenger Charges							
(a) Int. passengers	8,601	10,263	9,006	12,105	14,097	15,786	17,667
(b) Dom. passengers	1,878	2,001	2,142	1,989	2,358	2,505	2,658
	10,479	12,264	11,148	14,094	16,455	18,291	20,325
Total Traffic Income	19,158	22,461	20,736	25,479	28,812	31,755	34,896
2. Commercial Income							
(a) Duty/Tax Free	1,689	1,956	2,307	2,721	2,973	3,333	3,726
(b) Other	3,348	3,690	3,891	4,587	4,971	5,445	5,967
(c) Rents	1,524	1,665	1,911	2,070	2,160	2,277	2,367
Total Commercial Income	6,441	7,311	8,109	9,378	10,104	11,055	12,060
Total Operating Income	25,719	29,772	28,845	34,857	38,916	42,810	46,956
Operating Expenditure							
(a) Staff	8,343	9,444	10,410	12,117	15,003	16,101	17,373
(b) Premises	4,212	4,830	4,989	6,348	7,161	7,563	8,223

(c) Transport and plant	705	750	879	954	666	702	732
(d) Supplies and services	1,443	1,656	1,662	1,962	4,491	2,442	2,583
(e) Establishment expenses	1,059	972	1,143	1,377	1,386	1,445	1,521
(f) Agency services	1,521	1,539	1,677	1,767	453	411	393
(g) Misc. and contingency	102	174	201	405	231	240	249
(h) Recharges	−195	−261	−267	279	−348	−363	−378
(i) Depreciation					6,480	6,720	6,900
Total Operating Expenditure	17,190	19,104	20,694	24,651	33,327	35,271	37,596
Operating Profit before Interest and Tax	8,529	10,668	8,151	10,206	5,589	7,539	9,360
Interests on Investments	537	633	978	750	366	210	648
	9,066	11,301	9,129	10,956	5,955	7,749	10,008
Interest Payments							
(a) Short term borrowing					0	27	0
(b) Long-term borrowing					3,450	3,450	3,450
(c) Finance charges under lease payments					207	249	215
Total Interest Payments	0	0	0	0	3,657	3,726	3,675
Profit before Tax	9,066	11,301	9,129	10,956	2,298	4,023	6,333
Tax					804	1,407	2,214
Profit after Tax	9,066	11,301	9,129	10,956	1,494	2,616	4,119
Extraordinary Items							
Preliminary expenses					300		
Capital outlay from revenue	3	135	—	2,100			
Profit after Extraordinary Items	9,063	11,166	9,129	8,856	1,194	2,616	4,119
Debt Charges Met by Local Authority							
Repayment	1,224	1,164	1,464	1,818			
Interest	1,845	2,283	2,937	3,837			
	3,069	3,447	4,401	5,655	—	—	—

TABLE A10–2. Centralia International Airport—Balance Sheets

	Opening 4/1/89 $000s	At 3/31/90 $000s	At 3/31/91 $000s	At 3/31/92 $000s
Fixed Assets (Net Book Value)				
Land and buildings	76,426	74,877	72,597	70,914
Runways, taxiways and aprons	29,516	31,386	32,553	31,491
Vehicles, plant and equipment	13,413	15,507	17,175	16,488
Total fixed assets	119,355	121,770	122,325	118,893
Current Assets				
Stocks	435	450	471	489
Debtors	3,540	3,567	3,903	4,281
Short-term loan and deposits				
Cash at bank and in hand	8,100	495	2,793	11,898
Total current assets	12,075	4,512	7,167	16,668
Current Liabilities				
Creditors and accrued charges	11,661	3,009	3,078	3,219
Loan capital				
Lease capital	378	585	654	675
Tax payable				3,228
Short-term borrowing		250		
Dividend payable				7,908
Total current liabilities	12,039	4,344	3,729	15,030
Net current assets (liabilities)	36	168	3,438	1,638
Total capital employed	119,391	121,938	125,763	120,531
Financed by				
Deferred taxation	180	984	2,394	1,389
Long-term debt	30,000	30,000	30,000	30,000
Lease finance	1,359	1,908	1,707	1,266
Shareholders funds:				
Share capital	87,852	87,852	87,852	87,852
Profit and loss account		1,194	3,810	24
Reserves				
	119,391	121,938	125,763	120,531

TABLE A10–3. Centralia International Airport, 1986–1994—Capital Investment

	Actual Year to 3/31/86 $000s	Actual Year to 3/31/87 $000s	Actual Year to 3/31/88 $000s	Forecast Year to 3/31/89 $000s	Year to 3/31/90 $000s	Year to 3/31/91 $000s	Year to 3/31/92 $000s	Year to 3/31/93 $000s	Year to 3/31/94 $000s
Terminals									
New	—	—	—	6	—	—	—	—	—
Extensions	387	1,299	63	4,710	—	—	—	—	—
Refurbishment	60	654	7,050	687	777	105	—	180	2,988
Other operational buildings	1,635	402	69	36	516	1,551	477	270	27
Runways/taxiways/aprons	90	(15)	153	—	2,487	918	60	1,731	—
Car parks	228	447	6	1,623	474	1,836	1,221	132	—
Equipment	900	789	1,572	114	2,172	342	423	1,005	969
Vehicles	—	—	—	81	636	—	162	405	189
Land	3	(3)	—	—	450	450	450	450	450
Miscellaneous	495	243	51	603	1,383	2,073	675	534	201
Total	3,798	3,786	8,964	7,860	8,895	7,275	3,468	4,707	4,824

TABLE A10–4. Staffing Forecast, 1989–1990 to 1993–1994

Position	1989–1990	1990–1991	1991–1992	1992–1993	1993–1994
Senior Management and Support	10	10	10	10	10
Finance and System Development	25	25	25	25	25
Commercial Division:					
Divisional manager (Comm)	1	1	1	1	1
Terminal management	42	42	42	42	42
Cargo and development	3	3	3	3	3
Property management	4	4	4	4	4
Divisional manager (marketing)	—	—	—	1	1
Marketing and ext. relations	2	2	2	2	2
Administration and Personnel	28	28	30	30	32
Operations Division					
Divisional manager (Ops)	1	1	1	1	1
Air traffic control	45	45	45	45	45
Fire and rescue	70	72	76	78	80
Ramp services	240	244	248	252	254
Security	140	140	140	140	140
Engineering Division					
Divisional manager (Eng)	1	1	1	1	1
Tels	27	27	27	27	27
Electrical	36	38	40	40	40
Mechanical	75	75	78	78	80
Project control	—	—	5	5	5
Building services engineers	—	—	10	10	10
Total	750	758	788	795	803

Epilogue

With the extensive growth of air transport since World War II, airports have grown substantially in the last fifty years. In the case of many of the major airports in the United States, Europe, and elsewhere, the growth of traffic has been almost of two orders of magnitude. The increased size of the aviation industry has led to a public and political recognition that the sector should be self-supporting, with a minimum of public subsidies in the area of civil air transport.

In the absence of subsidy, airports tend to operate on commercial lines, rather than providing a public service, as was true in the fledgling industry. The growing development of airports operated on commercial principles has led to a need for a range of managers at various levels of responsibility who have some grasp of the financial aspects of airport management. The topics covered in this text could be expected to be of interest to those at the middle-management level of commercial transport airports. The approach has intentionally been of an international nature, partly because aviation is truly an international activity but mainly because the movement to world commercialization or privatization of civil aviation is a thrust that is internationally based.

The authors have intended to approach the subject in a basic and introductory manner so that a necessary range of topics could be introduced. Recognizing that it is necessary to deal with topics of current interest, we have attempted to avoid ephemeral issues; such matters are better handled by journals and the professional press.

In the closing years of the twentieth century, the financial factors of airport management are perhaps the most volatile and are, therefore, the most difficult to administer. The authors hope that this introductory text will provide a necessary framework on which the readers can build the understanding of the concepts of airport financial management needed to tackle the problems they will face in the course of their careers.

Index